The United States Military
in Limited War

The United States Military in Limited War

Case Studies in Success and Failure, 1945–1999

KEVIN DOUGHERTY

McFarland & Company, Inc., Publishers
Jefferson, North Carolina, and London

LIBRARY OF CONGRESS CATALOGUING-IN-PUBLICATION DATA

Dougherty, Kevin.
The United States Military in limited war : case studies
in success and failure, 1945–1999 / Kevin Dougherty.
p.   cm.
Includes bibliographical references and index.

ISBN 978-0-7864-7231-4
softcover : acid free paper ∞

1. Limited war — Case studies.   2. United States — Armed Forces —
Operations other than war — Case studies.   3. Miliary doctrine —
United States — History — 20th century.   4. United States —
History, Military — 20th century — Case studies.   I. Title.
UA11.5.D68 2012   355.02'15097309045 — dc23   2012037112

BRITISH LIBRARY CATALOGUING DATA ARE AVAILABLE

On the cover: Paratroopers of the 82nd Airborne Division descend on the
drop zone at Palmerola Air Base during Operation Golden Pheasant,
photograph by Tech Sgt. Bob Simons (Department of Defense)

Manufactured in the United States of America

*McFarland & Company, Inc., Publishers
Box 611, Jefferson, North Carolina 28640
www.mcfarlandpub.com*

Lovingly dedicated to my wife Rhonda who, like all good army wives, has fought and won many "operations other than war" of her own

Table of Contents

Preface

As a captain in the U.S. Army, I was assigned to Fort Benning, Georgia, as a tactics instructor for the Infantry Officer's Advanced Course and then a doctrine writer at the Infantry School and Center between 1992 and 1994. It was during that time that the army published the 1993 version of its capstone doctrinal manual, Field Manual (FM) 100-5, *Operations*. This manual included an entire chapter on "operations other than war" (OOTW), a new term for what had previously been called by such names as "small wars" and "low intensity conflict," and a type of operation that during the latter half of the twentieth century would become the one the United States most commonly faced. Both as an instructor and doctrine writer, I was a small part of the effort to incorporate this new OOTW doctrine into all aspects of the Infantry School and Center's activities. My interest in OOTW and the origins of this book can be traced to these formative experiences.

Part of FM 100-5's doctrine for OOTW was to identify objective, unity of effort, legitimacy, perseverance, restraint, and security as the six "principles of OOTW." A variety of studies, especially those generated by the U.S. military's senior service colleges, have since used these principles as an analytical tool to examine historical operations. For example, in his Naval War College study of Operation Earnest Will, the 1987–1988 tanker escort mission in the Persian Gulf, Michael Gurley connects the operation's success with his conclusion that "the operational commander effectively applied each principle of MOOTW."[1] Other authors who have used the principles of OOTW as a basis of analysis of case studies include Bernardo Negrete in "Grenada: A Case Study in Military Operations Other Than War" (Army War College, 1996), John Cowan in "Operation Provide Comfort: Operational Analysis for Operations Other Than War" (Naval War College, 1995), and Richard Brasel in "Operation Joint Endeavor: Operational Guidance from the Principles of Operations Other Than War" (Naval War College, 1996).[2] While these descriptive case studies illustrate the utility of the principles of OOTW to analyze a specific operation, they have not proceeded to then place the operation in the context of other OOTWs. This singular focus limits their ability to assess the overall utility of the principles as a predictor of mission outcome. Instead, their intent is largely to use the principles merely as an analytical framework to explain the given operation. Because of this singular focus, descriptive case studies such as these typically are underdeveloped in assessing linkages between the data and the theory and the criteria for interpreting the findings.[3]

I attempt to go beyond this limited objective and determine if a correlation exists between adherence to the principles of OOTW and the operation's outcome, and if there is any meaningful relation among the principles themselves. To do so I place individual operations in context by examining the entire era between 1945 and 1999, a time period not focused on by other studies, but which encompasses the transition from the Cold War to the post–Cold War environment. The sample for this study includes eight OOTWs, representing four successful (Greek Civil War, Lebanon, Dominican Republic, and Nicaragua/Honduras) and four failed (Vietnam, Beirut, Somalia, and Haiti) operations. In this case, success or failure was determined based on the operation's ability to achieve the immediate U.S. objective. In addition to a mix of successful and failed operations, selection criteria sought to represent the entire period. Two case studies come from the early Cold War period (Greek Civil War and Lebanon), two from the middle of the Cold War (Dominican Republic and Vietnam), two from the latter part of the Cold War (Beirut and Nicaragua/Honduras), one from the heady early days of the post–Cold War period (Somalia), and one from the more sober post–Somalia days (Haiti).

The resulting analysis indicates that the balanced application of the principles of OOTW is a reliable predicator of the operation's outcome and that there is a relationship among several of the principles themselves. These findings suggest the principles of OOTW are a useful planning tool for military commanders and staffs, an important factor in light of America's continued involvement in these types of operations in Iraq, Afghanistan, Libya, and elsewhere. Nonetheless, in an apparent effort to remove some of the perceived inappropriate uniqueness of OOTW from the doctrine, when the army rewrote FM 100-5 as FM 3-0 in 2001, it eliminated any specific principles of OOTW. Instead, the manual stated that "the nine [traditional] principles of war provide general guidance for conducting war and military operations other than war at the strategic, operational, and tactical levels."[4] Likewise when the army published FM 3-07, *Stability Operations and Support Operations* in 2003, it reiterated that "as in all operations, the principles of war outlined in FM 3-0 apply to stability operations and support operations," adding the small caveat that "the situation determines their degree of applicability."[5] The result was that although "many of the valuable ideas associated with the 1993 principles of operations other than war were salvaged as imperatives in the appropriate stability or support operations chapters," they appear in FM 3-0 only amid a much broader and diluted discussion of "considerations."[6] Given the findings, a more deliberate treatment of these considerations as principles may be appropriate.

I completed my army career in 2005 and entered the International Development doctoral program at the University of Southern Mississippi. This book is the result of that experience, and I would like to thank my dissertation chair, Dr. J. J. St. Marie, and the other committee members, Dr. David Butler, Dr. Tom Lansford, and Dr. Robert Pauly, for their advice and support throughout the duration of this project.

Introduction

Military theorists have long sought a set of principles upon which to base the military art. Inspired by the Enlightenment philosophy that emphasized rational objective analysis and the search for clarity in all fields, a series of military theorists, perhaps most notably Baron Antoine-Henri de Jomini, sought to uncover the natural scientific laws relating to the conduct of war, confident that the military art "like all others is founded on certain and fixed principles."[1] After twenty years of study, Jomini was convinced that "there exists a small number of fundamental principles of war, which could not be deviated from without danger, and the application of which, on the contrary, has been in almost all time crowned with success."[2] Drawing on the works of Jomini and Carl von Clausewitz, British military officer J. F. C. Fuller developed a list of principles for use by the British Army in World War I. The U.S. Army modified Fuller's list and published its first list of the principles of war in 1921.[3] The nine principles of war are objective, offensive, mass, economy of force, maneuver, unity of command, security, surprise, and simplicity.

These traditional principles of war have served the military well, but with the end of the Cold War, the army recognized it had entered "a new, strategic era" that would require that "Army forces operate across the range of military operations."[4] Observers began to speak of a "doctrinal renaissance of operations short of war."[5] By 1992, U.S. forces were increasingly being tasked with non-warfighting missions, such as support during the Los Angeles riots and Hurricane Andrew, and were being pressured to assume peacekeeping and peace enforcement operations in the Balkans. When the army rewrote its capstone manual, FM 100-5, *Operations* in 1993, it responded to this changed operational environment by devoting an entire chapter to "operations other than war" (OOTW).

FM 100-5 distinguished between peacetime (routine interactions between nations) and conflict (hostilities to secure strategic objectives) and war (the use of force in combat operations against an armed enemy). The manual classified activities during both the peacetime and conflict environments as "operations other than war" and cited non-combatant evacuation operations, arms control, support to domestic civil authorities, humanitarian assistance and disaster relief, security assistance, nation assistance, support to counterdrug operations, combating terrorism, peacekeeping operations, peace enforcement, show of force, support for insurgencies and counterinsurgencies, and attacks and raids as examples.[6]

While the traditional principles of war remained relevant to all military operations, the unique nature of OOTW, particularly its political considerations, suggested to many that a refined list of principles of OOTW separate and distinct from the traditional principles of war would be useful. Thus, the new FM 100-5 delineated six principles of OOTW: objective, unity of effort, security, restraint, perseverance, and legitimacy.[7] The first three of these principles were derived from the generic principles of war, and the remaining three were OOTW specific.[8]

FM 100-5 acknowledged that "Army warfighting doctrine has long been based on well-established principles of war that have withstood the tests of time and experience and remain embedded in our doctrine." However, it argued that "operations other than war also have principles that guide our actions." Part of the rationale for a separate set of principles of OOTW appears to have been based on OOTWs involving combat and noncombat actions. For OOTWs involving direct combat, the FM stated that the traditional principles of war applied. The principles of objective and security were considered to apply equally to combat and noncombat operations. The manual contended the traditional principle of war of unity of command required modification to unity of effort to meet the demands of OOTW. Three other principles — perseverance, restraint, and legitimacy — were added as being "more suited to the noncombat operations that comprise most operations other than war."[9]

A brief explanation of each of the six principles of OOTW follows:

Objective

The principle of objective requires commanders to "direct every military operation toward a clearly defined, decisive, and attainable objective." Commanders must understand the strategic aims, set appropriate objectives, and ensure that these aims and objectives contribute to unity of effort. Inherent in the principle of objective is the need to understand what constitutes mission success and what might cause the operation to be terminated before success is achieved.[10]

The importance of political considerations in OOTW is very apparent in the principle of objective. In many cases, the political objectives upon which military objectives are based may not specifically address the desired military end state. Therefore, commanders must translate their political guidance into appropriate military objectives through a rigorous and continuous mission and threat analysis. They should carefully explain to political authorities the implications of political decisions on capabilities and risk to military forces.

Although defining mission success may be more difficult in OOTW, it is important to do so to keep U.S. forces focused on a clear, attainable military objective. Specifying measures of effectiveness helps define mission accomplishment and phase transitions, but objectively assessing progress is problematic. Still, event-based objectives are far superior to time-based ones.

Measuring and achieving objectives is further compounded by a phenomenon known as mission creep or mission change. Changes to initial military objectives may occur because political and military leaders gain a better understanding of the situation or because the situation itself changes. Commanders must remain aware of shifts in the political objectives, or in the situation itself, that necessitate a change in the military objective. These changes may be very subtle, yet they still require adjustment of the military objectives. If this adjustment is not made, the military objectives may no longer support the political objectives, legitimacy may be undermined, and force security may be compromised.[11]

Unity of Effort

The OOTW principle of unity of effort is derived from the traditional principle of war, unity of command. It emphasizes the need for ensuring all means are directed to a common purpose. However, in OOTW, achieving unity of effort is often complicated by a variety of international, foreign, and domestic military and non-military participants, the lack of definitive command arrangements among them, and varying views of the objective. This dynamic requires that commanders rely heavily on consensus building to achieve unity of effort.[12]

Soldiers very familiar with the hierarchical nature of the military chain of command may be more challenged by the less formal relationship inherent in working with coalition partners, non-governmental organizations (NGOs), civilian agencies, other governmental agencies, and local authorities that permeates OOTW. The emphasis in such an environment is on unity of effort through cooperation rather than command.[13] Strong interpersonal skills usually are required to achieve this principle.

Security

The oftentimes nebulous, confusing, and changing nature of the threat makes security a particular challenge in OOTW. This OOTW principle requires commanders to never permit hostile factions to acquire a military, political, or informational advantage. In many OOTWs, this advantage comes from external support to an insurgent group. Commanders must be vigilant against complacency and be ready to counter activity that could bring harm to units or jeopardize the operation. All personnel should stay alert even in a non-hostile operation with little or no perceived risk. Inherent in this responsibility is the need to plan for and posture the necessary capability to quickly transition to combat should circumstances change.[14]

Operations other than war also pose particular operational security requirements based on media coverage as well as the need to provide security for civilians or participating agencies and organizations. The perceived neutrality of these protected elements may be a factor in their security. Protection of an NGO or Private Volunteer Organization (PVO) by U.S. military forces may create the perception that the NGO or PVO is pro–U.S. Therefore, an NGO or PVO may be reluctant to accept the U.S. military's protection.

Restraint

Restraint requires military capability be applied prudently. Especially in OOTW, a single act, even at the tactical level, can cause significant strategic military and political consequences. Restraint is closely tied to other principles of OOTW. It requires the careful balancing of the need for security, the conduct of operations, and the political objective. Excessive force antagonizes those parties involved, thereby damaging the legitimacy of the organization that uses it while possibly enhancing the legitimacy of the opposing party.[15]

Because of the importance of restraint, rules of engagement (ROE) in OOTW are generally more restrictive, detailed, and sensitive to political concerns than in war. Restraint is best achieved when ROE issued at the beginning of an operation address most anticipated situations that may arise. Rules of engagement should be consistently reviewed and revised as necessary. Additionally, ROE should be carefully scrutinized to ensure that the lives and health of military personnel involved in OOTW are not needlessly endangered. Even within the strictest ROE, the soldier's inherent right to self-defense must always be maintained.[16]

Perseverance

Perseverance means preparing for the measured, protracted application of military capability in support of strategic aims. Some OOTWs may require years to achieve the desired results. The underlying causes of the crisis may be elusive, making it difficult to achieve decisive resolution. It is important to assess possible responses to a crisis in terms of each option's impact on the achievement of the long-term political objective. This assessment does not preclude decisive military action but frames that action within the larger context of strategic aims.[17]

Often, the patient, resolute, and persistent pursuit of national goals and objectives, for as long as necessary to achieve them, is a requirement for success. This strategy will often involve political, diplomatic, economic, and informational measures to supplement military efforts.[18]

Legitimacy

Forces committed in an OOTW must sustain the legitimacy of the operation and of the host government, where applicable. Participants must be especially sensitive because legitimacy is a condition based on the perception by a specific audience of the legality, morality, or rightness of a set of actions. This perception may be completely different than the actual intention of the action. If an operation is perceived as legitimate, there is a strong impulse to support the action. If an operation is not perceived as legitimate, the actions may not be supported and may be actively resisted.[19]

Legitimacy may depend on adherence to objectives agreed to by the international community, ensuring the action is appropriate to the situation, and fairness in dealing with various factions. It may be reinforced by restraint in the use of force, the type of forces employed, and the disciplined conduct of the forces involved.

Domestically, the perception of legitimacy by the U.S. public is strengthened if there are obvious national or humanitarian interests at stake, and if there is assurance that American lives are not being needlessly or carelessly risked. The loss of domestic support can demand the termination of an operation, even in spite of battlefield success.

Another aspect of this principle is the legitimacy bestowed upon a government through the perception of the populace that it governs. Because the populace perceives that the government has genuine authority to govern and uses proper agencies for valid purposes, they consider that government as legitimate.[20]

The American withdrawal from Vietnam was precipitated by the loss of legitimacy on the home front as evidenced by anti-war protests, such as this 1967 march on the Pentagon, rather than any battlefield defeat. Photograph taken by Frank Wolfe. Lyndon Baines Johnson Library.

By one count, U.S. forces conducted eighty-one OOTWs between 1945 and 1999.[21] This book focuses on eight of these and analyzes them using the principles of OOTW found in FM 100-5. The cases represent a mix of successes and failures, and are drawn from various periods during and after the Cold War. Each example confirms the utility of FM 100-5's principles of OOTW as planning and analytical tools.

A brief introduction to each case study follows:

Greek Civil War (1947–1949)

In the chaos of World War II, a communist insurgency developed in Greece that threatened democracy there in the post-war era. In response to the Truman Doctrine, the United States established the Joint United States Military Advisory and Planning Group (JUSMAPG), a group of 350 advisors led by Lieutenant General James Van Fleet. As a result of the efforts of the JUSMAPG and the Greek Army, the communist insurgency was defeated, and Greece remained democratic.

Lebanon (1958)

In 1958, Lebanon was plagued by an internal crisis resulting from its factionalized society and from superpower regional competition. The pro–Western government of President Camille Chamoun was threatened and requested U.S. assistance under the Eisenhower Doctrine. The U.S. responded with a deployment of some 14,000 army troops and marines.

Dominican Republic (1965–1966)

On September 25, 1963, a coup deposed democratically elected Juan Bosch Gavino, president of the Dominican Republic, and replaced him with a civilian junta known as the Triumvirate, which came to be led by Donald Reid Cabral. Dissatisfaction with Reid and lingering loyalties to Bosch plunged the Dominican Republic into revolution in April 1965. The U.S. intervened with a force of over 40,000 army troops and marines to safeguard American lives and prevent the Dominican Republic from becoming communist. In 1966, former President Joaquin Balaguer, with the support of the U.S. government, was elected president, and the Dominican Republic entered a period of relative stability.

Vietnam (1967–1973)

Although, the U.S. formally had ground combat troop involvement in Vietnam from 1965 to 1973, this study will focus on the American pacification efforts in Vietnam. Accordingly, it will emphasize the period beginning in 1967 when the Civil Operations and Revolutionary Development Support (CORDS) was established in an effort to coordinate all pacification efforts. Pacification was viewed by many as a secondary effort that drew resources away from the "big war." It never was able to achieve its objectives of strengthening peasant support for the South Vietnamese government and seriously weakening the Viet Cong infrastructure. The U.S. withdrew from Vietnam in 1973, and North Vietnam ultimately defeated South Vietnam in 1975.

Honduras and Nicaragua (1980–1990)

In 1979, the Sandinista National Liberation Front overthrew pro–U.S. President Anastasio Somoza Debayle and initiated a leftist regime in Nicaragua with close ties to Cuba. Prohibited from direct combat action by a strong public sentiment to not enter into "another Vietnam," President Ronald Reagan executed a prolonged indirect campaign to strengthen Honduras and eliminate the communist threat in Nicaragua. The sustained pressure eventually persuaded the Sandinistas to agree to a cease fire, and President Daniel Ortega was forced to liberalize his government. He consented to hold a presidential election on February 25, 1990, and was defeated by Violeta Chamorro.

Beirut (1982–1983)

On September 29, 1982, the 32nd Marine Amphibious Unit (MAU) arrived in Beirut, Lebanon as part of a multinational peacekeeping force. The initial contingent received a warm welcome, but subsequent MAUs became caught up in the regional geopolitical rivalries and lost their perception of neutrality and legitimacy with segments of the local population. Pursuing a nebulous objective to "establish a presence," the adjustments made to the marines' mission, location, rules of engagement, force protection measures, and security posture were inadequate in light of the changing situation and made the Americans a vulnerable target. On October 23, 1983, 241 U.S. servicemen died in a terrorist attack on the marines' headquarters and barracks.

Somalia (1992–1995)

Ethnic violence, drought, and famine created a humanitarian crisis in Somalia, and in December 1992 the United Nations Security Council approved Resolution 794, which established Unified Task Force (UNITAF), a large, U.S.-led peace enforcement operation. UNITAF generally avoided provocative actions with the rival Somali warlords and succeeded in ending the humanitarian crisis. In mid–February 1993, U.S. Army forces began withdrawing, and on May 4, UNOSOM II took over operations from UNITAF. UNOSOM II attempted to take on a more ambitious mandate than UNITAF, despite having fewer and lower quality troops. In October 1993, a failed U.S. effort to capture warlord Mohammed Farrah Hassan Aideed ended in eighteen American deaths. The fiasco led to the Clinton administration's decision to withdraw U.S. troops by March 1994. The U.S. withdrawal compelled the UN to terminate UNOSOM II and withdraw all peacekeepers by March 1995. Somalia quickly returned to the chaotic state it had been in during mid–1992.

Haiti (1993)

On September 30, 1991, a military coup ousted Jean-Betrand Aristide, Haiti's first democratically elected president, and replaced him with Lieutenant General Raoul Cedras. Thousands of Haitians, seeking relief from Cedras's repressive regime as well as greater economic opportunity, fled in rickety boats seeking asylum in the United States. The United States began developing plans for either a forcible invasion to defeat the Haitian army or a deployment into a more permissive environment based on negotiations. As a result of the flawed Governor's Island Accord of July 3, 1993, a joint task force was deployed to Haiti to help facilitate a peaceful transfer of power from Cedras back to Aristide. On October 11 an unruly mob at Port-au-Prince prevented the USS *Harlan County* from unloading United Nations troops intended to retrain the Haitian Army and police. Unprepared to enter a non-permissive environment, the *Harlan County* withdrew, and the mission was abandoned. Although in October 1994, Cedras finally agreed to allow Aristide to return rather than face an imminent invasion, Haiti remains one of the world's most vivid examples of a failed state.

CHAPTER 1

The Greek Civil War: A Pretty Good Balance

With the end of World War II, erstwhile allies the United States and the Soviet Union entered a Cold War in which both competed to expand their influence. Greece proved to be the first battleground in this new era, and the Truman Doctrine articulated the U.S. interests there. Pursuant to these national security objectives, on February 7, 1948, Lieutenant General James Van Fleet was appointed commander of the Joint United States Military Advisory and Planning Group (JUSMAPG) and sent to Greece to help the Greek government battle a growing communist insurgency. This intervention highlights the OOTW principle of security because of the necessity of isolating the insurgents from their external bases of support. It also demonstrates the effective application of the principles of objective, unity of effort, and perseverance, as well as the satisfactory application of legitimacy and restraint. As a result of this OOTW, the U.S. accomplished its objective of securing Greece from the communist threat.

Background

The aftermath of World War II left Greece and many other European countries destitute and ideologically confused. The three and a half years of German occupation of Greece were ones of despair, collaboration, inflation, hunger, and oppression. In the process, the population suffered social, economic, and political disintegration. It was a situation that left Greece very vulnerable to the spread of communism.[1] This problem was exacerbated by the inadequate size of the 26,500-man British liberation force and Greece's proximity to countries that had fallen into the Soviet satellite system. The small size of the British force meant that it could physically station soldiers only in Athens, Piraeus, and a handful of other cities and communications centers to "show the flag." Otherwise, the country remained under the control of existing guerrilla armies.[2] The key communist organization that had developed during the German occupation was the EAM or National Liberation Front. The military arm of the EAM was the ELAS or National People's Liberation Army. As the Germans withdrew, ELAS had seized large quantities of arms and ammunition that were left behind.[3]

The ELAS benefited greatly from the Red Army's presence and Soviet influence around Greece. On the Albanian border, ELAS made contact with Albanian Communist Party resistance leader Enver Hoxha's guerrillas. In exchange for ELAS handing over some Albanian war criminals, a unit of Albanian guerrillas was placed under ELAS command. On the Yugoslav frontier, the ELAS moved forward into the old frontier posts and buildings wherever it could. To the east, four divisions of the ELAS northern corps moved into Thrace and Macedonia when the Bulgarian Army departed. Edgar O'Ballance notes that with these developments, "ELAS was in effective control of the greater part of northern Greece."[4]

At the time of liberation, ELAS strength was roughly 50,000 armed fighters. The communists quickly noted the inadequate size of the British liberation force and were successful in seizing physical possession of practically the entire countryside of continental Greece. The British were only able to control those cities where they could physically station troops.[5]

With this upper hand, the KKE, or Communist Party of Greece, decided that the time to strike for power had come, and it switched its strategy from one of infiltration and political intrigue to one of force. A massive EAM demonstration against the government was called for in Athens to be followed by a general strike. The demonstration took place on December 2, 1944, and two days later, ELAS and British troops were involved in shooting clashes in the streets of Athens. The British were woefully outnumbered, and within weeks they became isolated in the center of Athens.[6]

The desperate situation required Britain to send reinforcements, and, with the influx of this additional strength, conditions stabilized. By the arrival of the new year in 1945, the tide had turned in the British favor in Athens and Piraeus. The guerrillas' military setback was followed by a political one as two prominent socialist leaders in the EAM broke away from the coalition and formed their own parties.[7]

Thus weakened, the EAM was in a poor bargaining position when it met with British delegates in Varkiza on February 2. The Varkiza Agreement of February 12 included a provision to completely demobilize and disarm the ELAS. The main body of the ELAS was peacefully disarmed and disbanded, but thousands of ex–ELAS extremists escaped across the border into Yugoslavia, Albania, and Bulgaria. These embittered ex–ELAS leaders were the inspiration for and the nucleus of the DAS or Democratic People's Army which came into being as the result of a Politburo-level meeting in Bulgaria in December 1945. At this meeting, members of the Central Committee of the KKE and representatives of the Yugoslav and Bulgarian general staffs agreed to reorganize an insurgent army to fight the Greek government.[8]

Initial actions centered in the north, especially in Macedonia and Thrace, where the rugged mountains favored guerrilla tactics. The communist forces, which never surpassed 28,000, were overwhelmingly outnumbered by the 265,000 troops of the Greek National Army (GNA) and Gendarmerie, or national police force. To partially offset this numerical inferiority, the DAS received substantial military aid and advice from Yugoslavia, Albania, and Bulgaria. With this assistance, the guerrillas had an advantage in morale, tactics, terrain, and, to some extent, talent. They also benefited from the GNA pursuit of a static defensive strategy, which was inappropriate against a guerrilla enemy, and the often ineffective GNA leadership. Within seven months, the DAS claimed to dominate three-fourths of Greece, and the GNA was left in disarray.[9]

To achieve this string of victories, the guerrillas had made full use of their cross-border sanctuaries. They would often attack the Greek Army and then flee to Yugoslavia or Albania, while the GNA would dutifully halt their pursuit at the border. The guerrillas would then reappear only after the army had evacuated the area. In an even more dastardly exploitation of their sanctuaries, the guerrillas abducted as many as 30,000 Greek children in order to force villagers to follow them as they retreated across the frontier.[10]

The problem was clearly beyond the resources of Britain, which was suffering from its own post-war economic shortages. On February 21, 1947, the British informed the U.S. that they were pulling out of Greece, and on March 3 the Greek government formally requested U.S. aid. On March 12, President Harry Truman announced the Truman Doctrine, which stated that "it must be the policy of the United States to support free peoples who are resisting attempted subjugation by armed minorities or by outside pressures." On May 22, Truman signed a bill authorizing $400 million in aid to Greece and Turkey. Additional authorizations followed, and by 1952, Greek forces had received $500 million in U.S. aid.[11] The Greek insurgency had also been defeated.

Analysis of the Principles

Objective

The principle of objective is applicable at the strategic, operational, and tactical levels of war. At the strategic level, military activities are planned to support national security objectives — in this case, the containment of communism as articulated by the Truman Doctrine. The American interest in Greece was understood to be vital. Secretary of State George Marshall explained, "The crisis has a direct and intimate relation to the security of the United States.... If Greece should dissolve into civil war it is altogether probable that it would emerge a communist state under Soviet control." After explaining the effect of this outcome on neighboring countries, Marshall concluded, "It is not alarmist to say that we are faced with the first crisis of a series which might extend Soviet domination to Europe, the Middle East, and Asia."[12]

However, in spite of the urgency of the situation in Greece, the Truman administration was committed to securing this objective without committing U.S. combat troops. In fact, one poll showed that only 25 percent of Americans favored dispatching troops to Greece, even "if it appeared that Russia might get control" of Greece.[13] An American invasion of Greece was never considered a viable option.

Because accomplishment of the U.S. strategic objective was so influenced by the principle of restraint, Van Fleet's tactical objective was to train and reorganize the Greek Army to be an effective fighting force. Realizing that no significant progress could be made until this transformation was accomplished, Van Fleet made it his first objective to correct what C. M. Woodhouse, the British Army officer who had served as the commander of the Allied Military Mission to the Greek Resistance, described as a situation characterized by a mixture of "defeatism and complacency."[14] The British had incorrectly assumed a long period of peaceful transition in which most security problems could be handled by the police. Van Fleet would have to reverse what Woodhouse assessed as the resulting "half-hearted and misdirected" British training effort.[15] In the process, however, Van Fleet had to be extremely sensitive to the principle of legitimacy in order to avoid charges that the U.S. was merely using the Greeks to fight for U.S. interests. Once the Greek Army had been improved, Van Fleet could turn his attention to his operational objective of isolating the communists from their external support across the border. Van Fleet had astutely identified this capability as the communist center of gravity, and success in eliminating this situation would lead to ultimate victory.

Restraint

The U.S. adopted a pragmatic approach to the principle of restraint in Greece. The decision to dispatch just 350 advisors rather than a large combat force was an obvious reflection of restraint. Robert Mages boasts that JUSMAPG accomplished its mission "without the need of a single American rifleman."[16] It should be noted, though, that as the civil war proceeded, American advisors found themselves increasingly active and were often on the front lines. Van Fleet himself was twice lost in enemy territory, and an American pilot flying a reconnaissance mission was shot down and killed.[17] Still, the U.S. made a conscious decision not to commit sizeable numbers of ground troops to Greece.

One reason for this restraint was the fear that the Soviets would feel compelled to match any large U.S. presence, with the end result being "a big war."[18] In fact, the initial U.S. response was so restrained as to be ineffective. Major General William Livesay, the first JUSMAPG commander, was not allowed to even provide operational advice to the Greek Army. The U.S. effort became a largely logistical one, causing Queen Frederica to complain to Secretary of State Marshall that Greece needed a "fighting general" rather than a "supply sergeant."[19]

On other matters, the U.S. showed less adherence to restraint, such as its toleration of aggressive Greek population control measures. Before the U.S. arrival, Greek officials had begun effective but harsh tactics to separate the guerrillas from the people. Government-backed paramilitary organizations alternately had protected and terrorized the population to isolate it as a source of aid to the communists. Communist supporters were arrested by the thousands, and some were executed while others were sent to remote internment camps, often without trials. In areas of particular insurgent activity, entire populations were forcibly evacuated to eliminate the communists' base of support.[20]

The application of the principles of OOTW must be properly balanced, and in some cases trade-offs must exist among the principles. Many Greek military officials were willing to make some sacrifices regarding restraint in order to enhance security. After the watershed battle of Konista, which ended in a hard-fought government victory on January 4, 1948, there was a "moment of awakening" that resulted in "a total mobilization of resources." Men who thus far had evaded military service were conscripted, and communists were ruthlessly hunted down. Some fifty were executed in February alone.[21] By November, the Greek representative at the United Nations acknowledged that some 1,500 executions had occurred in the past two years.[22]

A good example of these strict measures is Operation Pigeon, which was initiated on December 19, 1948, to help curb the growing guerrilla presence in the Peloponnese. During the operation, the Greek corps commander "made his most decisive move" in ordering the arrest of some 4,500 suspected communist collaborators in the area. While the move showed little in the way of restraint, it had immediate positive effects on security. Freed from fears of guerrilla reprisals, the loyal local population began providing information to the Greek armed forces. Likewise, the arrests deprived the communist forces of their principal source of supplies and logistics.[23]

During the American Revolution, British officials believed that a similar circumstance existed in the Southern Theater. They assumed that a sizeable loyal Tory population was being intimidated by a small oppressive group of rebels, and if those rebels could be suppressed, the loyalists would publicly support the Crown, and pacification would accelerate. James Simpson reported to the British commander, "I am of the opinion whenever the King's Troops move to Carolina they will be assisted by very considerable numbers of the inhabitants.... If the terror [the rebels] have excited was once removed, a few months would restore this country to its former good government." However, Simpson cautioned, "Unless the government was to be so firmly established as to give security to them without protection of the Army ... the success would be far from complete. And if upon a future emergency, the Troops were withdrawn ... they should suffer."[24]

After some initial success, the British commander Lieutenant General Henry Clinton failed to heed Simpson's advice about maintaining a continued troop presence and departed South Carolina on June 5, 1780, returning to New York and taking about one-third of his force with him. He left Lieutenant General Charles Cornwallis behind with about 8,000 troops; far too few to control the large area.[25] To make matters worse, British excesses, such as those of Lieutenant Colonel Banastre Tarleton at the May 29, 1780, Battle of Wax-haws, alienated the local population and violated the principle of restraint. As a consequence, the insurgency grew rather than declined.

The Greeks and the U.S. avoided these pitfalls in obtaining an effective balance between security and restraint. Like the British in the American Revolution, the Greeks suffered from a paucity of forces, but they solved the problem by conducting Operation Pigeon in two sequential phases, clearing the Peloponnese region systematically from north to south in a deliberately slow and methodical manner. Furthermore, the Greeks resisted the temptation to divert units away from the Peloponnese to other areas such as Karpenissi in central Greece.[26]

Nonetheless, these efforts to improve security entailed some lack of restraint. Frank Abbott notes, "The mass arrests preceding the Peloponnese operation were certainly not in the best traditions of a democratic society. The arrests, however, were necessary for the people's sense of security, and thus necessary for the success of the operation."[27] The Greek people apparently were willing to accept the Greek government's taking some liberties with restraint in order to provide security, thus allowing the government to "reassert its control over the principal instruments of state."[28]

As far as the Americans were concerned, they were able to reap the benefits of this enhanced security at the expense of restraint without the loss of legitimacy that the British had suffered from the atrocities committed by Tarleton. Because the Americans practiced restraint in not involving their own troops in combat operations, they did not become the target of backlash that the British did. Instead, the U.S. enjoyed the best of both worlds, officially protesting the use of terror, mass arrests, and population relocation, but in many ways condoning the actions in the belief that drastic situations required drastic measures. Secretary of State Marshall, for example, felt "that stern and determined measures, although of course not excesses, may be necessary to effect the termination of the activities of the guerrillas and their supporters as speedily as possible."[29] Major General Stephen Chamberlin, whom the Pentagon had detailed to study the situation in Greece, believed that the "ruthless removal or destruction of food and shelter in the mountain villages would compel all but insignificant guerrilla forces to either retire to the frontiers or accept combat in the valleys and plains under adverse conditions."[30] Van Fleet was of the opinion that "the only good communist is a dead one," and he approved of mass arrests and population relocations.[31] The U.S. restrained itself by limiting the size and function of JUSMAPG and was able to disassociate itself from the less restrained actions of the Greek Army while still benefiting from the increased security. It was a delicate balance that had eluded the British when they were battling the American insurgency.

Legitimacy

The legitimacy of the U.S. intervention in Greece benefited from the presence of the United Nations Special Committee on the Balkans (UNSCOB), the first attempt by the UN to deploy an observation mission in the midst of an armed conflict. For the U.S., the UNSCOB was "a valuable opportunity to expose communist subversion and provide political support for the recently communicated Truman Doctrine."[32] Indeed in his March 12, 1947, message, President Truman attempted to give legitimacy to his policy by saying, "A Commission appointed by the United Nations Security Council is at present investigating disturbed conditions in northern Greece, and alleged border violations along the frontier between Greece on the one hand, and Albania, Bulgaria, and Yugoslavia on the other."[33]

Throughout its existence, the UNSCOB was the source of controversy between the democratic and communist UN members. The original proposal to establish an investigative commission to look into the violence along the Greek-Albanian border was vetoed by the USSR in August 1946. Then in December, Greece brought the complaint before the Security Council, and the U.S. repeated the earlier proposal. For reasons that remain unclear, this

United Nations Special Committee on the Balkans members observing the Yugoslav frontier area on May 1, 1949. British observer John Jeffrey is in civilian clothes looking through binoculars. Mr. Monsalve, a Mexican observer, is at left forefront. Behind an unknown soldier with rifle is a Greek liaison officer at left; person in background is unidentified. **Courtesy United Nations.**

time the USSR acquiesced to the commission. C. E. Black speculated that Soviet acceptance "may have been regarded as a necessary concession to public opinion."[34] In spite of this acquiescence, the USSR proceeded to repeatedly veto resolutions based on the commission's findings of Albanian, Yugoslav, and Bulgarian support to the Greek guerrillas.

In the ongoing diplomatic battle, the U.S. was able to move the matter from the Security Council to the General Assembly to avoid a Soviet veto, and on October 21, 1947, the UN created the eleven-member UNSCOB. The organization's legitimacy remained an issue as two of the nations appointed to the body, Poland and the USSR, refused to participate, and it was plagued by a lack of cooperation from the neighboring communist governments, which refused to allow it to operate in their territories. Nonetheless,

> UNSCOB observers demonstrated conclusively that Yugoslavia, Albania, and Bulgaria not only provided the Greek guerrillas with arms, ammunition, food, and other equipment and supplies, but that they also opened their borders to the guerrillas and permitted the [DAS] to conduct tactical maneuvers and even to support their operations by fire from positions located inside their territory.[35]

Such testimonies from a neutral international body served to validate the legitimacy of the American support for Greece in the face of external aggression. The UNSCOB functioned until December 7, 1951, when it was dissolved by the General Assembly and replaced on January 23, 1952, by a Balkan Sub-Commission of the standing Peace Observation Commission.[36]

While the UNSCOB helped the U.S. establish its international legitimacy, the latter also had to contend with legitimacy within Greece itself. In any civil war, the legitimacy of the government is being challenged by a rival internal group, and any assistance to the government that undermines its legitimacy, strengthens the rival's challenge to that legitimacy. The U.S. had to be careful, as it extended assistance, that it did not give the impression that Greece was merely a means to a larger American Cold War national security end. This potential threat to legitimacy was expressed by a Greek lieutenant who said, "This war in Greece is a battle between the United States and Russia. It happens that it's being fought here. That's our bad luck."[37]

Such opinions notwithstanding, from the very outset, the U.S. had a measure of legitimacy because its involvement came at the behest of the Greek government. Once Britain notified Greece that it could not provide the level of support the situation required, the Greek government formally asked American Ambassador Lincoln MacVeagh for U.S. support in March 1947. It was a delicate transition as the Greeks had become "accustomed to the British" and now faced the prospect of "an uncertain quantity" in the Americans.[38] Dwight Griswold, chief of the American Mission for Aid to Greece, assured Greece that, although the U.S. would be extending operational advice, American officers would "not be taking command" of Greek forces and that the American intent was to assist the Greeks "so that they can pick up the job and do it themselves."[39] Still, Woodhouse believed that, relative to the British, the Americans were "more inflexible, less adaptable, less willing to make allowances, more inclined to impose American methods regardless of national characteristics."[40] These tendencies would be a constant threat to legitimacy.

Realizing this situation, Griswold always considered legitimacy to be critical. He had the delicate task of making discreet recommendations to the Greek government while giving the outward impression that the Greeks themselves were the source of any policy reforms. Griswold had to be especially subtle concerning personnel actions. He would put quiet pressure on the Greeks to remove uncooperative and incompetent senior officials, but he had to avoid the public perception that he was subsuming Greek authority.[41]

When JUSMAPG was established on December 31, it was given the mission "to assist the Greek Armed Forces in achieving internal security in Greece at the earliest possible date."[42] The clear emphasis was on the U.S. effort supporting the Greek effort, rather than the U.S. assuming authority and responsibility for the situation. Forrest Pogue noted that "Van Fleet could observe and give advice, but he had no authority to command."[43]

Thus, Van Fleet recognized from the very beginning that the war had to be waged in such a way that victory would come from the efforts of the Greeks themselves. He facilitated the legitimacy of the Greek government in the eyes of its people by arguing that civil affairs programs had to be included in the anti-guerrilla effort. Even more specifically, he refused to build the Greek Army to be a miniature American Army, instead maintaining the character of the indigenous force while at the same time being sensitive to its inherent capabilities and limitations.[44]

Van Fleet's emphasis on civil affairs reflected a recognition of the importance of "winning the hearts and minds" of the Greek people. He believed it was critical that the Greek government "generate a furious love of freedom, a high morale among the civilians on the home front as well as within the armed forces ... at the front."[45] Van Fleet's assessment was consistent with a joint British/U.S. report from November 1947 that concluded "greater attention must be paid to the rapid rehabilitation of liberated areas, so that the people in these areas feel that the government has their well-being at heart."[46] Consequently, JUSMAPG recommended that once the Greek Army cleared an area of guerrillas, a robust civil affairs program follow to bring economic and social assistance to the area. With U.S. aid, the Greek government initiated a series of public works projects that provided employment and assistance to refugees. While the programs sometimes lacked the necessary scope and coordination to truly transform the Greek countryside, they did serve as a visible sign to the people that the government was acting on their behalf.[47]

In his care to create a Greek Army suitable for the specific conditions in Greece rather than modeling it after the U.S. Army, Van Fleet avoided a mistake made later by U.S. advisors in Vietnam. There, Lieutenant General John O'Daniel, the first chief of the American advisory effort, insisted on a U.S.-style organization in order to facilitate American logistical support. The result was "a nifty miniature copy of the U.S. military establishment."[48] This early emphasis on "Americanization" did not prove beneficial to the later requirement for "Vietnamization" and illustrated the dangers of assuming that what worked for the United States would also work for the nation the United States was assisting. A RAND Note entitled "Countering Covert Aggression" would indicate that this was not an isolated problem. The report cited general assistance shortcomings such as

> the US propensity to shape Third World forces too closely in the image of US forces, which have not been designed for counterinsurgency warfare; to provide Third World forces with high-technology weapons and equipment that are too costly for and ill-suited to local capabilities and likely battlefield requirements; and to make Third World a situation that could seriously impair local capabilities in the event of US aid cutbacks.[49]

Instead, in Greece, the U.S. provided mortars, machine guns, and pack artillery, which were suitable for mountainous operations, rather than tanks and heavy artillery, which would be of only limited utility. Van Fleet eschewed

Prior to becoming the US Ambassador to Greece, Henry Grady had a distinguished career as an economist and diplomat which included service as the assistant secretary of state, the vice president of the Allied Control Commission for Italy, and the ambassador to India. Photograph by Harris & Ewing. Library of Congress.

technology for its own sake and took such measures as reducing the number of motorized vehicles assigned to infantry battalions in order to prevent combat units from being road-bound. To facilitate the type of mobility needed in the particular environment of Greece, he equipped seven horse cavalry squadrons. In fact, the U.S. Army gave its Greek counterpart more mules than trucks.[50] Such actions indicate Van Fleet's careful adherence to the principle of legitimacy while assisting the Greek Army.

Unity of Effort

For some observers, the open-ended nature of the Truman Doctrine's commitment to Greece posed a threat to unity of effort. Shortly after replacing MacVeagh as U.S. Ambassador to Greece, Henry Grady noticed an assumption among the Greeks that they could "expect to live indefinitely on American bounty." When asked if he thought the Greeks were "holding back" in their war efforts "in order to get more dollars from the US," Grady tellingly replied, "No comment."[51] Woodhouse explained the Greek perspective as being that the need for resources and capabilities was so great, "the Greeks were tempted to meet them by demanding more aid from the USA, and by resigning the management of their affairs into American hands."[52]

Many Americans saw a similar situation in Iraq in 2007. As the Senate prepared to vote on a withdrawal timeline, Senator Ted Kennedy argued not only that the U.S. military "should not police Iraq's civil war indefinitely," but also that a deadline to withdraw U.S. troops was "the only realistic way to encourage the Iraqis to take responsibility for their future."[53] As did some observers in Greece, Kennedy saw an open-ended U.S. commitment in Iraq as being a disincentive to unity of effort, specifically to the Iraqis doing their share.

While Grady dealt with the problem of the Greeks' willingness to contribute, Van Fleet set out to improve their capability to do so by retraining and reorganizing the Greek Army.[54] To accomplish this objective, Van Fleet attached American officers to the Greek General Staff, to each corps headquarters, and to the headquarters of each fighting division. A major benefit of this dispersion was to ensure that general staff orders were being carried out. A contemporary report noted that previously, top level plans "invariably have been changed by politicians somewhere along the line. Political control of the 132,000-man army has been so great that members of Parliament often have vetoed military orders, had army units stationed in their own areas regardless of military need elsewhere."[55] This phenomenon had contributed to the defensive strategy thus far employed by the Greeks. Van Fleet and his men retrained the Greeks "to fight a mobile, offensive war instead of simply garrisoning key towns and villages — a policy which in the past had left most of the countryside at the mercy of hit-and-run raids."[56] His charge to the Greeks was "Get out and fight!"[57]

Van Fleet also endeavored to reorganize the GNA at the highest levels in order to decentralize command and to encourage greater initiative on the part of field commanders. The field army was reorganized into five corps instead of three. In the past, each corps commander had been directly responsible to the National Defense Council for operations. Now they would come under the control of the Chief of the General Staff. Van Fleet was "quick to see which of the Greek commanders were competent and which owed their appointments to political intrigue."[58] He was able to help generate a reshuffling of senior Greek officers, involving the gradual replacement of less efficient and less energetic commanders and staff officers.[59] In facilitating these changes, Van Fleet maintained the same inconspicuous but influential role pioneered by Griswold.[60]

Lieutenant General James A. Van Fleet (left-center) and Vice Admiral Forrest P. Sherman, Commander Sixth Task Fleet (right-center) join other dignitaries at a parade honoring the 128th anniversary of Greek independence at Athens, Greece, in March 1949. Naval Historical Center.

The most notable of these personnel moves occurred on February 25, 1949, when "with Van Fleet's hearty approval," General Alexander Papagos, the hero of the Greek victories in the Albanian campaign of 1940, became Greece's Commander-in-Chief.[61] Part of Papagos's conditions for accepting this post was a streamlining of the National Defense Council. With Papagos firmly in charge, GNA operations could proceed according to a coordinated central strategy that would allow "the country to be treated as a whole and to be swept through from south to north."[62]

Van Fleet also discovered that it was not just the hierarchy of the Greek Army that required attention. There was also a shortage of trained junior officers, and to correct this problem he set up training schools to increase the supply. In so doing, Van Fleet had to massage the Greek sense of pride, which was slow to admit that more training was needed.[63] To obtain unity of effort, Van Fleet would also have to maintain legitimacy, and through diplomatic yet persistent measures, he was able to build a Greek fighting force with which the Americans could cooperate. Woodhouse overstated the case, but it was a credit to Van Fleet's sensitivity to legitimacy that Woodhouse assessed that the Greek Army's tactical reformation was "devised by Greek initiative, with no more than moral support from JUSMAPG."[64]

Security

As a result of these efforts, Edward Wainhouse concluded that by the end of 1948, "the initiative had passed to the GNA and a confident, more experienced, and better trained national army was ready to launch its offensive in the spring of 1949."[65] With this improved Greek fighting force, Van Fleet could pursue his operational objective of moving to seal off the guerrillas from their lines of communication on Greece's northern border.[66] Such external support has historically been a condition essential to the success of an insurgent movement.[67] The ability of the communists to move freely back and forth to their cross-border sanctuary represented a failure to adhere to the principle of security. To correct this situation, Van Fleet and the Greeks launched an offensive in the fall of 1948, which involved clearing operations beginning in the south and moving northwards. This process would drive the guerrillas back to their main base in the Grammos-Vitsi region, where the final blow would be struck.[68] The campaign began with Operation Pigeon when Greek army, navy, and police forces cleared much of the Peloponnese and deprived the communists of critical logistical and intelligence support.[69] The operation was conducted with the utmost secrecy, including such precautions as cutting telephone wires to Athens and arresting 4,500 suspected communists.[70]

With this development, the Greek Army could now secure its lines of communication and prevent the enemy from re-infiltrating areas that had already been cleared.[71] The results were dramatic. By March 16, 1949, the Greek government was able to announce that the Peloponnese was completely clear of guerrillas and the Greek Army could thus be released for operations on the mainland. This capability was first exercised in the mountain ranges to the north and northwest of Athens. The GNA units were used to seize and hold passes and peaks while the LOK (mountain commando companies) and other infantry battalions trained in antiguerrilla warfare spread outwards in movements to contact.[72] As a result, the Peloponnese to the south and the Roumeli region of central Greece were now "cleared ... once for all."[73]

In the meantime, the conflict between Yugoslav President Josip Tito and Soviet Premier Joseph Stalin greatly benefited the Greeks, so much so that Andreas Papandreou calls it "the turning point in the civil war."[74] As soon as it became clear that Moscow was in control of the Greek Communist Party, the independent-minded Tito wanted no part of the fight. On July 10, 1949, he announced his intention to progressively close his borders with Greece, a decision that greatly reduced the guerrillas' freedom of maneuver and caused Nikolaos Zachariadis, head of the KKE, "to turn from insurgent tactics to positional warfare."[75] Papandreou writes that this development "more than anything else doomed the guerrillas."[76] Zachariadis's decision was actually the end result of a long struggle between Zachariadis and military leader Markos Vafiadis. While Vafiadis wished to align the Greek communists with Tito, Zachariadis favored an association with Stalin. However, underlining their political differences was also a longstanding dispute over tactics.[77] Vafiadis favored waging a guerrilla war using hit and run tactics and avoiding decisive combat while Zachariadis advocated converting the DAS into a conventional force. The disagreement led to the relief of Vafiadis and six other high ranking DAS officials in January 1949.[78] While unity of effort was increasing among the Greeks and Americans, serious internal and external fissures were developing on the communist side.

With the departure of Yugoslav support, the guerrillas received increased assistance from Bulgaria and Romania, but the main center of DAS activity was Albania. Given this situation, Zachariadis massed 7,000 troops in the Vitsi Range region and another 5,000 to the south in the Grammos Range, hoping to launch offensive operations from these positions.[79] But since most of the other parts of Greece were now clear, the Greeks were able to concentrate six of their eight field divisions against the guerrillas in these areas. Sensing the changing circumstances, Van Fleet stated on June 23 that he was "very optimistic" about the situation and that he was "confident that [the Greek Army] can do the job by winter."[80]

On August 5, the Greeks initiated their attack on the Grammos Range, and on August 10 they attacked the Vitsi. Initially there was little progress. Then, slowly but surely, and largely thanks to fifty-one Curtiss Helldivers supplied by the U.S. to the Greek Air Force, the guerrillas fell back. By August 16, the last organized resistance in the Vitsi area had been overrun. On August 19, with support from the Helldivers, the GNA attacked the Grammos.

There the Greek communists had built a virtual "state of Grammos" with its own system of administration, education, justice, and communications.[81] The area was absolutely critical to the insurgency. Key to the attack was the seizure of the Starias and the Baroukas, the two main passes from the Grammos into Albania. These routes had been used so extensively by the communists during the previous few months that they were nicknamed the "Twin Boulevards to Athens." Placing blocking positions along likely avenues of approach to fix the guerrillas, on August 28 the Greeks seized the Starias and the Baroukas, and by August 30 they controlled the Grammos. Nonetheless, some 8,000 communists managed to escape into Albania.[82]

Curtiss SB2C-3 "Helldiver" bombers like this one played a small but critical part in supporting Greek attacks against communist strongholds. Naval Historical Center.

Although this victory was incomplete, the changing political landscape began to greatly benefit the Greeks. With Yugoslav aid drying up, the guerrillas had become dramatically dependent on Albania. However, Albania now had on its border a Greek Army that

> with US aid ... had been converted over-night from an ill-equipped, dispersed, and not-too-efficient army, into a formidable, well-equipped, competently led fighting force with guns, trucks, tanks, and over fifty modern aircraft. If Greece chose to swoop into Albania to try and encircle the Greek insurgent elements sheltering there, there was nothing the tiny, rag-tag Albanian Army could do to stop her.[83]

Being a pragmatist, Enver Hoxha, who by this time was the Albanian Prime Minister, announced on August 26 that all Greeks found in Albania would be disarmed and detained.[84] With their once formidable external support gone, on October 16, 1949, from a secret radio station in Romania, Greece's communist guerrilla leaders announced a "cease-fire" in order to "prevent the complete annihilation of Greece."[85]

Perseverance

This outcome reflected a U.S. willingness to persevere where the communists would not. As the communist insurgency had grown in Greece, the Soviet Union had been confident that, given time, the situation would deteriorate to the point where it was beyond the Greek government's ability to control. Often in an insurgency, time is on the side of the insurgents, who need merely to practice a strategy of exhaustion to wear out the limited government resources. Stalin understood this advantage, advising, "If it cannot be done today, it can be done tomorrow."[86] However, the decisive American action, articulated by the Truman Doctrine and practically manifested by JUSMAPG, played havoc with the Soviet timetable. The U.S. understood the Soviet attempt to use perseverance as a delaying tactic in the United Nations and thwarted the communist design by American perseverance.[87]

For Stalin, the Greek Civil War was one small battle in a larger Cold War and also was a subordinate concern in the Balkans to his power struggle with Tito.[88] Stalin was unwilling to commit excessive resources to an unsure endeavor, and pragmatically confided to Yugoslav leaders in early 1948, "What do you think, that Great Britain and the United States — the United States, the most powerful state in the world — will permit you to break their line of communication in the Mediterranean! Nonsense. And we have no navy." Stalin was willing to pluck low hanging fruit, but not willing to risk Soviet security in an uncertain and dangerous confrontation with the U.S.[89] When it came time to determine priorities, Yugoslav communist leader Svetozar

"Tempo" Vukmanović contended that the Soviet Union "had no interest what-ever in a victory of the people's revolutionary movement in Greece."[90] In fact, Woodhouse concludes his history of the struggle for Greece from 1941 to 1949 saying, "The rank and file of the KKE, and in particular its leaders, were expendable. Without a trace of compunction, Stalin let them go to their doom."[91] On the other hand, the Truman Doctrine had made Greece a priority, and by perseverance, the U.S. was able to sustain a commitment that the com-munists would not.

This is not to say that the American will to persevere was never in doubt. The most tenuous period occurred after the two principal operations of the spring and summer of 1948, Operations Dawn and Crown, failed to destroy the communist forces operating near Rumeli in central Greece and in Gram-mos near the northern border. When the bulk of the enemy was able to with-draw into Albania, both American and Greek enthusiasts had to count it as a "bitter disappointment."[92]

In the wake of this setback, many in Congress began calling for significant cuts in U.S. aid to Greece. Van Fleet knew the GNA still needed improving, but he also knew that he did not have the time to proceed slowly. It was this recognition that U.S. support would not be indefinite that led Van Fleet to develop his decisive strategy to isolate the guerrillas from their cross-border base in Albania with his attacks on the Grammos and Vitsi ranges in August 1949.[93] While the U.S. was willing to support Greece via the Truman Doctrine, it also wanted to see results. Van Fleet was politically aware enough to know that there were limits to the U.S. perseverance, and he developed a timetable that could accommodate U.S. resolve.

Conclusion

The U.S. intervention in Greece was a successful OOTW. It represents a mix of consistently strong adherence to some OOTWs and satisfactory adherence to others. It contained no cases of strong failure to adhere to any one principle. Because the JUSMAPG mission was advisory only, much of the adherence to the principles was dependent on the host nation. The com-bined effort of the Americans and the Greeks presents a strong case for a rela-tionship existing between the balanced application of the principles of OOTW and operational success.

American and Greek forces during the Greek Civil War exhibited strong adherence to the principles of objective, security, unity of effort, and perse-verance. The U.S. strategic objective was clearly articulated by the Truman Doctrine, and General Van Fleet and JUSMAPG adeptly derived operational and tactical objectives from it. With American support and advice, the Greek Government exhibited strong adherence to the principle of security by conducting military operations that, in conjunction with political developments in Yugoslavia, isolated the insurgents from their external support. The U.S. forces also adhered to the principle of security by eschewing a combat role themselves and maximizing force protection. General Van Fleet displayed exceptional interpersonal skills in establishing unity of effort between the advisors and their hosts, as well as encouraging the Greeks to make the personnel and tactical adjustments necessary to coordinate meaningful action. Because of the clearly stated national interest at stake and the acceptable cost of the American contribution, the U.S. was able to adhere to the principle of perseverance and sustain its commitment in Greece longer than the Soviets.

Adherence to the principles of legitimacy and restraint was satisfactory. Because the U.S. objective in Greece was so clearly based on U.S. interests, the intervention was subject to perceptions of illegitimacy in some circles in Greece. Van Fleet mitigated this vulnerability by conscious efforts to limit the U.S. role to an advisory one and ensure all actual decisions were made by the Greeks themselves. While the U.S. practiced restraint by not committing combat troops and by encouraging moderate behavior on the part of the Greeks, the Greeks themselves were willing to infringe on the population's civil liberties in pursuit of military operational expediency. Because the aggressive behavior came from the host nation and because most of the Greek citizens were willing to make sacrifices for the cause, there were few negative consequences associated with this loose application of restraint.

This analysis suggests relationships among several of the principles, both in terms of correlation and balanced application. The clearly stated and accepted strategic objective and the acceptable costs generated by restraint facilitated perseverance. The strongly U.S.-centric objective posed a challenge to host nation perceptions of legitimacy, but this threat was mitigated by a deliberate emphasis on unity of effort within Greece. The Greek forces made sacrifices with regard to restraint in order to enhance security. The U.S. support to the Greek Civil War is a good example of how the balanced application of the principles of OOTW can result in success.

CHAPTER 2

Lebanon: Following the Principles, but by Chance or Design?

Arab nationalism and the threat of communist expansion posed a threat to stability and U.S. interests in the Middle East. When Lebanon appeared ready to collapse into civil war, the Eisenhower Doctrine provided the justification for the deployment of a U.S. force, beginning on July 15, 1958. This intervention highlights the OOTW principle of security because the massive show of force served to thwart any significant unrest before it had a chance to develop. It also demonstrates the effective application of the principle of restraint. Adherence to the principles of objective, unity of effort, legitimacy, and perseverance were mixed. As a result of this OOTW, the U.S. accomplished its objective of preventing a civil war in Lebanon.

Background

The Suez Crisis of 1956 served both to diminish Western influence in the Middle East and to strengthen the forces of Arab nationalism led by Egypt's president, Gamal Abdul Nasser. When Nasser began accepting Soviet aid, Cold War sensibilities demanded an American response. The resulting diplomatic counteroffensive produced the Eisenhower Doctrine, a geographic extension of the Truman Doctrine that promised military and economic assistance to nations in danger of a communist-sponsored invasion or subversion. However, anti–Western and Pan-Arab sentiment were so high that the new policy received a decidedly cool reception in the Middle East. Only Lebanon agreed to the American offer, and even this acceptance was not without controversy. Many felt Lebanese President Camille Chamoun's support of the Eisenhower Doctrine was motivated more by a desire to facilitate an extra-constitutional move to succeed himself as president than by a genuine fear of foreign threat to Lebanon.[1]

Lebanon had a history of religious and ethnic divisions, and the current political suspicion certainly was nothing new. When Lebanon gained its independence in 1943, the republic's new leaders had hoped to accommodate its sectarian diversity with a "confessional system" by which popular representation was based on religious affiliation. Out of this arrangement emerged the traditional practice of selecting a Maronite Christian president, a Sunni Moslem premier, and a Shi'ite speaker of parliament. Allocations of parliamentary seats were likewise derived from the relative numerical strength of the religious communities in each electoral district. However, the system was based on percentages calculated from obsolete census data that did not reflect current increases in the Moslem population. The result was an over-representation of the Christian population that created a considerable imbalance of power and left any sitting government vulnerable to the major factions.[2] The Chamoun government was not immune to this dynamic and faced a serious challenge from the National Union Front (NUF), which was powerful enough to be considered "another government, existing side-by-side with the legally constituted authorities."[3]

After the Suez crisis, the Middle East continued to be rocked by a series of developments that were contrary to American interests. On April 13, 1957, within a month of Congress approving the Eisenhower Doctrine, King Hussein of Jordan thwarted a pro–Nasser coup attempt. On February 1, 1958, Nasser and President al-Quwwatli of Syria announced the merger of their countries with Yemen to form the United Arab Republic (UAR), and Pan-Arabism rallies and riots broke out throughout the region, including Lebanon. On July 14, Iraq's King Faisal and Crown Prince Abdul Illah were assassinated in a coup led by General Abdel Karem Kassem, an Arab nationalist and UAR sympathizer. Simultaneously, rumors began circulating that another plot against King Hussein was developing. Fearing that he might be the next target, Chamoun appealed to Ambassador Robert McClintock to invoke the Eisenhower Doctrine. At 6:43 P.M. that same day, President Eisenhower directed that the initial marine contingent of a U.S. intervention force arrive at Beirut no later than 9:00 A.M. on July 15. Army troops would follow, and the total force on the ground would eventually number over 14,000 men.

Analysis of the Principles

Objective

The Eisenhower Doctrine provided the general strategic objective for the deployment of U.S. forces to Lebanon. In his January 5, 1957, message to Congress, Eisenhower had identified the need to provide "assistance and cooperation to include the employment of the armed forces of the United States to secure and protect the territorial integrity and political independence of [the nations of the Middle East], requesting such aid, against overt armed aggression from any nation controlled by International Communism."[4] Beyond this overarching objective, however, there was little in the way of a specific operational objective to help direct military action.

The deployment launched by President Eisenhower on July 14 was based on CINCAMBRITFOR OPLAN 1-58. This contingency plan was code-named Operation Bluebat and had two versions: The first involved American and British ground forces operating in concert and the second substituted U.S. Marines for the British contingent.[5] However, the planning emphasis of Bluebat appears to have been largely focused on building and deploying the force. "Beyond that," according to historian Roger Spiller, "little attention had been paid to what specific missions the force might be called upon to accomplish."[6] Such a mentality was not unusual at the time. Walter LaFeber puts the specific Bluebat situation in the larger Cold War context by arguing, "The problem would always be less a proper choice of the military means than a wise understanding of the objectives. In postwar American foreign policy, the debate over the nature of the communist threat usually lagged behind the debate over which weapons to use against the threat."[7] The result, according to Lawrence Yates, was that the "American troops [that] intervened in Lebanon ... had no clear mission."[8] Initial planning envisioned establishing a beachhead south of Beirut, seizing the international airport, and advancing on the capital. "What would follow," surmises Yates, "would be anyone's guess."[9] Indeed at one point, Brigadier General David Gray, the commander of Army Task Force (ATF) 201, was left confiding to one group of infantrymen from the 187th Airborne Infantry, "At this time I cannot tell exactly what our future mission may be."[10]

The imprecise understanding of objective was not limited to the military. Even after a high-level meeting in June, U.S. Ambassador to the United Nations Henry Cabot Lodge was left asking Secretary of State John Foster Dulles, "How are we going to get our troops out once we have got them in? How long shall they remain? What will the formula be for getting them out? What will the formula be for holding elections in Lebanon while our troops are there? What happens if the elections should go definitely against us?"[11] Lodge's queries today would be called questions of end state, exit strategy, and measures of effectiveness, and they continue to beguile OOTW planners. In May, Dulles already had pointed out to President Eisenhower, "Once our forces were in, it would not be easy to establish a basis upon which they could retire and leave behind an acceptable situation; that might create a wave of anti–Western feeling in the Arab world comparable to that associated with the British and French military operation against Egypt, even though the circumstances were quite different."[12] Now, on the eve of the deployment of U.S. forces to Lebanon, all Dulles could tell Lodge was that these "hard questions" had been given a great deal of thought but remained unanswered.[13] Thus, according to Spiller, Bluebat was a plan "innocent of the political nuances" that shape the objective of any mission, especially an OOTW.[14]

Ambassador Robert Murphy also reported an ambiguous and loose definition of the operation's objective. President Eisenhower dispatched Murphy to serve as an advisor to Admiral James Holloway, who as the Commander in Chief, Specified Command, Middle East (CINCSPECOMME), was in overall command of the U.S. forces deployed to Lebanon, but Yates argues, "Eisenhower himself had little idea of what the troops would be required to do."[15] Thus it is not surprising that Murphy describes his instructions from Eisenhower as being "conveniently vague, the substance being that I was to promote the best interests of the United States incident to the arrival of our forces in Lebanon." Murphy writes that when Eisenhower "elaborated a little on his purpose in ordering US Marines to land in Lebanon," the President explained that a sentiment had developed in the Middle East that the U.S. was "capable only of words, [and] that we were afraid of Soviet reaction if we attempted military action." Thus Murphy felt Eisenhower "believed that if the United States did nothing now, there would be heavy and irreparable losses in Lebanon and the area generally." In language similar to that about a later generation of marines' mission to "establish a presence" in Lebanon in 1983, Murphy felt Eisenhower "wanted to demonstrate in a timely and practical way that the United States was capable of supporting its friends."[16] Details of what that practical support might entail were conspicuously underdeveloped. The result of the operation may have been success, but according to Yates, it was "success without a plan."[17]

Perhaps the best explanation of this ambiguity surrounding Bluebat's objective stems from the fact that President Eisenhower and Secretary Dulles viewed "Lebanon almost completely in terms of the global communist threat and largely ignored the development of Arab nationalism."[18] In reality, however, based on their perspective from on the ground, both Ambassador Murphy and Admiral Holloway ultimately concluded "that much of the conflict concerned personalities and rivalries of a domestic nature, with no relation to international issues. Communism was playing no direct or substantial part in the insurrection."[19] Eisenhower and Dulles certainly understood that America had a vital interest in the region, but they did not comprehend the true threat to that interest. Thus, "they tended to attribute the troubles they were facing to the wrong causes, and, as a result, may have sought the wrong remedies."[20]

Security

If the object of the U.S. intervention was to defeat the internal Lebanese resistance movement, the size of the U.S. force appears completely out of proportion to the threat. Although Saeb Salem (alternately "Saib Salam"), the rebel leader in Beirut, had boasted, "You tell those Marines that if one Marine sets foot on the soil of my country, I will regard it as an act of aggression and commit my forces against them," the Americans had little to worry about. The total rebel force consisted of some 10,000 irregulars, but they were dispersed throughout the country in groups of 400 to 2,000 lightly armed men. There was no central leadership, and each band owed its loyalty to an individual personality like Salem.[21] The day before the marine landings, General Fuad Chehab (alternately "Shihab"), the neutral and broadly respected commander of the Lebanese Army, had met with rebel leaders and was confident they had no plans to initiate new actions against the government.[22]

Instead, the "only immediate effective threat" was from outside Lebanon in the form of the Syrian First Army which consisted of 40,000 soldiers and over 200 Russian-built T-34 medium tanks. To guard against interference from this direction, securing the airport and the approaches to the north of Beirut was critical.[23] Indeed, the original plans to defend Beirut by blocking off the main roads suggest that rather than any rebel uprising, the Americans considered "the real threat was going to reveal itself in the rather conventional form of a foreign, communist-dominated army, probably from Syria, marching from Damascus to invest Beirut."[24] Any intervention from Egypt was considered much less likely.[25] In the end, all fears of outside invasion proved to be highly exaggerated, leading one observer to quip that the Americans "had effectively secured the country from a Syrian invasion that never was."[26]

Thus, in many ways the intervention in Lebanon achieved security, just as it achieved objective, in spite of itself. Spiller concludes his study of the operation by noting, "Virtually every official report opens with the caveat that had Operation Bluebat been opposed, disasters would have occurred."[27] For example, Lieutenant Colonel Henry Hadd, who commanded the initial marine landing force, reported that "the delay in the breaching of the causeway and the unloading of the LSTs would have been disastrous if the landing had been opposed."[28] Spiller goes so far as to say the disjointed nature of the American organization would "have been welcomed by a determined and professional enemy."[29] Instead, the "deployment of large numbers of troops ... created a climate of intimidation conducive to the reduction or cessation of hostilities."[30] The result was that, given the lack of serious opposition, the U.S. forces "quickly found themselves in a role limited to showing force instead of using it."[31]

In part, the large force committed to Lebanon was a result of the prevailing attitude of "massive retaliation" among the Joint Chiefs of Staff. President Eisenhower and General Maxwell Taylor were in the process of creating a Strategic Army Corps which would provide a light strike force to give the military a "flexible response" capability, but this transformation was not complete in time for the Lebanon crisis.[32] President Eisenhower had initially sought to avoid intervention at almost any cost, but he now settled on a plan "to send in everything we've got and this thing will be over in forty-eight hours if we do so."[33] There seemed to be few options in between the two extremes.

Another reason for the large force was the Cold War context in which Lebanon unfolded. President Eisenhower and Secretary of State Dulles intended to send the Soviet Union a clear message that the U.S. would "meet head-on the challenges of the new Middle East."[34] American military forces were placed on worldwide alert in the event the Soviets tried to interfere with the operation. Chairman of the Joint Chiefs of Staff General Nathan Twining assured President Eisenhower the military could deal with any such threat, crowing, "The Russians aren't going to jump us. If they do jump us, if they do come in, they couldn't pick a better time, because we've got them over the whing whang and they know it."[35]

The uncertainty of the initial situation, to include the unpredictable response of other nations in the Middle East, also suggested the need of a force strong enough to meet any contingency.[36] However, the initial marine battalion landing teams met little opposition, and joint Lebanese-American jeep patrols soon calmed whatever tension had existed in Beirut. With the situation on the ground now defying the dire assumptions that predicated the creation of the large Marine-Army force, one correspondent felt that, given this new development, "the best course might be to sit down with some ice packs and think out a realistic objective for the operation."[37] Spiller agrees that at this point, prior to the commitment of the Army contingents, "local circumstances certainly warranted no more ground troops."[38]

Instead, decision-makers remained wedded to the original plan that called for the deployment of General Gray's ATF 201 of some 8000 men, currently prepositioned at a forward staging base at Adana, Turkey. Spiller suggests there may have been a mentality that "now that the Army had moved a task force 2,100 miles, it had to have a part to play in the intervention," and ATF 201 was ordered forward. Likewise marine battalions continued to arrive on schedule until July 20, when, Spiller reports, "reason triumphed" and additional marines were considered unnecessary. Nonetheless, five days after the initial landing, there were more than 10,000 men concentrated in less than four square miles south of Beirut.[39] The Army of Lebanon boasted only 6,000 men.[40]

By July 22, General Gray had determined ATF 201 had reached its saturation point, and he attempted to halt the planned deployment of a battalion of seventy-two medium tanks from Bremerhaven, Germany. While insisting at least a company of armor was needed for mounted patrolling, Admiral Holloway's staff agreed to request that United States Army Europe (USAREUR) reduce the contingent, but USAREUR felt sending the whole battalion was necessary in order to preserve "tactical integrity." Spiller laments that Gray was forced to accept the fact that "the armor was coming, whether he needed it, wanted it, or not."[41]

The same "worst-case planning" impacted logisticians as well. In anticipation of heavy fighting, supplies were pushed forward automatically. Andrew Birtle asserts, "Zealous logisticians soon buried the small intervention force under nearly 50,000 tons of supplies."[42] Because the fighting never materialized, the supplies were not consumed as rapidly as planned, creating "waste and piles of unused supplies." In his logistical study of the operation, Gary Wade concludes only "the lack of fighting (a best-case situation) freed man-

The 13,600 ton heavy cruiser USS *Boston* steaming off Beirut, Lebanon, while serving with the Sixth Fleet, on July 18, 1958. Naval Historical Center.

power to handle massive resupply shipments.[43] Still, the "tooth-to-tail" ratio was staggering, with 47.1 percent of the Army troops involved in support activities.[44]

Security is not merely a function of numbers, and in spite of the large size of the Bluebat force, there were numerous potential security disasters. The rapid decision to intervene in Lebanon found the U.S. Sixth Fleet geographically unable to support Bluebat's plan of landing three marine battalions simultaneously. Instead only the 2nd Battalion of the 2nd Marine Regiment, commanded by Lieutenant Colonel Harry Hadd, was sufficiently close to Beirut to arrive with the required alacrity. The result was "the Marine contingent [was] committed piecemeal into an altogether confused—and therefore very dangerous—situation."[45] Birtle has the benefit of hindsight when he chides the initial troops "faced nothing more dangerous than bikini-clad women and boys aggressively hawking bottles of soda pop," but the fact remains that had the Lebanese Army chosen to defend Lebanon's territorial sovereignty, Hadd would have been in a tight spot.[46] According to the Marine Corps' official history of the operation, this vulnerability had occurred because military security had been sacrificed for political expediency in order to meet President Eisenhower's promise of a rapid deployment. This decision "dramatized the political nature of the Lebanon operation," a common characteristic of OOTWs.[47]

Aircraft also flowed into the forward staging base in Adana, Turkey in a piecemeal and poorly synchronized fashion that threatened security. The result, according to Spiller, was that "unarmed, fully loaded transport aircraft [closed] at an area of potential combat before fighter squadrons had established air superiority, certainly a violation of the most basic canon of air strategy." It made Adana "a wonderful target for anyone who wished to take advantage of it."[48]

The combination of the large size of the force and the successful conclusion of the Lebanon intervention in 1958 has been used to explain the decision to commit a similarly large force to the Dominican Republic in 1965.[49] However, observers should be careful in drawing a direct correlation between the large force and the security outcome in Lebanon. It is true that throughout the 102-day operation, only one American soldier was killed by hostile fire, but this result was largely a function of the lack of resistance.[50] Proponents of large forces will certainly argue that the impressive show of force was instrumental in keeping opposition low, but Birtle is also correct in his conclusion that "a good deal of luck" also played a big part.[51]

Restraint

The low threat allowed the Bluebat forces to adhere to the principle of restraint so much so that Ambassador McClintock could boast the intervention proved to be "that rarest of military miracles: the making on an omelet without breaking the eggs."[52] In a situation that one Pentagon spokesman described as "not war, but like war," American troops and their commanders, as well as diplomats like McClintock, sought to tread cautiously. In the final analysis, they were rewarded for their disciplined and measured approach that eschewed military action in favor of a political settlement.[53]

James Shulimson describes the landing on Red Beach as "perhaps one of the most colorful in the long history of Marine Corps landings." Bikini-clad sunbathers, horseback riders, soft drink vendors, and beach workmen waved and some even cheered as "fully armed Marines charged over the sand." A few young boys even offered to help the marines carry their heavy equipment ashore. One marine described the strange reception as being "better than Korea, but what the hell is it?"[54]

As the initial marine battalion landing teams made their way inland, they were subjected to only a few instances of harassing fire around the airport and only in one case felt compelled to open fire themselves. The situation was calm enough that when two marines became lost and were taken captive in the Basta, the Arab quarter of Beirut and center of government opposition, they were released unharmed. Even their weapons were soon returned.[55]

Amid such conditions, strict rules of engagement were possible and practical. Of equal note, Ambassador McClintock recognized that the spectacle of American troops killing Moslems could inflame the already volatile Middle East. While Chamoun pressed the U.S. to not only stabilize Lebanon but also to militarily eliminate threats in Iraq, Egypt, and Syria, Secretary of State Dulles countered that there would be no "preventive war," and that the Lebanese situation would be resolved by "patience." Likewise, the recommendation of Vice Admiral Charles Brown, commander of the U.S. Sixth Fleet, to have forces fan out from the capital to other areas of the country was dismissed by Admiral Holloway and Ambassador McClintock as being "counterproductive."[56] This exercise in geographic restraint also was influenced by the need to foster legitimacy. President Eisenhower explained the decision by saying if the Lebanese Army could not control the countryside, "I felt we were backing up a government with so little popular support that we probably should not be there."[57]

Even before the deployment, General Gray had impressed upon his soldiers his intent that they "conduct themselves in such a restrained, alert, highly professional manner that they would not inadvertently involve themselves, and the Lebanese would not want to get involved with them either." He made it clear that the mission would require "strict discipline."[58] Once the low nature of the threat became apparent, American soldiers were prohibited from firing unless they were fired upon, and then only if they could clearly identify

An American paratrooper cleans his rifle at an army base camp in Beirut in July 1958. Photograph taken by Thomas O'Halloran. Library of Congress.

the source of the shooting and engage it without unduly endangering non-combatants.[59]

Shulimson explains that such precautions were useful counters to attempts by the rebels to use harassment "to provoke the Marines into rash retaliation." However, like their army counterparts, "The Marines were under strict orders to maintain fire discipline, and to shoot only in self-defense."[60] Lieutenant Colonel Hadd testified to the delicacy and wonder of the situation, saying,

> The conduct of the individual Marine in holding his fire when he can see who is shooting in his direction must be mentioned. When a youngster lands all pre-pared and eager to fight and finds himself restricted from firing at a known rebel who he sees periodically fire in his direction and in every instance restrains him-self from returning fire, it is felt this is outstanding and indicated good small unit discipline. The situation had to be thoroughly explained to the individual Marine and they understood why the restriction on fire was necessary. Many innocent people could have been killed.[61]

Additionally, detailed codes of conduct minimized the likelihood of neg-ative contacts with Lebanese citizens, and property owners were compensated for any damages or inconveniences.[62] General Gray went so far as to eliminate calling cadence during physical fitness training once he learned "that the local inhabitants didn't particularly appreciate being awakened at 0500 every morning to the sound of pounding feet and the airborne chant."[63] The results were worth the effort. Shulimson concludes, "This successful restraint of the troops proved to be an important stabilizing feature of the American intervention."[64]

The lone American casualty to hostile action occurred on August 1 when Sergeant James Nettles was killed by sniper fire near the Basta. On August 21, another soldier was wounded close to the Basta. The next day, employees at the American Embassy were pinned down by machine gun fire from the same part of the city, but there were no casualties. In a remarkable testimony to the restraint demonstrated by the Bluebat forces, there was no military reaction to any of these incidents.[65]

American restraint was tested again after September 23, the day General Chehab was inaugurated as the new president of Lebanon. In response to the inclusion of former rebel leaders in the cabinet, supporters of former President Chamoun called for a general strike and the dissolution of the new government. Rather than intervening, the U.S. forces established a contingency force to meet any emergency and allowed President Chehab to deal with the present situation. On September 24, the Lebanese Army effectively broke up a clash between Chamoun loyalists and rebels. Shulimson concludes, "Both sides, impressed by the determination of the Lebanese Army to end the fighting, commenced negotiations to end the political stalemate."[66]

Nonetheless, in early October, the Phalange, a right-wing Maronite Christian militia group associated with Chamoun, launched a series of demonstrations. After several U.S. soldiers were captured and released near the Basta, the Americans sent an armored show of force to the edge of the opposition stronghold. There was no fighting, and the warning seemed to have the desired calming effect.[67] In these instances and throughout Operation Bluebat, restraint served the U.S. forces well.

Unity of Effort

Although one branch of the Bluebat contingency plan envisioned a cooperative American and British effort, little progress was made in pursuing the combined option. British sources allude to participating in some "unobtrusive planning" with the Americans, but there is scant evidence of active British participation.[68] Bluebat was destined to be a unilateral U.S. operation.

British reluctance to become more involved may have been a function of their perception that the Eisenhower Doctrine and the U.S. response to the situation in Lebanon represented hypocrisy. Prime Minister Harold Macmillan complained, "The new American policy could hardly be reconciled with the Administration's almost hysterical outbursts over Suez."[69] Macmillan also expressed some concern that direct British action might result in attacks on British oil installations which would "inflict great loss upon the international companies and particularly upon us who depend on sterling oil."[70] For whatever the actual reason, when it came time to act, the Joint Chiefs of Staff directed execution of only "the US portion of Bluebat."[71] President Eisenhower felt the U.S. force would be sufficient and that the 3,700 British troops in Cyprus would form a formidable reserve if necessary. Ultimately, Britain responded to a request from King Hussein and dispatched troops to Jordan on July 17.[72]

The unfolding drama quickly made its way to the UN Security Council. On July 17, the Soviet Union submitted a draft resolution by which the Council would call upon Britain and the United States "to cease armed intervention in the domestic affairs of the Arab States and to remove their troops from the territories of Lebanon and Jordan immediately." The proposal was rejected by majority vote. The United States proposed its own draft resolution, which would request the Secretary General "immediately to consult the Government of Lebanon and other Member States as appropriate with a view to making arrangements for additional measures, including the contribution and use of contingents, as may be necessary to protect the territorial integrity and independence of Lebanon and to ensure that there is no illegal infiltration of personnel or supply of arms or other matériel across the Lebanese borders." This proposal was vetoed by the Soviet Union.[73] Bluebat would remain a unilateral U.S. operation, but that did not mean it would be without unity of effort challenges.

As an early joint operation, Bluebat experienced some difficulties in achieving unity of effort among the services. On the other hand, although the U.S. military entered Lebanon without a status of forces agreement, the American and Lebanese forces quickly settled into a mutually cooperative relationship. This remarkable development was realized in no small part by the efforts of seasoned diplomats like McClintock and Murphy. Political-military unity of effort rose to the occasion in Lebanon's fluid and uncertain environment.

At the operational level, joint unity of effort in Bluebat was frustrated but what Spiller calls "a wave of 'provisionalism' which dominated military planning as well as a certain parochialism in the services." The result he claims, in spite of several joint planning conferences, was three separate marine, army, and air force organizations rather than a unified task force.[74] Attempts at coordination were further frustrated by high security classifications that "impeded planning and made execution even more vexatious than it would have been otherwise."[75] It would be a fair assessment that the lack of unity of effort among the services in Operation Bluebat was reflective of an era when joint operations had not yet become the order of the day.

Nonetheless, in spite of the absence of the joint protocols that have by now become routine, cooperation among the services was established. As Commander in Chief, Specified Command Middle East, Admiral James Holloway had authority over all U.S. forces in the area. The maritime component was commanded by the commander of the U.S. Sixth Fleet, Vice Admiral Charles Brown, and the air component was commanded by Brigadier General James Roberts. Command of the land component was slightly more complicated. On the day of the initial landings, marine Brigadier General Sidney Wade had been designated the Commander, American Land Forces. When Brigadier General David Gray arrived with ATF 201, a decision had to be made as to how best to coordinate the marine and army activities. Admiral Holloway had requested the Joint Chiefs of Staff provide an army or marine corps major or lieutenant general for this purpose, and the marine corps had expected their Lieutenant General Edwin Pollock to be tapped for this assignment. Instead, on July 23, army Major General Paul Adams was designated Commander in Chief, American Land Forces, Lebanon. General Wade was then relegated to Commander, U.S. Marine Corps, Troops Assigned, Lebanon. The appointment of an army land component commander was likely based on the fact that army troops in Lebanon would soon outnumber their marine counterparts. Although the decision came as somewhat of a disappointment to the marines, Wade confessed, "I think that General Adams, as commander, was as fair to the Marine Corps as any Army general I've ever dealt with."[76]

Unity of effort between the American and Lebanese militaries was still another issue requiring attention. The fact that President Chamoun had requested the U.S. intervention did not ensure cooperation, and although General Chehab was, like Chamoun, a Maronite Christian, the Lebanese Army was plagued by the same sectarian divisions that epitomized the country. Chehab was determined to keep the army out of the political dispute. "If the army moved against the rebels," he declared, "it would have little difficulty in reestablishing order.... But if it cleared the Moslem quarters of Beirut and Tripoli, knocking down a few houses in the process, the army — which is predominantly Christian — would in fact be destroying the structure of Lebanon as a political entity."[77] Thus, Chehab intervened only to keep certain essential lines of communication open and to prevent rebel forays from their strongholds in Tripoli, the Chouf, and the Basta area of Beirut.[78] Although the Lebanese Army would take no sides and act as what Spiller describes "as a passive sort of constabulary," this outcome could not have been predicted as the marines came ashore.[79] The marines had been instructed to treat all Lebanese Army units as friendly unless proven otherwise, but Ambassador McClintock worried the Lebanese Army might oppose the marines' line of march simply as a matter of honor.[80]

McClintock's fears almost came to fruition as Lieutenant Colonel Hadd's battalion advanced on Beirut. After landing at Red Beach, the marines had taken control of the international airport. The Lebanese Army troops that Hadd encountered there offered no resistance, and the Americans and Lebanese worked out liaison relationships and arrangements for both guarding the airport and air traffic control.[81] After this promising beginning, however, the next morning when the marines started moving to Beirut proper, they ran into a roadblock of Lebanese tanks with gun barrels pointed directly at the lead vehicles of the marine column.[82] Ambassador McClintock reached the roadblock just in time to superintend arrangements with General Chehab to have the Lebanese Army escort the marines into town. With McClintock, Chehab, and Holloway riding together in the same vehicle to lead the way and a jeep carrying Lebanese Army officers at the head of each section of marine vehicles, Ambassador Murphy reported that "what might have been a tragic episode was narrowly averted."[83] Instead, McClintock and Chehab began to develop plans for future cooperation between the American and Lebanese military forces.[84] McClintock was astute in determining Chehab to be key to a peaceful solution in Lebanon, believing if "General Chehab decided to throw in the sponge, the Lebanese army will fall apart."[85] Fortuitously for the Americans, McClintock was able to secure Chehab's cooperation, and

A U.S. marine mans a foxhole with his machine gun oriented towards Beirut in July 1958. Photograph taken by Thomas O'Halloran. Library of Congress.

Yates credits this action with setting the stage "for US forces and the Lebanese army to work together as partners."[86]

Building on this positive encounter, it was mutually agreed that most Americans would remain outside Beirut, with Lebanese forces assuming positions between the Americans and the parts of the city controlled by radical Moslem elements. General Wade felt this arrangement gave General Chehab improved peace of mind, and, with this matter settled, "the tension was lifted and he was more or less cooperative."[87] The resulting buffer zone did much to reduce conflict and allowed the Americans to confine their activities to garrisoning key facilities. An integrated military police force was formed composed of Lebanese, and American army, navy, and marine personnel, and combined Lebanese and American patrols maintained security and communication between American outposts. Lebanese Army liaison officers were attached to battalion headquarters, and one, Major Alexander Ghanem, proved especially effective. According to one marine colonel, after a phone call of "only a few seconds," Ghanem could make a rebel roadblock "melt away."[88] In other cases, Lebanese guides pointed out rebel positions to marine battalions.[89] In spite of these instances of operational cooperation, however, the Lebanese politely declined most American offers of training assistance.[90] Overall, Birtle calls the Lebanese Army's support "indispensable," and, on this level, unity of effort during the intervention in Lebanon was exceptional.[91]

Cooperation between the American diplomatic and military efforts also ended up being a positive aspect of the operation. A pre-deployment agreement between the Department of State and the Pentagon had declared, "In case of difference between the military commander and the local United States diplomatic representative in regard to political matters relating exclusively to Lebanon, the views of the latter shall be controlling."[92] Still, an early misunderstanding between Ambassador McClintock and Lieutenant Colonel Hadd caused some consternation, and to ensure unity between the American military and diplomatic efforts, President Eisenhower dispatched Deputy Under Secretary of State Robert Murphy to Lebanon as his special representative.[93] Murphy was billed a "five-star diplomat," which allowed him to oversee both Ambassador McClintock and Admiral Holloway who carried four-star rank. Murphy found "close cooperation between the diplomatic and military sides of the American house," a fact that he believed "contributed greatly to the success of our Lebanese undertaking."[94] Since McClintock and Holloway had already established a cooperative rapport, Murphy was free to immerse himself in the intricacies of Lebanon's internal crisis, and he met once or twice daily with President Chamoun as well as with leaders representing other Lebanese factions such as Moslems Saeb Salem and Rashid Karami, Christian Raymond Edde, and Druze Kamal Jumblatt.[95] Murphy believes his diplomatic tour de force among Lebanese leaders "contributed in the end to the peaceful settlement" of the crisis, and Birtle credits Murphy with "unifying the politico-military effort."[96] It was an effective combination. With the strong military show of force providing the needed motivation, American diplomats were able to encourage the contending factions to reach a negotiated solution.[97]

Legitimacy

The American intervention was afforded a small amount of legitimacy by the fact that on May 22, the Lebanese government had requested a meeting of the United Nations Security Council to consider its complaint "in respect of a situation arising from the intervention of the United Arab Republic in the internal affairs of Lebanon, the continuance of which is likely to endanger the maintenance of international peace and security." On June 11, the Security Council adopted UNSCR 128, which formed the basis of the establishment of the United Nations Observation Group in Lebanon (UNOGIL). The first UNOGIL members arrived in Beirut on June 12 and began their mission "to ensure that there is no illegal infiltration of personnel or supply of arms or other matériel across the Lebanese borders." However, UNOGIL was not tasked to interdict illegal infiltration. Instead, it was hoped that its presence alone might deter any such traffic.[98]

UNOGIL had little time to make an impact and proved to be unable to salvage the deteriorating situation. It did not obtain full freedom of access to all sections of the Lebanese frontier until mid–July. In the meantime, however, the coup in Iraq had exacerbated the situation, leading President Chamoun to request U.S. intervention.[99] As the crisis unfolded, UN Secretary General Dag Hammerskjold had cautioned Secretary of State Dulles against U.S. action, but he had conceded that if the UN or Lebanon failed to resolve the matter, Western intervention at the request of the Lebanese government would be "legal."[100]

Such a tepid UN endorsement carried little international resonance, and from its very inception, Operation Bluebat faced a challenge to its perceived legitimacy from those who saw it as "meddling in Lebanon's internal affairs."[101] President Eisenhower offered some slight defense against this argument in citing the need to protect the 2,500 Americans living in Lebanon, but it was debatable if these citizens were really in immediate danger that exceeded the capabilities of local authorities.[102]

By far the "thorniest" problem regarding legitimacy for Eisenhower was to prevent an overthrow of the Lebanese government without committing American forces to directly supporting any of Lebanon's political factions.[103] Allaying fears that the Americans were exclusively tied to President Chamoun was high on Ambassador Murphy's agenda during his personal meetings with the leaders of the various segments of Lebanese society. He assured them the U.S. military was not in Lebanon to keep Chaumon in power, and he felt this effort "cleared away much information about American intentions."[104]

An even more definitive demonstration of legitimacy occurred when the U.S. refused to endorse Chaumon's bid for a second term.[105] Ambassador Murphy astutely ascertained that the best solution to the current unrest was to form a new government.[106] Focusing on this task had the added benefit of indirectly enhancing Bluebat's legitimacy by diverting the attention of some Lebanese Parliament members away from protesting the American intervention and instead redirecting their efforts to the problem of electing a new president.[107]

The U.S. contributed to this process by helping persuade Chaumon to not only step aside but also lend his support to his rival General Chehab, whose family background, Maronite religious affiliation, conciliatory attitude, and reputation for neutrality while commanding the Moslem-Christian army made him a logical candidate. Chehab was elected president on July 31 and took office on September 23. Ambassador Murphy contends Chehab did not seek the position and accepted it "only as a compromise essential to peace in Lebanon."[108] As a testimony to this character, the Chehab government included many members that would have previously been considered "rebels."[109]

A second challenge to Bluebat's legitimacy was that, with their country's long history of foreign invasion, some Lebanese were "deeply opposed to the presence of foreign troops on their soil" and saw the American forces as an army of occupation.[110] To combat this perception, within days of the initial landings, American planes dropped a million leaflets all over Lebanon that bore a picture of President Eisenhower and his message that the troops had come at the request of the Lebanese government to protect the country and that the U.S. forces would withdraw as soon as security was ensured.[111] At General Chehab's request, special care was taken to position the marines so they "would not give the appearance of being occupation troops."[112] Indeed, Shulimson quips, "The American forces were in the unusual predicament of having to negotiate in order to establish their positions in lieu of seizing them."[113] The result was that, as Spiller notes, "the Americans showed no inclination to stay very long in Lebanon and so gave hope to all that their influence would be fleeting."[114] In fact, the marines began withdrawing toward the end of August, and all American forces had left Lebanon by October 15.

Perseverance

Such a brief intervention was never intended to resolve Lebanon's deep social and sectarian fissures.[115] Operation Bluebat averted the immediate crisis, and Lebanon remained at peace for seventeen years, but as a later generation of

American marines would learn, the underlying causes of the conflict remained. This broader reality was not lost on U.S. officials in 1958. Even as he praised the successful conclusion of the American intervention from Lebanon, Secretary of State Dulles noted that the overall problem in the Middle East was not solved.[116]

Perhaps in recognition of this situation, Ambassador Murphy was dispatched on a tour of the Middle East after his departure from Lebanon. He visited Jordan, Israel, Iraq, and Egypt, hoping to "convince leading officials that our intervention would exercise a stabilizing effect in the Middle East."[117] There were, in fact, some positive developments in the region. Robert Divine believes Eisenhower's "determination to make Lebanon a display of America's resolve in the Middle East impressed Arab leaders," adding that Iraq's General Abdul Karim Kassem "was quick to reassure the European leaders that there would be no interruption in the flow of oil."[118]

Even of greater note, shortly after the crisis, Nasser became alienated from the new Iraqi leadership, the Soviet Union, and his Syrian partner in the UAR. These setbacks caused Nasser to seek better relations with the U.S., and the Eisenhower administration, realizing it could not destroy Nasserism, was willing to settle for an accommodation with it. This conciliatory tone on both sides allowed for improved U.S.–Egyptian relations throughout the remainder of Eisenhower's presidency and into the 1960s. If John Marlowe's argument is accepted that the Eisenhower Doctrine was aimed not just at communism, but was also "directed ... in appearance and in effect against Egyptian imperialism," Operation Bluebat can be viewed as part of a larger adherence to the principle of perseverance.[119] However in the specific context of the operation, Yates is quick to note that the U.S. "had not planned for all this at the time American troops intervened in Lebanon."[120] It would be incorrect to attribute too much "perseverance" to an operation that lasted only 102 days, but Operation Bluebat did last long enough to see Lebanon through its immediate crisis.

Conclusion

Operation Bluebat adhered to the principle of security by both chance and design. The massive size of the force was designed to handle any eventuality, but it was by chance that no resistance developed to challenge the marines during Bluebat's early awkward moments. As a result of the large force and low threat, the Americans were able to adhere to the principle of restraint. Admiral Holloway captured the effective combination of potential strength and practiced restraint in noting that "patience, consolidation of strength, acclimating the Lebanese to our presence, and restraint characterized our actions accompanied by our great potential military strength are paying dividends."[121]

Adherence to the principles of legitimacy and unity of effort began problematically but progressed to satisfaction. Initial fears of U.S. imperialism, meddling, and occupation were quickly allayed by tangible signals of intent to withdraw as soon as possible. Early miscommunications between U.S. diplomatic and military entities were overcome by the dispatch of Ambassador Murphy and the interpersonal skills and efforts of a number of individuals. The early uncertain status of relations between the American and Lebanese militaries was quickly reversed by personal effort, notably by General Chehab, and routine liaison at all levels. Most certainly, American ongoing restraint and improved legitimacy helped foster unity of effort and cooperation with the Lebanese, suggesting a relationship among those principles.

Adherence to the principle of objective was initially flawed but ultimately not detrimental to the operation. The overarching objective to thwart the threat of communist expansion pursuant to the Eisenhower Doctrine proved to be irrelevant. Ambassador Murphy helped focus a more appropriate objective by concentrating on the forming of a new government, and the American security presence helped provide the stability needed for this process. The refocused objective also served to enhance Bluebat's legitimacy.

Adherence to the principle of perseverance was a qualified success. The American forces remained in place long enough to facilitate the immediate objective of a transfer of power to the new Chehab government but certainly not long enough to address the underlying cause of instability in Lebanon, let alone the Greater Middle East. Part of this outcome may be attributed to the imprecise assessment of the original situation, which framed the objective in terms of responding to a communist threat that never materialized. Had the intervention been based on a more nuanced understanding of Arab nationalism and been designed to address this much broader phenomenon, a much more significant commitment than Bluebat's 102 days would clearly have been required.

This analysis suggests relationships among several of the principles, both in terms of correlation and balanced application. The emphasis on security represented by the large force size allowed the Americans to practice restraint. The strategic objective's being based on miscalculations about the external communist threat generated some challenges to legitimacy, which were mitigated by a concerted military and diplomatic emphasis on unity of effort within Lebanon. This case study also suggests that perseverance is a function of objective in that perseverance must be assessed in the context of being directed toward a specific objective. American adherence to the principles of OOTW was far less deliberate in Lebanon than it had been in Greece, but the result was the same: the balanced application of the principles of OOTW led to a successful operation.

CHAPTER 3

The Dominican Republic: Security Allows Restraint

A civil war in the Dominican Republic threatened American citizens there and also generated fears of communist expansion in an area of traditional American influence. In response to these twin threats, particularly the latter one, the United States began the deployment of a substantial invasion force on April 27, 1965. This intervention highlights the OOTW principle of restraint because U.S. forces demonstrated remarkable discipline that helped facilitate a negotiated solution to the crisis. It also demonstrates the effective application of the principles of security and perseverance. Adherence to the principles of objective, unity of effort, and legitimacy were mixed. As a result of this OOTW, the U.S. accomplished its objective of preventing communism from gaining another foothold in the Caribbean, and increasing the stability of the Dominican Republic.

Background

Rafael Trujillo ruled the Dominican Republic like a feudal lord for thirty-one years from 1930 until his assassination in 1961. When Trujillo was killed, his puppet, President Joaquin Balaguer Ricardo, remained in office, but his association with the dictatorship of Trujillo made him unpopular and weak. The country soon fell unto general unrest, and Balaguer was forced from office by a coup. The coup, however, could not establish the authority necessary to rule because of popular protest in the Dominican Republic and opposition from the United States. An election was held on December 20, 1962, and, with significant support from the urban lower class, Juan Bosch Gavino, a scholar and poet, became president.

The Bosch Administration represented something new to the Dominican

Republic, and its moves toward liberalization, secularization, and concern for the poor soon placed it at odds with the traditional elites. There was also concern that Bosch's leadership was making the Dominican Republic vulnerable to communism by such actions as legalizing the previously outlawed communist parties. Amid the backdrop of Fidel Castro's rise to power in Cuba in 1959, such seemingly innocent gestures were highly scrutinized. On September 25, 1963, a coup deposed Bosch and replaced him with a civilian junta known as the Triumvirate, which came to be led by Donald Reid Cabral. However, the Triumvirate failed to establish its authority over competing conservative factions both inside and outside the military or to convince the majority of the population of its legitimacy. Dissatisfaction with Reid and lingering loyalties to Bosch plunged the Dominican Republic into revolution in April 1965.

Bosch's supporters and like-minded revolutionaries took the name *Constitutionalists* in reference to their support for the 1963 constitution. The Constitutionalists also came to be known as the rebels. Conservative forces who called themselves *Loyalists* struck back under the leadership of General Wessin y Wessin, commander of the elite Armed Forces Training Center (CEFA). On April 28, the United States intervened in what had become a civil war.

Operation Power Pack, as the U.S. intervention was named, began with the deployment of the U.S. Marines to protect Americans in the Dominican Republic. Portions of the 82nd Airborne Division soon joined the marines, and the situation expanded beyond its initial nature as a non-combatant evacuation operation (NEO) to become part of the Cold War struggle against communism. In all, the operation lasted sixteen months, and it serves as a useful case study of the interaction among the various principles of OOTW, especially security and restraint.

Analysis of the Principles

Objective

As the situation in the Dominican Republic deteriorated into civil war, rebel paramilitary groups descended on the grounds of the Hotel Embajador, where U.S. citizens had gathered in anticipation of evacuation. Rebels lined up Americans outside the hotel and fired shots over their heads. Other rebels riddled the building's upper stories with bullets.[1] By this point the Joint Chiefs of Staff (JCS) had already begun contingency planning to protect American lives.[2] Shortly after noon on April 27, Chairman of the Joint Chiefs of Staff General Earle Wheeler received President Lyndon Johnson's order to begin the evacuation.[3]

Because Power Pack began as a NEO, the objective of the original marine landings was expressed solely in terms of "protecting American lives," and President Johnson broadcast that message to the nation in a television address the night of April 28.[4] However, from the very beginning the operation had the ulterior motive of preventing a "second Cuba."[5] This agenda was in part facilitated by John Bartlow Martin, former U.S. Ambassador to the Dominican Republic, whom President Johnson dispatched to Santo Domingo as his special emissary early in the crisis. Martin quickly became convinced that the rebellion had taken a communist turn, and his reports to Johnson reflected this assessment.[6] Thus, General Wheeler informed Lieutenant General Bruce Palmer, the newly appointed Power Pack commander, "Your announced mission is to save American lives. Your unstated mission is to prevent the Dominican Republic from going communist. The President has stated that he will not allow another Cuba.... You are to take all necessary measures ... to accomplish this mission."[7]

It was not until May 2, when it became necessary to justify additional troop deployments, that President Johnson publicly revealed his fears of a second Cuba by announcing that "the American nations cannot, must not, and will not permit the establishment of another communist government in the Western Hemisphere."[8] Thus, from early in the operation, the American intervention suffered from an ambiguous objective that presented some challenges to its legitimacy. Additionally, Palmer was not provided the unequivocal mission statement routinely sought by military commanders.

A contributing factor in this failure was President Johnson's decision to rely more on Secretary of Defense Robert McNamara than the Joint Chiefs of Staff for military advice.[9] While this technique reinforced the national value of civilian control of the military, it also contributed to inadequate representation of the military point of view on the Dominican Republic. Such a state of affairs led Palmer to lament that political decisions were made "without taking into account important military considerations."[10]

One aspect of the objective that was clear was that tactical control of Santo Domingo was critical to success. The city lay on the south central coast and was the country's capital and largest city. Moreover, Palmer considered it "the heart and brain of the republic." An old saying proclaimed, "As goes Santo Domingo, so goes the Dominican Republic."[11] As Beirut was for Operation Bluebat in 1958, Santo Domingo would be the site of almost all of Power Pack's activity.

Legitimacy

The base issue of legitimacy associated with Power Pack was overcoming the stigma of America's history of interventions in the Caribbean, none of which, Palmer knew, had "ever claimed general approbation."[12] President Theodore Roosevelt's Corollary to the Monroe Doctrine had provided the justification for America assuming control of Dominican financial and political affairs, and in 1916, the U.S. even established a military government under a navy and marine occupation that lasted eight years. President Franklin Roosevelt's Good Neighbor Policy had led to the last of the American forces in the region being withdrawn in 1934, but the legacy of American imperialism remained.[13] This phenomenon caused the Organization of American States (OAS) to proceed cautiously with any measure that could "lend legitimacy to a US return to an interventionist policy and be interpreted as one Latin nation acting against another at the behest of the United States."[14]

Palmer found that one development that helped take some of the edge off the latest American intervention was the fact that black soldiers comprised about 30 percent of the average battalion in the 82nd. He felt that this demographic, as well as some Spanish-speaking soldiers, "helped establish friendly relations between our troops and the people of Santo Domingo" that survived "even the sustained efforts of the rebel opposition to arouse the people against us."[15]

In contrast to Palmer's good fortune in establishing legitimacy at the tactical level was the impact of Power Pack's ambiguous objective on its perceived operational and strategic legitimacy. The guise of U.S. neutrality and the focus on the objective of securing American citizens could be maintained tenuously as long as the operation was limited to the marines. However, the introduction of the 3rd Brigade of the 82nd Airborne destroyed this fiction by appearing unrelated to the NEO. Specifically, the brigade landed at San Isidro Airfield, a location nominally held by Loyalist forces, while the marines were in Santo Domingo, the site of the U.S. Embassy and the American citizens that the deployment was supposed to safeguard. These developments led some observers to characterize Power Pack as "a political-military intervention ... disguised ... behind a humanitarian act."[16] In fact, 76 percent of the American population initially supported the marine NEO, but less than half supported the subsequent introduction of the army.[17] Even the 82nd had to admit that "the current and planned disposition of ... [its] forces did not appear to substantiate the stated mission of protecting American and foreign nationals."[18]

Another part of the problem with legitimacy was that President Johnson's abrupt announcement of a communist threat in the Dominican Republic had little evidence to support it. Johnson had hoped that establishing a link to communism would win him support both domestically and abroad, but his claims were so spurious that they only weakened his case. For example, when Speaker of the House Sam Rayburn told Johnson there were not many "commies" in the Dominican Republic, the president replied that Rayburn "just wasn't looking hard enough." Then when the CIA released to the press lists of "Current Rebels Who Had Cuban Training" and "Rebels Who Are Known Leftist Activists," the lists were found to contain several people with only loose associations with the communists, as well as duplicate names within each list. Such incidents damaged President Johnson's credibility with both Congress and the press.[19]

Regarding the ambiguity of the operation's purpose, the JCS ordered that "Military commanders should respond to press queries relative to deployment of 82nd Airborne troops that they are to reinforce Marines for the purpose of protecting lives of Americans and other foreign nationals. No other response or conjecture should be offered." This inconsistency initiated difficulties with what had heretofore been a friendly news media.[20]

In fact, problems with the press had begun to develop even before the 82nd was deployed. The military shared the political arm's value of thwarting communism, but some commanders were less attuned to the requirement for legitimacy. Commodore James Dare, the naval task group commander, told reporters that the marines would stay ashore as long as necessary to "keep this a non-communist government," just one day after President Johnson had justified the landings solely in terms of "protecting American lives." Similarly, military briefers soon began referring to the Loyalists as "friendlies" and the Constitutionalists as "unfriendlies." The press reported the discrepancy between such statements and the official proclamations of U.S. neutrality, and a credibility gap developed.[21] This failure to provide accurate information created the first crack in the bipartisan consensus that had provided the underpinning of U.S. foreign policy thus far in the Cold War.[22] In fact, a report issued by the Center for Strategic Studies concluded, "The reasons for US landings were ineptly explained to the public. The failure to communicate effectively the rationale for its actions had damaging effects in the United States and throughout Latin America."[23] It also set the stage for even greater difficulties for the administration and the military in their dealings with the media during the Vietnam War, a war in which the legitimacy of U.S. military actions was fiercely attacked.[24]

Unity of Effort

In addition to problems with legitimacy on the domestic front, the U.S. struggled with international perceptions as well. Several hours before the OAS passed a resolution calling for a ceasefire and the establishment of an International Security Zone (ISZ) through the diplomatic quarter of Santo Domingo, U.S. Marines had already entered the area of the proposed ISZ.

Moreover, President Johnson also had already committed the 82nd, elements of which were in the process of landing at San Isidro at the time of the OAS resolution.[25]

Although Palmer noted that "the timing of these troop movements ... would prove awkward at best for the US government, particularly in its Latin American relations," the initial urgency of the NEO aspects of Power Pack largely justified the U.S. taking unilateral action rather than working through the OAS.[26] As Secretary of State Dean Rusk explained, "As presently organized, the OAS does not have standby forces or the political machinery for the immediate decisions required to deal with such contingencies."[27] However, even such necessary unilateral action clashed with the American values of collective security and nonintervention, and threatened the legitimacy of the operation in international eyes.[28] As the U.S. military build-up continued and the mission took on a more and more anticommunist nature, charges of "gunboat diplomacy" made unity of effort within the context of the OAS necessary to legitimize the operation.[29] Realizing that unity of effort can provide "an organizational dimension to military legitimacy," President Johnson instructed Secretary of State Rusk "to make it look good" in the OAS; a remark Palmer interpreted as meaning "to get OAS acceptance and participation."[30]

The Latin American ambassadors to the OAS had been informed of the unilateral U.S. action on the evening of April 28, after the order had been issued to land the first contingent of marines. American diplomats were now playing catch-up to bring the OAS on board. Meetings and negotiations continued, and on May 6, the day after the corridor between the marines and the 82nd was secured as a buffer zone, the Tenth Meeting of Consultation of Ministers of Foreign Affairs of American States passed a resolution creating the Inter-American Peace Force (IAPF). The IAPF was established to act

> in a spirit of democratic impartiality, that (purpose) of cooperating in the restoration of normal conditions in the Dominican Republic, in maintaining the security of its inhabitants and the inviolability of human rights, and in the establishment of an atmosphere of peace and conciliation that will permit the functioning of democratic institutions.[31]

Ultimately a Brazilian general, Hugo Panasco Alvim, assumed command of the IAPF, with Palmer serving as his deputy. Although Palmer reported that the two "soon established a warm and close relationship," he nonetheless felt that turning over field command of U.S. combat forces to a foreign officer was a "serious error," and from a purely military point of view, his argument makes sense.[32] Diplomatically, however, an international peacekeeping force under OAS control was far more palatable in Latin America than one under U.S. control. Conveniently, the IAPF would also be working toward the same goals as the United States: to end the violence and to prevent a communist takeover.[33] In effect, the move simultaneously reinforced the principles of objective, legitimacy, and unity of effort.

One factor that facilitated cooperation among the IAPF's combined staff was that many of the Latin American officers were graduates of the U.S. Army's Command and General Staff College or the U.S. Army–operated School of the Americas, then located in the Panama Canal Zone. Palmer reports these shared experiences "gave us a common understanding with respect to military terms and procedures, and accelerated our progress as an effective and reliable staff."[34] At the same time, Palmer applauded General Alvim's decision to organize the Latin American troops into a separate brigade in order to "preserve the integrity of [the Latin American] troops as an entity, which was important psychologically and enhanced their pride and spirit."[35]

With the creation of the IAPF, the legitimacy of U.S. intervention was enhanced.[36] The military's need for security wrought by unilateral action and U.S. command was forced to accommodate the U.S. government's need for the legitimacy that could be gained by international unity of effort. In spite of his concerns, Palmer understood the bigger issue. "On the balance," he wrote, "the 6 May resolution was timely and useful. It clearly came as a relief to many nations of the hemisphere and provided the United States an umbrella of legitimacy."[37]

Such an understanding was achieved in large part because of Palmer's acknowledgement of the need for the diplomatic and military efforts to "work hand in glove."[38] He understood the principle that "in any given operation, one individual should be charged with planning and carrying out approved actions and programs, especially in the field," and in the Dominican Republic, Palmer recognized that "Ambassador Bunker was clearly in charge."[39] When Palmer received his initial assignment, the only advice General Wheeler gave him was "to seek out the US ambassador and stick to him like a burr." Palmer noted "it was good advice that was to pay off."[40] As the operation progressed, he had a direct phone line installed between his desk and Ambassador Bunker's to provide secure and private access.[41] The two men soon established an excellent working relationship.

Wheeler's assessment and Palmer's response are especially noteworthy given the lack of reciprocity in some political circles. President Johnson, for example, excluded all military officials, to include the Chairman of the Joint Chiefs of Staff, from the executive deliberations in the first five days of the developing the crisis.[42] Palmer mused, "It seems obvious that a responsible senior military individual should have participated in those earlier decisions."[43] Still, he recognized "an integration of effort means that there must be close civilian-military relations at high decision-making levels."[44] Since that appeared unlikely at the presidential level, Palmer actively pursued a synergistic relationship with Ambassador Bunker.[45] Rather than creating a power struggle between the diplomatic and military agendas, Palmer submitted to civilian authority, and, largely thanks to his professionalism, the U.S. achieved unity of effort.

Security

While the political and military communities had some trouble coordinating the issues of legitimacy and unity of effort, they did agree on the principle of security as it applied to the wisdom of the initial introduction of sufficient combat power. Nonetheless, motivations for the large force structure varied, and not all can be explained by purely operational military necessity. Michael Grow argues President Johnson intended "to send an unmistakable message to multiple audiences, foreign and domestic: that under the Johnson administration, and under Lyndon Johnson's personal presidential leadership, the United States was fully prepared to project its power internationally in defense of its interests."[46] The end result was that, for a variety of reasons, security was a major initial planning concern.

The operational problem in the Dominican Republic was that, before the U.S. intervention, whichever side thought itself to have the military advantage showed little inclination to submit to negotiations.[47] President Dwight Eisenhower had been faced with a similar situation in the early phases of the 1958 Lebanon crisis, and his decision to deploy a large number of troops had succeeded in creating a powerful show of force that encouraged a negotiated settlement. It seemed like a good example to follow. Conversely, the recent Bay of Pigs fiasco showed the dangers of a less resolute course, and Johnson, Rusk, McNamara, and other veterans of the Kennedy administration appear to have been affected profoundly by that experience. Palmer, too, felt that a large force was justified because "in the beginning no one was sure what the internal situation might bring, especially whether the revolt might spread to the countryside."[48] Thus President Johnson "urged the relevant military advisors to review the Dominican Republic contingency plan to assure that there would be enough troops in Santo Domingo to deal with any foreseeable eventuality."[49]

Palmer concurs with the wisdom of a decisive response. "Sending too small a force," he explains, "can backfire by accomplishing only a stalemate or, worse, failing the mission entirely.... The presence of ample force is more likely in the end to result in fewer human casualties, combatant and noncombatant, and less material damage as well; sending an inadequate force is more likely to have the opposite effect." Once the decision to intervene has been made, Palmer cautions against "sending a boy to do a man's work."[50] The results, he argues, speak for themselves. "It was clearly demonstrated," according to Palmer, "that the rapid troop buildup in the Santo Domingo area allowed us to stabilize the situation on land quickly, which in turn permitted a significant and rapid phasedown of US troop strength."[51]

Domestically, Johnson had other incentives to provide a decisive force because he feared that a setback in the Caribbean would weaken his political base and endanger his Great Society program. Arthur Schlesinger, Jr., warned Johnson that failure "to avert a communist takeover" in the Dominican Republic would "probably" mean "losing the House of Representatives next year."[52] Moreover, any weakness against communist expansion would alienate the powerful congressional conservatives who were critical to the passage of Johnson's civil rights, anti-poverty, and medical care reforms. Peter Felten believes Johnson, by his strong response in the Dominican Republic, was likely trying "to appease conservatives on foreign policy in order to win their tolerance of reform at home."[53]

Strategically, the looming crisis in Vietnam helped recommend a strong response as well. Criticizing what he calls a case of "Texan overkill," Undersecretary of State George Ball claims, "Johnson's excessive use of power and effort in the Dominican Republic reflected a wider preoccupation. We were just on the verge of committing large numbers of American combat forces to Vietnam and the President feared that a disaster close to home might lead more Americans to challenge our adventure ten thousand miles away."[54] Palmer dismisses such criticisms, writing, "In my opinion the hindsight judgment of too much force is neither fair nor accurate, because the use of overwhelming force, properly controlled, can save lives and reduce collateral material damage."[55]

Johnson obviously agreed with Palmer, and the president had even considered sending a more robust force, initially authorizing the commitment of not just the 4th Marine Expeditionary Brigade and the entire 82nd, but the 101st Airborne Division as well.[56] However, Johnson later opted against deploying the 101st in order to lend credibility to his desire for a negotiated settlement.[57] Reducing the size of the force helped Johnson shore up the weakness the operation had regarding legitimacy. It was a relatively easy decision. Even without the 101st, the U.S. contingent was adequate for the task at hand, and the principle of security was met in terms of available forces.

Restraint

This accommodation of the principle of security, however, would be mitigated by considerations regarding restraint. The large force would not be allowed to act with a free hand. Palmer astutely described Operation Power Pack as being "more political than military," and early in the operation, he recognized that it was "inevitable that Washington is going to take direct control."[58] Sensing President Johnson's sensitivity to casualties, Palmer ensured that "in all our operations the minimizing of loss of life and of property damage was an integral part of our planning."[59] That the U.S. military could successfully perform its mission under these circumstances is a testimony to the military's outstanding discipline, a characteristic so prevalent that Lawrence Yates describes it as "the critical element in the performance of the US troops in the Dominican intervention."[60]

The marines initially established an ISZ around the American and other embassies in western Santo Domingo, and the 82nd secured the San Isidro Airfield, the San Isidro Highway, and the Duarte Bridge. The area between the two forces, however, was firmly in the hands of the rebels. On May 3, the 82nd established a line of communication (LOC) linking the marine and army forces. Palmer directed the operation be conducted in darkness, in part to "minimize civilian noncombatant casualties and property damage."[61] With the establishment of the LOC, the ever-present political concerns became even more pronounced, and the principle of restraint began to eclipse the principle of security.[62]

The most obvious manifestation of these considerations was in the tactical rules of engagement (TACROE). Because one of President Johnson's stated goals for Power Pack was "to save the lives of all people," the initial TACROE for the Dominican Republic served both a humanitarian and political purpose.[63] The main battleground was Santo Domingo, which was a congested and explosive city with a population of half a million people. Former Ambassador Martin increasingly was concerned with the danger of "a US 'Hungary'—a frontal assault on the 'rebel' stronghold in Ciudad Nueva, with US troops slaughtering thousands of Dominicans, including innocents."[64] Thus the military was limited in its use of tanks and indirect fire to prevent collateral damage. With this consideration in mind, the 82nd redeployed all but one of its artillery batteries by the end of May 1965 and did not even bring its tanks. The marines did, in fact, bring tanks but did not use them. Few argued the merits of these restrictions.[65]

Less palatable was the injunction not to fire unless fired upon. However, this too proved to be a necessary measure because of the initial difficulties in friend or foe identification, an aggressive spirit amongst the troops, and imperfect fire discipline. Needless casualties caused by any of these factors would have seriously hindered the conclusion of a diplomatic solution and the legitimacy of the operation.[66]

However, as the intervention progressed, control from Washington became even more complex and confusing to the soldier on the ground. The general rule not to fire unless fired upon gradually became stricter and stricter until the end result was a prohibition against firing unless the soldier's position was in imminent danger of being overrun. Of course, the rebels took full advantage of this situation. It was not uncommon for an openly armed sniper to stroll down the middle of the street past an American position, fire his weapon, and then depart as nonchalantly as he came — often pronouncing his exit with an obscene gesture directed at the Americans.[67] American soldiers also were subjected to frequent harassing fire from a tall hospital building, conspicuously draped in Red Cross flags.[68] Under these conditions, sniper fire eventually accounted for the majority of the American casualties in the Dominican Republic.[69] In other cases, soldiers were required to watch passively as rebels unloaded a freighter of ammunition within plain view of the American positions.[70] Obeying such rules endangered both soldier safety and morale, but disobeying them would violate the sanctity of the chain of command and risk court martial. Many commanders developed ingenious ways of walking a thin tightrope between compliance and military necessity, but in general, they followed the rules.[71]

Higher headquarters were involved in all details of the TACROE to include restrictions on the use of tear gas and flamethrowers, and the designation of no-patrol areas. When one unit emplaced a string of lights on their perimeter to deter nighttime sniper attacks, the Constitutionalists protested, resulting in an order to remove the lights. Such circumstances moved Army Chief of Staff General Harold Johnson to remark, "One thing that must be remembered ... is that the command of squads has now been transferred to Washington and is not necessarily limited to the Pentagon either."[72]

The astute Palmer called the more restrictive TACROE a "logical step," because he understood that although the situation was a difficult one, restraint actually served the ultimate objective.[73] The U.S. military's goal was an effective ceasefire, but Palmer knew "a quiet, stabilized situation in Santo Domingo was the last thing the rebels wanted." Fomenting unrest and continuing the fighting met their political agenda. Thus, Palmer endeavored "to improve our own discipline and discourage firing on the part of our troops unless there was sufficient and good provocation."[74]

Palmer's philosophy received perhaps its toughest test when the rebels made one last effort to expand out of their Ciudad Nueva stronghold on June 15. Elements of the 82nd quickly checked the rebel progress and were in the midst of a counterattack, but Palmer knew that "wiping out the rebel zone would leave the OAS and the United States open to the charge of perpetuating 'the Budapest of the Western Hemisphere.'"[75] Calling it "the most disagreeable task I ever had to do," Palmer halted the successful operation midstride and ordered the 82nd to consolidate its position "in the most defensible locations available."[76]

The Ciudad Nueva operation presented the IAPF an opportunity to "take matters into its own hands," but instead it acted with political sensitivity and military restraint. The IAPF used enough force to halt the uprising and seriously weaken the rebels militarily, but it remained "responsive to OAS political guidance and control." As a result, Palmer reports, "the negotiating position of the OAS Ad Hoc Committee was immeasurably strengthened." Because a negotiated outcome is what was ultimately desired, Palmer was confident "we did the right thing."[77]

As much operational sense as this approach made, for many soldiers such a situation was highly unnatural. According to Sam Sarkesian, "Once committed, the military professional expects to employ the resources at hand to quickly prevail; it is unconscionable not to use the most effective weaponry and tactics to subdue the enemy."[78] In the Dominican Republic, the military would not be allowed to act in accordance with this expected premium on security. Nonetheless, the U.S. soldiers conducted themselves in concert with the situation's political demands for restraint. When Palmer issued the difficult order to halt the Ciudad Nueva operation, he reports, "To their great credit, the division leaders understood and accepted the orders without complaint."[79]

A variety of observers share Palmer's assessment of the exceptionally measured conduct of the American soldiers. For example, Yates notes that "if restraint provided the key to a political solution to the crisis, discipline provided the key to restraint."[80] Peter Chew, after observing a rifle platoon from the 82nd· noted that "the 'don't fire until fired upon' conditions require[d] the sternest discipline."[81] Likewise, Charles Moskos, Jr., who also accompanied elements of the 82nd, noted that "their exceptional personal discipline had been a major factor in the successful accomplishment of their mission."[82] Moskos cited examples in which soldiers resisted taunts from young Dominicans, took steps to avoid injuring noncombatants though this "consideration was not conspicuously evident within the opposing 'rebel' and 'junta' forces," and ignored enemy efforts to "provoke US soldiers into creating incidents that could be used for propaganda purposes."[83] Echoing Moskos' remarks, Chew relates having observed a Dominican woman openly giving instructions to a concealed sniper. The woman chanced such blatant belligerence because, as one paratrooper explained, "I guess she knows we don't shoot women. We don't play by those rules."[84] Moskos concluded that the Americans "exhibited grace under pressure."[85] Soldier discipline and Palmer's political awareness were critical to this process, but without the operation's inherent adherence to security afforded by the large force size, such restraint would have been much more difficult to achieve. Still, of all the principles, restraint was the one most required in the Dominican Republic, and one the American soldiers executed quite admirably.

Perseverance

This high degree of restraint worked hand in hand with the principle of perseverance. Palmer knew that the Washington-imposed rules clashed with military expediency, and he was a tireless advocate for the military's point of view. Still he appreciated the need for perseverance in stability operations and recognized that, in the long-run, a negotiated political settlement, rather than a heavy-handed military one, was in the best interests of both the U.S. and the Dominican Republic.[86] "Diplomacy and force are not black-and-white alternatives," he explained, "but must be closely intermeshed for the best prospects of success."[87] Rudolph Barnes contends that mission success in OOTW "requires military leaders who can combine military proficiency with the finesse of a diplomat," and to this end, Yates describes Palmer as one of a handful of U.S. officers who truly grasped the "political-military" nature of Power Pack.[88] As a testimony to Palmer's character, Yates speculates that "had a general officer not possessed of Palmer's 'political sensitivity' been in charge of the US forces, the outcome of the crisis might have been decidedly different."[89]

One of Palmer's initiatives to help boost the negotiation effort was a series of information programs and a daily news bulletin for the 82nd troops to help them understand why they were in the Dominican Republic and thus prevent incidents between them and the often hostile rebel-inspired crowds.[90] The American soldiers had been trained to fight and had not been adequately sensitized to political-military considerations when the deployment began.[91] As soon as Palmer had the military situation relatively stable, he began placing greater emphasis on civil affairs and humanitarian aid. Palmer's command climate and political acumen helped his soldiers adopt a more patient and measured approach.

The end result of the combined military and civic actions was that in just three weeks the Power Pack forces had separated the combatants and imposed a military stalemate that ensured the situation would be resolved by negotiation and compromise rather than armed conflict. Once the LOC had been established, Palmer noted increased chances of success "in achieving a political settlement because US troops were in a position to prevent either side from defeating the other."[92] Time was now working against the belligerents and in favor of the U.S. and international peacekeeping effort.[93] Perseverance was working.

Nonetheless, given the rather contentious nature of the intervention and the growing involvement in Vietnam, the U.S. was eager to get its forces out of the Dominican Republic as soon as some sense of stability had been reestablished. This condition would require finding and imposing a political solution that occupied what Palmer called "the 'practical middle ground' between the extreme Left and Right."[94] Such a solution would be very complicated to achieve. As a contemporary news report assessed, in the Dominican Republic, the U.S. was finding "it is easier to move into a country with military force than to get out again."[95] Success would depend on the U.S.'s ability to practice the principle of perseverance in the face of mounting pressure to bring Power Pack to a conclusion.

Complicating the situation was the U.S.'s continuing awkward attempts to maintain neutrality, now as part of the IAPF. Up to this point, the U.S. had found itself providing foreign aid to both the junta and the rebels, although the majority went to the junta.[96] In the long term, Ambassador Bunker favored establishing a "middle road" government, not necessarily associated with either the Constitutionalists or the Loyalists.[97] The solution finally came on September 3, when Hector Garcia-Godoy, a Dominican businessman and diplomat, and the OAS's hand-picked moderate candidate, took the oath of office as president. With this development, the IAPF shed its neutrality and became the protector of Garcia-Godoy's Provisional Government.[98]

With Garcia-Godoy's inauguration, violence in the Dominican Republic dropped to the point that the U.S. could resume the troop withdrawals that it had begun two months earlier. Still, the continued presence of the IAPF proved essential to Garcia-Godoy's survival, and the IAPF and Palmer were instrumental in removing General Wessin, who, as the leader of the archconservative military faction that had ousted President Bosch in 1963, posed a serious threat to Garcia-Godoy. With Wessin gone, the IAPF also demilitarized the rebel stronghold of Ciudad Nueva.

The adherence to the principle of perseverance in the Dominican Republic is consistent with Roland Paris's prescription for "institutions before liberalization" (IBL). The key elements of Paris's strategy are to wait until conditions are ripe for elections, to design an electoral system that rewards moderation, to promote good civil society, to control hate speech, to adopt conflict-reducing economic policies, and to produce the common denominator of rebuilding effective state institutions.[99] Ambassador Bunker seems to have intuitively understood Paris's logic and also knew the process would take time. Fortunately, Bunker by nature was able to remain patient and unhurried, even under great stress.[100] To provide the time he needed, "the IAPF settled down for a 'long, hot summer' of keeping the peace and holding the belligerents apart, while the protracted OAS negotiations continued."[101]

Paris argues that elections are inherently competitive processes that may, in fact, merely result in the rise to power of forces "dedicated to the violent destruction of their rivals."[102] Thus, he argues that elections must be delayed until a time when they can be held not only in a free and fair manner, but also in a way that advances the development of a stable democracy and reduces the risk of renewed violence. This outcome requires an assessment of the political parties likely to participate in the election and the institutional setting in which the election will take place.[103]

Ambassador Bunker addressed these conditions by visualizing elections in the Dominican Republic as coming as the result of two separate stages. The first was establishing a third-force government, and the second was laying the foundation for the electoral process.[104] Garcia-Godoy was an effective choice for the first condition because he had no direct ties with either of the civil war's belligerent parties.[105] The second condition was facilitated by two principal documents: "The Institutional Act" and "The Act of Reconciliation." The Institutional Act established the parameters of Garcia-Godoy's provisional government, outlined the conditions for the elections, and delineated the power and authority of elected officials. The Act of Reconciliation addressed issues such as amnesty, demilitarization, public order, reintegration of ex-rebels or their safe voluntary departure from the country, and the withdrawal of the IAPF.[106]

Paris also considers the situation to be particularly dangerous in cases "in which the principal contenders for election are the very individuals or organizations that recently fought the civil war."[107] He encourages "peace-builders" to employ "a variety of means" to combat this threat, and in the Dominican Republic a very effective solution was to "persuade the Dominican military leaders of the crisis period, loyalist and constitutionalist, to leave the country voluntarily for an indefinite period of time as a patriotic act."[108] Key departures included rebel leader Francisco Caamano and loyalist Caminero Rivera.[109] Even staunch anti-communist Wessin was subjected to a rather "unceremonious removal," which was troubling to Alvim, but which Palmer considered "on the balance ... for the best."[110]

As a result of this groundwork, when the elections were held on June 1, there was "a record voter turnout and a minimum of untoward incidents."[111] A variety of international observers monitored the proceedings and declared them free and honest.[112] The moderate candidate, Joaquin Balaguer, emerged with almost 57 percent of the vote compared to 39 percent for Bosch.[113] Palmer took great pride in the fact that "the new government assumed power under a constitution and electoral process that had not been imposed from without but had been drawn up by Dominicans."[114] Allowing the people of the Dominican Republic to take a measure of ownership of their own destiny was a key to the successful transition.

Balaguer held power for twelve years, and his rule certainly cannot be considered a liberal democracy. Yet while he restored much of the authoritarianism of the Trujillo era to the presidency, Balaguer was "beloved for his beguiling, parental embrace of the country's most destitute people."[115] His successor, Antonio Guzman, ushered in a transition to a more liberal, democratic style of politics and government, and, given the tradition of authoritarianism in the Dominican Republic, it is perhaps fair to take the long view of this process as being a part of a continuum.[116]

Another piece of Paris's IBL strategy that was adhered to in the Dominican Republic is the necessity of controlling hate speech. He advocates regulating the activities of news media that incite hatred and violence as well as developing responsible news outlets that provide accurate sources of information.[117] Radio Santo Domingo had become the "primary weapon" of the rebels in launching a "psychological offensive" against the United States and the OAS.[118] The transition government launched a military strike on several Radio Santo Domingo sites on May 13 and 14, 1965, which reduced the rebels' ability to broadcast outside the capital.[119] Garcia-Godoy ultimately got some control of the facility, but it was still dominated by leftists who broadcast inflammatory messages. In October, a clandestine "Radio San Isidro" also began transmitting anti-government programs.[120]

Radio Santo Domingo remained problematic until December when Garcia-Godoy was able to install a more moderate and neutral director and staff.[121] Resolving this issue well before the June 1966 elections was critical because, as Palmer notes, "In a civil war, propaganda is a deadly weapon, and words can at times be more effective than bullets."[122] In the Dominican Republic, Yates considered the propaganda generated by Radio Santo Domingo to be "the 'biggest thorn' in the side of the Americans."[123] It could not simply be ignored. In answer to critics who see targeting such opposition sites as an infringement on free speech, Samuel Huntington notes that "authority has to exist before it can be limited,"[124] and Paris observes that in 1997, NATO forces in Bosnia seized control of a key transmitter belonging to a Bosnian Serb radio station that had been broadcasting inflammatory propaganda.[125]

A final aspect of Paris's model that can be highlighted by the experience in the Dominican Republic is his contention that the "first task of peacebuilding is to restore [the Weberian monopoly over the legitimate use of force] as a foundation and precondition for all further institution-building efforts."[126] This requirement was problematic in the Dominican Republic because the Dominican National Police (DNP) had become demoralized and disorganized. Palmer oversaw the DNP's slow restoration to effectiveness and began their limited use in patrolling the ISZ, which lay in the "better part" of the city. He restricted them from the rebel sector and prohibited them from making any political arrests.[127] By the time Garcia-Godoy took office, the OAS Ad Hoc Committee was confident enough to grant the DNP full police powers under the authority of the new president.[128] As a testimony to the rejuvenation of the asset, a special element of the DNP, equipped with helmets, armor vests, and heavier weapons on loan from the Americans, spearheaded the move to demilitarize downtown Santo Domingo by moving into Ciudad Nueva and taking over police jurisdiction. Half of this force was comprised from the regular police and the other half from ex-rebels who had police experience.[129] The restoration of the DNP was a necessary step in establishing the credibility of the new Dominican government.

Paris notes that proponents of the "quick and dirty" approach may argue that IBL takes too long. He counters that "the danger of prolonged deployment is one that must be faced and accepted if the goal of peacebuilding is to foster a stable and lasting peace." He adds that "the IBL strategy does not preclude the judicious use of timetables to maintain the forward momentum of a peace-building mission."[130] Palmer concurs that the military commitment must make steady progress to conclusion. "The intervening forces should get in and get out as soon as possible," he argues. "Stability operations of this nature are, in a sense, deadly situations: the longer the forces stay, the worse things are likely to become."[131] Thus, there appears to be a useful tension between staying long enough and not staying too long. Power Pack, with its willingness to build institutions before rushing to hold elections, but at the same time having the pressure of Vietnam to provide a sense of urgency, appears to have satisfied Paris's vision.[132]

Events have proved the wisdom of the measured and long-term approach advocated by Paris and practiced by Palmer and his colleagues. Power Pack helped set the stage for decades of relative peace in the Dominican Republic. Especially in sharp contrast to the chronic instability of neighboring Haiti, the Dominican Republic has been relatively calm.[133]

Conclusion

Throughout its duration, Operation Power Pack demonstrated extremely strong adherence to the principles of security and restraint. The American force was massive in size and capability, but the rules of engagement were strict, and soldier discipline was exemplary. The American involvement was also characterized by an adherence to the principle of perseverance in efforts to help transition the Dominican Republic to a new government. In this regard, the U.S. demonstrated some of the characteristics of Paris's "IBL" strategy.

Operation Power Pack suffered from an ambiguous objective that was potentially problematic for the military. This deficiency was mitigated by the political sensitivity of General Palmer and the military's willingness to sub-ordinate itself to civilian authority.

Adherence to the principles of legitimacy and unity of effort began problematically but progressed to satisfaction. The unilateral nature of the initial deployment and America's legacy of imperialism in the Caribbean posed a serious challenge to the operation's legitimacy. The subsequent significant role of the OAS and IAPF helped reverse this deficiency as well as enhancing international unity of effort. The breach in unity of effort between the American political and military establishments was in large part repaired by the close interpersonal interaction between Palmer and Bunker.

This analysis suggests relationships among several of the principles, both in terms of correlation and balanced application. Like Operation Bluebat in Lebanon, Operation Power Pack highlights the opportunity for restraint that is facilitated by adherence to the principle of security. Security "complements and complicates" restraint, and too much of one can be problematic for the other.[134] Palmer was able to strike the proper balance, noting "although large and powerful forces were deployed to the region, the United States showed great restraint, using only the minimum force appropriate to the situation — a basic principle in dealing with a problem such as the 1965 Dominican case."[135] Also like Operation Bluebat, the U.S.–centric anticommunist strategic objective negatively impacted legitimacy, but the U.S. accepted this risk in pursuit of its Cold War agenda and perception of national interests. The requirement for security generated by the operational objective of the NEO recommended unilateral action at the expense of unity of effort. Once this immediate objective was accomplished and the strategic objective of transitioning the Dominican Republic to a stable country that was safe from communist threat gained dominance, the U.S. exhibited the prerequisite perseverance. Like Operation Bluebat, this OOTW suggests that perseverance is a function of objective in that perseverance must be assessed in the context of being directed toward a specific objective. Also like Operation Bluebat, the balanced application of the principles resulted in operational success.

CHAPTER 4

Vietnam Pacification: The Primacy of Objective

In a "people's war," the center of gravity is the people. The U.S. only belatedly realized this to be the true nature of the Vietnam War and then embarked on a dizzying array of initiatives and organizations that collectively represented the "pacification program." America's lackluster and haphazard pursuit of pacification highlights the objective principle of OOTW because of the program's perceived competition with an alternative strategy that saw victory as coming from more conventional battlefield victories. In part as an extension of its problems with objective, pacification also failed to adhere to the principles of security and legitimacy. It demonstrated an evolving adherence to unity of effort, and its adherence to restraint was mixed. Like the rest of the war effort, pacification suffered from a critical lack of perseverance, and America withdrew from Vietnam in 1973. As a result of this OOTW, the U.S. failed in its objective of securing South Vietnam from a communist insurgency.

Background

After the defeat of the French at Dien Bien Phu, the 1954 Geneva Accords divided Vietnam in two halves, one led by Ho Chi Minh in the north and the other by Emperor Bao Dai in the south. Elections that would ultimately unify Vietnam were scheduled to occur two years later. In October 1955, Ngo Dinh Diem became the first president of the newly formed Republic of South Vietnam, and the U.S. established the Military Advisory and Assistance Group for Vietnam (MAAGV) to support the fledgling ally. When the date set by the Geneva Accords passed without the promised countrywide elections, Ho launched a protracted war to realize his vision of a united, communist Vietnam. By 1958, an estimated 12,000 Vietcong (VC) or Vietnamese Communists were operating in South Vietnam, creating a Viet Cong Infrastructure (VCI) that would enable Ho's insurgency.

The VC's primary target was South Vietnam's peasantry, and the pacification campaign was designed to shield them from this threat while at the same time strengthening their commitment to the South Vietnamese government. Of all the situations that made the South Vietnamese rural population vulnerable to VC exploitation, perhaps the most frustrating was the critical need for land reform. The Agroville Program was an early pacification initiative intended to address this condition.[1]

Beginning in 1958, the Diem government used a combination of direct force and incentives to relocate peasants scattered throughout the countryside into large communities called Agrovilles. The initial focus area for the effort was the Mekong Delta where the dispersed pattern of settlement exacerbated the security problem. Villages were strung out for miles along canals and waterways, making them vulnerable to communist infiltration. In a classic example of denial and oversimplification, President Diem felt that it was this geographic isolation that made the peasants easy prey rather than considering that the VC might actually be appealing to the people by meeting their needs. Thus, in Diem's mind, relocation would free the people from the clutches of the enemy and the problem would be solved.[2]

In addition to relocating the population, Diem wanted to secure the people's allegiance by making them aware of their larger national identity. To accomplish this goal, he emphasized collective action, self-help, and hard work — ideas that were all subject to abuses. Provincial officials conscripted thousands of peasants for construction work without pay, drafting many more than were actually needed. The construction interrupted the farmers' efforts to bring in their harvests, and a scarcity of construction equipment forced the projects to be completed largely by manual labor. Rather than correcting this problem, the government boasted that because of the absence of machines, "the people should feel that this was something they had done themselves."[3] In another selfish manipulation, Diem argued that the peasants had to build the Agrovilles themselves in order to free Vietnam from foreign dependence. In the process, he was able to protect the project from the American oversight that he feared would limit his options.[4]

Diem characteristically set a rushed pace for the Agrovilles in spite of providing only limited resources. The government allocated the equivalent of $13,000 for each settlement, although estimates for some centers were two-thirds greater than that. The pressure of limited time and money led to additional conscriptions as officials emphasized signs of physical progress rather than peasant satisfaction. Of course, these increased demands only served to alienate the peasants further and clearly demonstrated the program's lack of adherence to the principle of legitimacy. In the end, the Agroville Program served more to exacerbate the problem rather than help it.[5]

Under pressure from the Americans, Diem finally agreed in March 1960 to slow down the construction of Agrovilles in order to alleviate the program's excesses, and this deceleration eventually turned into a gradual abandonment of the program. With only twenty centers having been built and further construction lagging far behind, Diem announced in September that the program would be halted. He explained his decision by citing monetary difficulties, but U.S. Ambassador Elbridge Durbrow, recognizing the program's lack of legitimacy, speculated that "perhaps [Diem] has finally been convinced that the 'real cost' is the loss of popular support for his regime."[6]

The failure of the Agroville program left the pacification effort somewhat adrift. Not only had the Agrovilles failed to stem the insurgency, they seemed to have contributed to it. Diem now found himself under increasing pressure to adopt the U.S.–styled policies he had hoped to avoid. In response, Diem's brother Nhu began plans for a successor to the Agrovilles that became known as the Strategic Hamlet Program. Based on a program that had worked well for the British in Malaya, the idea was to concentrate the rural population in a limited number of fortified villages to provide them physical security against the VC. By focusing on existing settlements, rather than attempting to build new ones, the Strategic Hamlet Program hoped to avoid some of the construction problems that had plagued the Agrovilles. Once security was established, social programs that would hopefully foster government allegiance were planned to follow.[7]

The Strategic Hamlet Program was largely a failure. Unlike the Chinese immigrant squatters who were the subject of the British relocations in Malaya, the Buddhist South Vietnamese had ancestral ties to the land, and moving interrupted their practice of veneration of ancestors. Additionally, the relocations caused the peasants to abandon generations of hard work and took vital, arable land out of production, which hampered economic progress. In the new hamlets, the peasants had to start over from scratch, without compensation for their labor or loss. These factors obviously led to a disgruntled population that was ripe for VC exploitation, a situation facilitated by the fact that many VC secretly relocated to the new hamlets with the rest of the population. Many peasants were so alienated by the entire ordeal that they slipped away from the hamlets and returned to their ancestral lands. This development greatly hindered one of the goals of the relocation, which was to create free fire zones in the vacated areas based on the assumption that anyone there now was a VC.[8]

As part of the program, the VC-controlled areas that could not be penetrated by the government were subjected to random bombardment by artillery and aircraft in order to drive the people into the safety of the strategic hamlets. This process created tens of thousands of refugees, which Diem advertised as a show of political support — the population voting with its feet — as the people fled the VC to government-held territory. In actuality, the refugees were angered by this dangerous disruption to their lives, and they resented the government as the instrument of it.[9]

The relocations created other problems as well, including the perception that if relocation was necessary in the first place, then security must be weak. Many peasants were left with the impression that if the South Vietnamese government was not able to secure even its allies, fully supporting the government would be dangerous. Finally, by moving the population away from the countryside, a significant, if imperfect, source of intelligence was lost.[10] Summing up the Strategic Hamlet's failure to address the needs of the South Vietnamese people, Dave Palmer concludes the program was "executed with too little real feeling for the human beings involved."[11]

All these problems were exacerbated by reporting inaccuracies that served to further weaken perceptions of the program's legitimacy. By the summer of 1962, the Diem government claimed to have established 3,225 strategic hamlets, which held over four million people or one-third of South Vietnam's population. When the Diem regime collapsed in October 1963, it became apparent that many of these hamlets existed on paper only, and the reporting was part of a South Vietnamese misinformation campaign to deceive the Americans. As a case in point, the number of "secure" hamlets in Long An Province was revised downward from over two hundred to about ten after Diem's death.[12] Accurately measuring the success of the effort would be a common difficulty throughout the pacification program and a continual challenge to its legitimacy.

As with the Agrovilles, the result of the Strategic Hamlet Program was "less rather than more security in the countryside."[13] Still searching for a solution, Henry Cabot Lodge, who was Durbrow's successor as U.S. Ambassador in Saigon, proposed another pacification program called Hop Tac in June 1964. In this effort, pacification would spread outward from Saigon like a "giant oil spot" or concentric "rings of steel." In this way, the capital city would be safeguarded because the enemy could never reach it through the secured outer rings. By September, South Vietnamese troops were implementing Lodge's plan, but a year later, little progress had been made.[14]

Part of the difficulty was that the Americans were still having problems understanding the situation in Vietnam and determining the correct objective. Language such as "rings of steel" reflected an attitude that the war could be won by isolating the population from the enemy rather than addressing the fundamental problems that made the population vulnerable in the first place. Progress in these areas would be difficult, however, because of the weak commitment of the South Vietnamese government to real reform. In fact, Hop Tac revealed the Army of the Republic of Vietnam (ARVN) to be a largely political organization structured more as a private force designed to protect the regime from a coup than a professional army motivated to protect the population from the VC. The result was that ARVN "evinced little enthusiasm or aptitude for taking on the 'village war.'"[15]

Hop Tac also suffered from a lack of unity of effort. The South Vietnamese clearly desired to run the pacification program without outside interference, and they perceived Hop Tac almost exclusively as an American plan. Thus, there was little incentive for them to execute it enthusiastically since, even if it succeeded, the credit would go elsewhere. On the other hand, while increased South Vietnamese autonomy potentially would help pacification's legitimacy, it had also been shown to lead to inefficiency and a lack of accountability. South Vietnamese government officials thus far had demonstrated a reluctance to support reforms if compliance would weaken their power, and their self-serving execution of many pacification programs actually drove some South Vietnamese to the VC side. Hop Tac showed that the Americans and South Vietnamese still had not achieved an appropriate level of cooperation and common purpose in their battle against the communists.[16]

Hop Tac also failed to recognize the essentially decentralized nature of Vietnamese society. While it seemed logical and businesslike to the American mind to work from the center out and to look to government for centralized solutions, such an attitude was antithetical to the severely localized nature of rural Vietnamese society. The end result was almost a reverse oil spot model. First, the VC were able to defeat and displace ARVN units. Then, VC political cadres worked out from previously held areas into the newly available territory to expand VC control and influence at the expense of the South Vietnamese government.[17] In this regard, Hop Tac had clearly failed to adhere to the principle of security. With this latest disappointing effort, the pacification problem continued to appear to defy solution.

Analysis of the Principles

Legitimacy

Recognizing sufficient progress was not being made, President Lyndon Johnson convened a meeting with South Vietnamese leaders including new President Nguyen Van Thieu and Premier Nguyen Cao Ky in Honolulu, Hawaii in February 1966 to discuss the status of economic, social, and political projects for South Vietnam. Johnson made it clear that he expected a massive increase in pacification productivity in the upcoming year, and he expressed his mounting impatience with the need to develop an effective American organization for pacification support. The Honolulu Conference sent a clear message that Johnson considered business as usual to be sufficient.[18]

As a result of the meeting, the South Vietnamese decided to give a new face to the pacification program by calling it Revolutionary Development. At the core of this new program were teams of fifty-nine South Vietnamese specially trained and financed by the Central Intelligence Agency (CIA). Thirty of the team members were self-defense experts and the other twenty-nine were specialists in every kind of village need. The teams, dressed in peasant garb, would move into a hamlet, identify and eliminate the VC secret political cadre, remove corrupt South Vietnamese officials from office, organize democratic institutions, and create a hamlet defense force. Once these objectives were accomplished, the team would move on to another hamlet while the South Vietnamese government developed programs in education, health, land reform, and financial credit in the original hamlet. To supplement these teams, several U.S. civilian agencies worked at various levels in information, agriculture, and public health programs.[19]

Such an effort was consistent with "PROVN — The Program for the Pacification and Long-Term Development of South Vietnam," a U.S. Army report commissioned in 1965 and completed in March 1966 that called for a greater focus at local levels. The study argued that "the crucial actions are those that occur at the village, district and provincial levels. This is where the war must be fought; this is where the war and the object which lies beyond it must be won."[20] Nonetheless, while appearing promising at first, Revolutionary Development belied a basic flaw in connection with the principle of legitimacy. The South Vietnamese government was not at all committed to the reforms the programs envisioned. In fact, it viewed a better educated and empowered peasantry as a threat to its power.[21]

Moreover, such a strategy lacked legitimacy in the eyes of many American officials because it conflicted with General William Westmoreland's vision for "the big war" fought by battalion-sized conventional operations. The enemy would be defeated by fighting, not by civic action, according to this school of thought. While Robert Komer and other pacification advocates favored a "clear, hold, and rebuild" strategy, Westmoreland favored a traditional military solution to the war by using large unit search and destroy operations. Knowing he lacked the forces to conduct both a war of attrition and pacification, Westmoreland relegated pacification to a second tier status as "the other war." The recommendations of PROVN would be largely ignored until General Creighton Abrams replaced Westmoreland as Commander, MACV in 1968.[22]

Against such resistance, pacification officials attempted various ways to use statistics to not only measure results, but also to boost the program's legitimacy with an often-skeptical military command. Major General Lewis Walt, commander of the III Marine Amphibious Force, developed an early model based on five "progress indicators": destruction of enemy units, destruction

President Johnson and President Thieu confer at the President's Suite, Royal Hawaiian Hotel during the Honolulu Conference in 1966. Photograph by Yoichi Okamoto. Lyndon Baines Johnson Library.

of the Viet Cong infrastructure, South Vietnamese government establishment of security, South Vietnamese government establishment of local government, and degree of development of the New Life Program (a successor to the Strategic Hamlet Program). Each indicator represented a possible total of twenty points and was broken down into related subdivisions. A village that accumulated sixty points reflected "firm South Vietnamese/U.S. Government influence," while a score of eighty points indicated pacification. Critics questioned Walt's formula, arguing that it was possible for a village to gather enough points to be declared "pacified" even if the VCI, the most important of the indicators, remained virtually undisturbed.[23]

Within a year, the CIA developed a more sophisticated "Hamlet Evaluation System" (HES), which, while it "borrowed freely" from Walt's system, sought to "provide a uniform measure of progress throughout Vietnam."[24] Under HES, American advisors made monthly assessments on worksheets that were then sent to Saigon for computer processing into composite scores. Like Walt's system, however, HES was susceptible to challenges to its objectivity and legitimacy. The evaluations took place at the district headquarters, far away from rural hamlets. A senior advisor normally visited just one-fourth of the district hamlets in a month. Visits to individual hamlets usually lasted only a few hours, and during that time most advisors were completely dependent on interpreters. The result was evaluations based largely on surface appearances or historical data. To make matters worse, these advisory positions were not considered career enhancing jobs. Thus, many military officers cycled through them as quickly as possible in pursuit of the more prized combat positions.[25]

The result was that, in spite of efforts to make the evaluation as objective and legitimate as possible, assessment was still subject to manipulation. For example, in October 1968 the U.S. faced the disconcerting prospect of being subjected to demands for concessions at the Paris Peace Conference based on a communist claim of representing a large segment of the countryside. To preempt this possibility, MACV inaugurated the Accelerated Pacification Program (APP) in November.[26] The APP modified the criteria, attempting now to establish a minimal government presence in as many hamlets as possible. Some 1,000 additional hamlets were earmarked, but to accommodate these increased quantities, the quality of the effort was diminished. Where cadres once stayed six months, they now only stayed six weeks. One American adviser said, "The name of the game is planting the government flag."[27] Using these new standards, the number of "relatively secure" hamlets shot up to 73.3 percent, an all-time high.[28] In the process though, legitimacy suffered.

The pacification effort received a boost when Abrams replaced Westmoreland as Commander, MACV in 1968. Abrams not only was more committed to the "one-war concept" than his predecessor, but the reality of the phased American withdrawal and Vietnamization limited opportunities for large combat operations. Instead, Abrams emphasized that "the key strategic thrust is to provide meaningful, continued security for the Vietnamese people in expanding areas of increasingly effective civil authority."[29] He was especially interested in neutralizing the VCI and separating it from the population, considering the infrastructure to be the "eyes" for the enemy main forces. Without this asset, Abrams figured the main forces "cannot obtain intelligence, cannot obtain food, cannot prepare the battlefield, and cannot move 'unseen.'"[30] What Abrams hoped to do was to implement the essential provisions of the PROVN study that had been largely ignored when it had been announced in 1966. He insisted that population security, not enemy destruction, was the definitive mission. One observer called the new approach "Son of PROVN."[31]

Vietnamization also helped to belatedly convince the South Vietnamese government to get behind pacification, as President Nguyen Van Thieu realized that he had to secure a popular base before the American withdrawal.[32] He actively promoted the return of village elections that Diem had abolished in 1956 and promulgated what the *New York Times* called "probably the most imaginative and progressive non-communist land reform of the twentieth century."[33] While admitting Thieu had many critics in other aspects of his performance, Komer assessed Thieu as "personally the most pacification-minded of all top [South Vietnamese] leaders and did more than any other person to promote its growth."[34] Komer praised Thieu for chairing the Central Pacification and Development Council and using his personal leadership to make the 1970 Pacification and Development Plan a primarily South Vietnamese drafted document.[35] The South Vietnamese assumption of ownership for the pacification strategy did much to enhance its legitimacy, but this significant development was far too late in coming.

Objective

Like Thieu, the Americans were slow to realize and accept the fact that the true objective in the war was the winning of the hearts and minds of the Vietnamese people. Thoroughly schooled in Mao's doctrine of protracted war, the communists, however, understood this key to victory and waged the war accordingly. They gained deep inroads into the South Vietnamese rural population thanks in large part to the work done by the VC during the initial phases of Mao's model, and the establishment of a VC "shadow government" throughout the South Vietnamese countryside had helped solidify this hold. This shadow government consisted of communist cadres who were secretly assigned positions as village chiefs; police officers; postal workers; and district-, province-, and national-level officers. These officials levied taxes, regulated trade, drafted men, and punished criminals on behalf of the communist cause. The VC hoped to have a complete government in place when their victory was finally won, and these individuals then could step forward and formally claim their offices.[36]

The pacification program was designed to weaken this control the VC had on the countryside and simultaneously strengthen the confidence the people had in the South Vietnamese government. The first goal would protect the rural population from the insurgents and also help deprive the insurgency of its rural support base. The second goal would be brought about by a host of reforms that would address the needs of the people and thus win their loyalty to the government. Thus, pacification had a logical concept for the principle of objective, but one that proved difficult to measure and assess in a practical sense.[37]

Komer realized that the chaotic nature of a half-formed country at war with an ever-present enemy created a difficult environment for dramatic progress. Knowing that no one program could achieve success by itself, Komer opted for quantity over quality. His efforts can be roughly divided into four categories. The first involved a massive effort to produce and disseminate propaganda. Second were initiatives focused on distributing food and other supplies to the countryside. Next were paramilitary programs designed to control the rural population by improving physical security. Finally, there was a whole host of new ways to measure progress and assess effects in order to statistically determine what percent of the population had been pacified.[38]

Ever since the conference in Honolulu, there had been increasing calls to conceptualize pacification in terms of incremental results.[39] As a result, Komer introduced a variety of means to measure the effort in order to determine if pacification was producing "an acceptable rate of return for [the] heavy investments."[40] The HES was an example. It used a five letter scoring system to assess progress via eighteen security and development indicators. Security indicators were in the categories of VC military activity, VC political and subversive activities, and security based on friendly capabilities. Development indicators were in the categories of administrative and political activities; health, education, and welfare; and economic development. An "A" hamlet was excelling in all areas of security and development. A "B" hamlet was still considered high-grade with effective 24-hour security, adequate development, and no VC presence or activity. A "C" hamlet was relatively secure day and night. Viet Cong military control had been broken, and there were no overt VC incidents, although VC taxation was perhaps continuing. Economic improvement programs were underway. In a "D" hamlet, the VC frequently entered or harassed at night, and VC infrastructure was largely intact. The

South Vietnamese program was in its infancy, and control of the hamlet was still strictly contested. An "E" hamlet was definitely under VC control, and American and South Vietnamese officials entered only as part of a military operation. Most of the population in an "E" hamlet supported the VC.[41] When Komer began the HES there were 12,600 hamlets. He was able to assign U.S. senior military advisors to 222 of the 242 South Vietnamese districts.[42]

One criticism of HES was that because the advisors had a vested professional interest in the results, the system was prone to manipulation. When William Colby replaced Komer as head of CORDS, Colby built on his prior experience with the Strategic Hamlet Program to create a new evaluation system designed to remove some of the subjectivity that affected HES. As part of this process, the army contracted with Control Data Corporation to develop a new survey called "HES 70." HES 70 was billed as "a highly integrated man-machine interface" which would solve the problem of subjectivity by being "objective and uni-dimensional."[43] The new survey counted such things as TV sets, organized activities for youths, motorized vehicles, self-defense forces, and other key indicators of security and development. However, in a marked departure from the old system, advisers no longer did the rating, and all scoring was done in Saigon using a formula not known to the advisers. The idea behind this arrangement was to remove the impression that the advisers were actually evaluating themselves. While HES 70 improved the system, it remained better suited to measure quantifiable factors such as control and suppression of the opposition rather than the less tangible but more significant ideas of popular allegiance and the strength of commitment to the South Vietnamese government.[44]

Current military doctrine uses the term *measures of effectiveness* (MOEs) for techniques such as the ones used by Komer and Colby. A MOE is "a criterion used to assess changes in system behavior, capability, or operational environment that is tied to measuring the attainment of an end state, achievement of an objective, or creation of an effect."[45] While all MOEs can at best offer incomplete assessments of the overall situation, the tools used by Komer and Colby did much to quantify progress toward the achievement of pacification's objective.[46]

Unity of Effort

The Hamlet Evaluation System, however, was just one of the many often competing and disjointed initiatives that comprised what can only be loosely called the pacification "program." At the time American ground troops were introduced to Vietnam in 1965, a variety of civilian agencies had developed their own pacification programs which they were coordinating through the

U.S. Embassy. The rapid expansion of military forces added military advisory teams to the pacification effort in all of South Vietnam's provinces and most of its districts. There was, however, no formal system of combining the civilian and military initiatives.[47]

One of the obstacles to unity of effort was that pacification meant different things to different people. Because the word stemmed from the French period in Vietnam, to many Vietnamese pacification smacked of colonialism and outside interference. Komer admitted "the term often had unfortunate connotations."[48] Nonetheless the Americans continued to use the phrase, reflecting a failure to fully understand the Vietnamese situation.

Within the American ranks, many considered pacification to be "the other war," contrasting it with the strategy of defeating the enemy by battle and attrition. Perhaps reflecting their diverse historical experiences, the marines and the army viewed pacification differently, and early marine initiatives "quickly involved key Marine officers in a stormy debate with the Army-dominated US Military Assistance Command Vietnam (MACV) over the appropriate strategy for winning the war."[49] Even MACV commanders William Westmoreland and Creighton Abrams came to represent different strategic approaches.

In such an environment, unity of effort was elusive. Because "pacification is an imprecise term," Thomas Scoville explains, "there was never agreement among Americans in Vietnam on just what pacification was and how it might be achieved. Some saw it as controlling the population; others as winning the people's allegiance. Some viewed it as a long-term process of bringing in addition to security, economic, political, and social development to the people."[50] The result was a disjointed and fragmented approach to pacification and a myriad of programs that often were not synchronized or synergistic.[51]

Pacification could make little progress under such conditions. In January 1966, Westmoreland wrote, "It is abundantly clear that all political, military, economic, and security (police) programs must be completely integrated in order to attain any kind of success."[52] President Johnson also saw the need for greater coordination and wanted a single manager to head the entire pacification program. In March, he appointed National Security Council member Robert Komer his special assistant for pacification and tasked him with coming up with the solution.[53]

One problem facing Komer was defining the roles of the Department of Defense and the Department of State. He succeeded in convincing the military, which he argued controlled 90 percent of the resources, to lead the effort, but the civilian agencies uniformly opposed this plan. As an ill-conceived compromise, Ambassador Lodge was directed by Washington to create a new organization called the Office of Civil Operations (OCO) in November

1966 in an attempt to bring more efficient management to the effort. Expressing high hopes, President Johnson told Lodge, "I intend to see that our organization back here for supporting this [pacification] is promptly tightened and strengthened and I know that you will want to do the salve at your end ... I suggest that your designation of [Deputy Ambassador William Porter] as being in total charge, under your supervision, of all aspects of the rural construction program would constitute a clear and visible sign to the Vietnamese and to our own people that the Honolulu Conference really marks a new departure in this vital field of our effort there."[54]

The results fell far short of these high expectations, in part because of Lodge's recalcitrance in embracing Johnson's vision. Unwilling to appreciably relinquish his control over pacification, Lodge unified the civilian agencies but excluded the military aspects from Porter's charge. For his part, Porter saw his job merely as being to coordinate existing pacification efforts, rather than trying to establish direct command over different bureaucracies. Although Porter understood "the basic idea is to place total responsibility on one senior individual to pull together all of the civil aspects of revolutionary development," he saw his role "primarily as a coordination effort" and did not intend "to get into the middle of individual agency activities and responsibilities." When he did interact with an agency, he endeavored "to suggest rather than criticize."[55] The result was that, although Komer considered it "a step in the right direction," the OCO did little to correct the existing problem of unity of effort.[56] Like its predecessor Revolutionary Development, the OCO was short-lived and would be the last attempt to have pacification run by the U.S. mission in Saigon.[57]

In May 1967, the U.S. replaced the OCO with CORDS, an acronym for Civil Operations and Revolutionary Development, which combined the names of the last two pacification efforts and represented a unification of the previously fragmented pacification effort. While CORDS was under the MACV command, it included representatives from a host of civilian agencies including the Agency for International Development (AID), the Department of State, the CIA, the United States Information Agency (USIA), and the White House. The military and civilian efforts were now fully integrated at all levels in a single chain of command. At its peak strength at the end of 1969, CORDS had approximately 6,000 military and 1,100 civilian personnel.[58] Although late in coming, CORDS represented a dramatic step in the pacification effort, but even with this improved unity of effort, pacification still consisted of a mind-boggling quantity of initiatives that, although prioritized, even Komer assessed as "admittedly inefficient."[59]

Komer was a former CIA official who had served in both the Kennedy and Johnson administrations as an aid expert. When President Johnson appointed him Deputy to the Commander USMACV for CORDS, Komer

President Johnson and Ambassador Komer at a meeting in the Oval Office of the White House in 1966. Photograph by Yoichi Okamoto. Lyndon Baines Johnson Library.

assumed ambassadorial rank and became the first ambassador to serve directly under a military command and also have command responsibility for military personnel and resources. The relationship between Westmoreland and Komer was replicated throughout MACV. Each of the four corps commanders was partnered with a CORDS chief who had direct responsibility for the province advisory teams in the corps area and coordinated military and civil plans as well as military civic action. The resulting unity of effort infused the pacification program with a new sense of purpose and urgency.[60]

Komer found common cause with Ellsworth Bunker, who had replaced Maxwell Taylor as ambassador in Saigon in March 1967. Bunker objected to those who called pacification "the other war," protesting that "to me this is all one war. Everything we do is an aspect of the total effort to achieve our objective here."[61] Komer and Bunker represented a new philosophy that pacification would no longer be relegated to a subsidiary role in the war. Komer in particular also sought to improve the South Vietnamese Regional Forces and Popular Forces (RF and PF) and police who were participating in pacification.[62] He provided these forces additional training and equipment, to include M16 rifles, and greatly expanded advisory attention. He established a program to field 353 Mobile Advisory Teams (MAT), each of which consisted of two American officers and three non-commissioned officers, to give what he called "on-the-job training" to the RF and PF units. By these steps, Komer demonstrated he understood that the South Vietnamese would have to be active, capable, and willing participants in the pacification process.[63]

Komer also improved unity of effort and accountability by establishing unified civilian-military advisory teams that worked with each of the South Vietnamese ministries associated with pacification at all levels from hamlet to national. Part of their function was to contribute to periodic reports on the progress of various programs and on the impact of military operations on pacification. Among the benefits of these "report cards" was the ability to identify corrupt and incompetent South Vietnamese officials and to increase U.S. leverage to eliminate those who were not meeting the standard.[64]

Komer noted that "there was no one pacification technique that could of itself and by itself be decisive if we just put all our resources behind it. So as a practical matter we pulled together all the various programs then in operation — civilian and military — that looked as though they could make a contribution."[65] It was not a system that reflected efficiency or rigid unity of effort, but it did seek to lend some order to a very fluid situation. Through CORDS, Komer hoped by trial and error, time, and cumulative effect to make gradual progress.[66]

Komer saw CORDS as "the organizational key" to the pacification effort.[67] Prior to its creation, Komer assessed that "everybody and nobody had been responsible" for pacification.[68] He claimed that "CORDS not only unified the US support and advisory effort but provided impetus to getting the GVN (Government of South Vietnam) to move in the same direction."[69] It was CORDS that brought some belated measure of unity of effort to pacification.

Security

Komer and other proponents of pacification knew there could be "no civil progress without constant real security," and as numerous observers noted, the fundamental problem was an absence of that security.[70] Recognizing this prerequisite, Komer pragmatically argued, "Until the GVN regained dominant control of the countryside and provided credible semipermanent protection to the farmers, it would hardly be feasible to proceed with other aspects of pacification."[71] In the same vein, Ambassador Taylor stated, "We should have learned from our frontier forbears that there is little use planting corn outside the stockade if there are still Indians around the woods outside."[72] The 1966 PROVN study had urged this same philosophy.

The program that probably came closest to the intent of PROVN, and the one that best adhered to the principles of both security and unity of effort, was the Combined Action Program or CAP. Beginning as a small experiment to secure U.S. military bases around Phu Bai and Da Nang in 1965, CAP soon became the linchpin in the marines' strategy for winning the war.[73] It also came to exemplify Westmoreland's negative attitude toward pacification.

A CAP platoon was a combination of a fourteen-man marine corps rifle squad and one navy medical corpsman, all who were volunteers, and a locally recruited Popular Forces (PF) platoon of about thirty-five men. The resulting CAP was assigned responsibility for a village, which typically consisted of five hamlets spread out over four square kilometers with an average population of 3,500 people. The American marines lived with their Vietnamese PF counterparts and become integral parts of the unit. The effect was synergistic. The marines gained intelligence from the South Vietnamese soldiers' knowledge of the local terrain and enemy, while the PF benefited from the marines' firepower, tactical skills, and discipline. The CAP was a solid and mutually beneficial combination.[74]

Perhaps most important, the constant marine presence sent a powerful message that the Americans were there to stay. They did not fly in by helicopter in the morning and fly out at night to leave the villagers at the mercy of the VC. This continued presence was critical because the peasant who cooperated with the government had to carefully weigh the risk of VC reprisals against himself, his family, his friends, and his community with the benefits of improved clothing, food, education, and medical assistance. When the Americans flew in and flew out, the risks to the Vietnamese villager often outweighed the benefits. However, under CAP, the marines shared the same fate as the South Vietnamese soldiers and people. In fact, CAP marines took 2.5 times the casualties of the PF in the CAP. The CAP was a strong testimony of American commitment and partnership, and gave the Vietnamese people a sense of enduring security.[75]

The CAP program expanded steadily, and in 1966 there were fifty-seven CAP platoons. By the end of 1967, the number had grown to seventy-nine. Despite these increases and demonstrated success, Westmoreland was unwilling to adopt the program, arguing that he "simply had not enough numbers to put a squad of Americans in every village and hamlet; that would be fragmenting resources and exposing them to defeat in detail."[76] While there is some merit to Westmoreland's argument about numbers, his genuine objection lay more in a fundamental strategic difference. Westmoreland viewed the CAPs as static and defensive employments of his resources. Instead, he favored the aggressive pursuit and destruction of enemy forces. The focus of CAP at the small unit level also violated Westmoreland's quest for the mass he needed to gain a conventional battlefield victory.

On the other hand, CAP advocates argued that the real battlefields were the villages, and the real enemy was the VC in them. Lieutenant General Victor Krulak had served as the Special Assistant for Counterinsurgency and Special Activities during the Kennedy administration before becoming the commanding general of Fleet Marine Force Pacific. He argued that "if the enemy cannot get to the people he cannot win." In an effort to "comb the guerrillas out of the people's lives," Krulak argued that protecting the South Vietnamese population must be "a matter of first business."[77] Once the villages were secured, the repelling of enemy main forces would be an easy matter, given the American superiority in firepower and mobility. Furthermore, the main enemy forces would be severely weakened by denying them the logistical support they enjoyed from the unsecured villages. Such arguments fell largely on deaf ears.[78]

In the end, Westmoreland never put the CAP concept fully to the test and ultimately vetoed the strategic concept. Perceived as competition with "the big war," CAP was never allocated the manpower resources it required, and, lacking a grand strategic direction, its local successes were never able to be replicated on a larger scale. For many, CAP showed that the marines, building on their experience in Cuba, Haiti, the Dominican Republic, Nicaragua, and Panama, seemed to understand pacification better than their army counterparts.

The philosophical difference between the two services is exemplified by Krulak and army Major General Julian Ewell. Krulak insisted that the big force engagements "could move to another planet today, and we would still not have won the war because the Vietnamese people are the prize."[79] In contrast, Ewell, commander of the 9th Infantry Division and a major proponent of the body count, had his staff draw up a report that concluded "the most relevant statistical index of combat effectiveness was the average number of Viet Cong losses inflicted daily by the unit in question."[80] Ewell explained, "I guess I basically felt that the 'hearts and minds' approach can be overdone."[81] "In the 9th Division," he wrote, "we always stressed the military effort."[82] By and large, the army high command shared Ewell's point of view.

Another effort to enhance security was *chieu hoi*, an open-arms amnesty program designed not just to woo VC defectors without reprisal, but to then train them to become productive members of the South Vietnamese economy. It was not a popular program with the South Vietnamese government, which considered the VC better candidates for prison than schooling. Nonetheless Komer pressed ahead, dropping millions of leaflets by airplane and artillery shells that promised, "We will be happy to welcome you, feed you well, not put you in prison."[83]

The *chieu hoi* program drew large numbers of defectors, as many as

27,178 by early 1968. After being interrupted by Tet, an additional 17,000 VC took advantage of *chieu hoi* from 1969 to 1970. However, when the North Vietnamese saw that the program was beginning to bear fruit, they countered by unleashing a terrorist campaign that reduced defections from 5,000 to 500 a month.[84]

In part as a response to these communist reprisals, the U.S. turned to perhaps the most controversial pacification program — Phoenix or Phung Hoang. The initiative had been envisioned under Komer's tenure, but its activation fell to his successor at CORDS, William Colby, who brought a more offensive approach to the pacification effort. Phoenix's objective was to eliminate the Viet Cong infrastructure and its shadow government in South Vietnam. It was designed to enhance security, but in the process it would compromise the principle of restraint.

By 1967, some 70,000 to 100,000 VCI cadre wielded considerable influence in South Vietnam, offering a viable communist alternative to the government in Saigon. The VCI provided a variety of persuasive services to win support, including medical treatment, propaganda, and education. If these tactics failed, the VCI would resort to a terror campaign aimed at selected village leaders to increase the incentive to comply. On the other hand, the South Vietnamese government was rarely able to establish a permanent presence, especially at night, in the villages. Pacification could not succeed without countering this grip the communists had on the population. The task was so crucial that Dale Andrade and James Willbanks describe the VCI as "nothing less than a second center of gravity."[85]

The roots of the Phoenix program can be traced to the Intelligence Coordination and Exploitation Program (ICEX), which began in July 1967 and mainly served as a clearinghouse for information on the VCI. In December, the focus on the VCI was intensified, and ICEX gave way to Phoenix. Phoenix was much more decentralized than ICEX, and district intelligence and operations coordinating centers (DIOCCs) were built in regions where the VCI operated. Also, with the new emphasis came a great increase in resources, and by 1970, there were 703 American Phoenix advisors throughout South Vietnam.[86]

With CIA and CORDS assistance, Colby tasked the South Vietnamese to target the VC leadership through arrest, conversion, or assassination. In its first year of operation, Phoenix eliminated 16,000 VC cadres, most by defection or capture. By forcing high-ranking VC to move to safer areas, Phoenix made control more difficult for the communists and severed the link between the population and the mid-level VC that called the shots in the villages.[87] Even General Tran Do, the North Vietnamese deputy commander in South Vietnam, admitted Phoenix was "extremely destructive."[88]

In spite of these successes, Phoenix's detractors claimed it was a rogue operation that perpetrated murder and torture, and abuses certainly existed due to the decentralized nature of the program. Andrade and Willbanks counter that most advisors understood that only VC captured alive could provide the intelligence Phoenix needed. The numbers seem to support their claim. Colby testified before a congressional committee that between 1969 and 1971, Phoenix had reduced the insurgency by 67,000 people. Of that number, approximately 21,000 were killed, and the rest had surrendered or been captured. Andrade and Willbanks argue that with statistics showing more than two-thirds of the neutralized VC were captured not killed, Phoenix can hardly be called "an assassination bureau."[89]

Corruption and political infighting was a less debatable problem with the program, as some South Vietnamese politicians identified their political enemies as VC and used the Phoenix hit squads, properly known as "provincial reconnaissance units," to go after them. In a development reminiscent of the body count, pressure to eliminate VC led to a quota system that erroneously labeled many innocent people as VC.[90] Such practices led Ivan Arreguin-Toft to consider Phoenix to be a strategy of "barbarism," which he defines as "the systematic violation of the laws of war in pursuit of a military or political objective."[91]

Setting aside the different characterization offered by Andrade and Willbanks (and even Arreguin-Toft admits Phoenix represents "barbarism at the mildest end of the violations spectrum"), Arreguin-Toft uses Phoenix to demonstrate the hypothesis that "when strong actors employ barbarism to attack weak actors defending with a GWS [guerrilla warfare strategy], all other things being equal, strong actors should win."[92] He argues that Phoenix successfully "eviscerated the VC command infrastructure in the South [and] may have even provoked the North into its premature and disastrous direct confrontation with US regular forces during the 1968 Tet Offensive."[93] This analysis certainly depicts the compromise Phoenix made with the principle of restraint in its pursuit of security as being an efficient one.

Although it was the most aggressive of the pacification programs, Phoenix reflected the philosophy of the PROVN, Krulak, and others who had long argued the need of protecting the South Vietnamese rural population. Like pacification writ large, however, the small measure of security provided by Phoenix was too little and too late and was unable to break the communist will to persevere. Seriously hurt, the communists responded to the twin setbacks of Phoenix and Tet by "sharply curtailing the level of military activity in the south and withdrawing some of [their] troops back across the demilitarized zone."[94] Andrade and Willbanks note, "While enemy main forces and guerrillas licked their wounds, they were less able to hinder pacification in the villages," but Arreguin-Toft captures the bigger picture: "Certain that American public opinion would eventually force Nixon to withdraw from Vietnam, the North Vietnamese were prepared to wait him out, no matter what additional suffering it might entail."[95] Against such a determined enemy, even drastic increases in security may not be enough to produce the desired strategic results.

Restraint

In spite of demonstrating Phoenix's tactical and operational successes, Arreguin-Toft is quick to note his findings "do not imply the necessity of creating a force capable of barbarism" in a counterinsurgency.[96] Indeed, the pacification program reflected the principle of restraint by a variety of programs designed to reach the South Vietnamese population by means much less violent than Phoenix. The previously discussed CAP is one such program that Arreguin-Toft offers as an example, but aid and information were two other efforts.

In an attempt to facilitate what is now called "human security," Komer had at his disposal a $1.7 billion economic aid fund that he could distribute to the population. Multi-crop miracle rice, soya-bean seeds, fertilizer, cooking oil, pharmaceuticals, cement, corrugated tin, medical and dental supplies, and hygiene items all sat in warehouses waiting to be shipped to the countryside. In the first half of 1967, American officials distributed 12,044 tons of food, performed 4,843,396 medical treatments, and administered 1,381,968 immunizations.[97] But what made this aspect of the pacification program difficult was that physical security had to precede distribution. The last thing Komer wanted was for his efforts, designed to win the hearts and minds of the South Vietnamese people, to end up as logistical support for the VC. In addition to this problem with security, the American largess also eroded the legitimacy of the South Vietnamese government that "had neither the resources — nor in many cases the inclination — to shower gifts upon its own people."[98] As in all aspects of the pacification effort, balancing the principles of OOTW was problematic.

A second initiative that modeled restraint was an intensive propaganda campaign. Between 1965 and 1972, over 50 billion leaflets were distributed in North and South Vietnam and along the Ho Chi Minh Trail in Cambodia and Laos. In 1969 alone, over 10.5 billion leaflets, 4 million pamphlets, 60,000 newspaper articles, over 24.5 million posters, and almost 12 million magazines were produced in the attempt to influence Vietnamese opinions.[99] Based on volume, the Americans appeared to recognize the importance of persuasion and information in a people's war.

Oftentimes, however, the propaganda efforts seemed to be more appropriate for an American than a Vietnamese audience. For example, one program

A sailor from Team Six of the U.S. Naval Support Activity, Da Nang, conducts "sick call" for Vietnamese children of the Tam Toa village in November 1967. Photograph by Bob Young. Naval Historical Center.

in 1968 involved distributing brown paper grocery bags to merchants. Each bag had a political message on it. The problem was that the Vietnamese traditionally used plastic netting or cloth squares rather than paper bags to carry their groceries. Paper was used to wrap purchases. Therefore, rather than using the bags for their intended purposes, merchants often shredded them to use as wrapping material before the customer even had a chance to read the message.[100]

While the American propaganda campaign struggled to overcome such cultural differences, the VC proved highly skilled in using the combination of agitation and propaganda ("agitprop") "to arouse the people to the [South Vietnamese] Government's oppressiveness and lack of responsibility." They tapped into the local grievances, using songs, skits, and speeches to deliver their message "in terms the people could understand."[101] Once again, the communists demonstrated their superiority in reaching the center of gravity in Vietnam.

Perseverance

The pacification effort suffered from a lack of perseverance on a variety of levels. Tactically, there was little resolve to commit forces to the long-term presence that was necessary to bring real security to a village. Secretary of Defense Robert McNamara noted this aspect of the problem, saying, "the most enduring problems are reflected in the belief of the rural Vietnamese that the GVN will not stay long when it comes into an area, but the VC will."[102] Strategically, Komer thought victory in protracted war would come "by patient and prolonged effort to outlast as well as counter" the enemy.[103] He referred to the build-up of pacification resources as a "painful gradual process."[104] The program would take time to produce results and require a commitment that could not be sustained by a nation that was rapidly losing its interest in the war. According to Colby, "CORDS's gradual success after Tet 1968 fatally lagged behind the American public's rapidly growing perception that the Vietnam enterprise was an exercise in futility."[105]

In a field in which the marines showed a certain superiority, perhaps the army unit that showed the most potential for pacification at the tactical level was the 25th Infantry Division. In the fall of 1966, a battalion from the division executed Operation Lanikai in the Hau Nghia province. The battalion's report of the operation noted that U.S. units on pacification missions

> must be prepared to live in the pacification area until the people have been made to feel secure and their cooperation has been won.... The full benefits of pacification type operations in an area can only be realized through vigorous and constant efforts to sustain the favorable conditions created until such time as the local Vietnamese officials and military leaders are prepared to accept the full gamut of civil and military responsibilities.[106]

After highlighting the work of the 25th Infantry Division, Samuel Smithers cautioned that "no one can say how long U.S. troops will be required to remain in any particular province before it can be declared capable of protecting itself." Writing in 1967, Smithers cited commentators who predicted a U.S. presence "may well be required in Vietnam for as long as 20 years."[107] This open-ended commitment and need for some sort of permanent security, however, required manpower that Westmoreland did not think he could spare from "the big war." "Had I had at my disposal virtually unlimited manpower, I could have stationed troops permanently in every district or province and thus provided an alternative strategy," he mused.[108] Instead, less proficient ARVN and local force units were left to provide the bulk of population security while U.S. units conducted search and destroy operations. This American failure to adhere to the principle of perseverance left the VCI free to wield its considerable control over the South Vietnamese population.[109]

Edwin Chamberlain, one of the hard-working military advisors, confessed, "There is little glory and much weariness in pacification."[110] America eventually reached the same conclusion about the Vietnam War in general and lost its will to continue the effort. Sir Robert Thompson had cautioned,

"If one tries to talk about speed in pacification, it must be remembered that it will take as long to get back to the preferred status quo ante as it took the other side to get to the new position."[111] Given the huge head start enjoyed by the communists, the American public simply had no stomach for such a lengthy endeavor. Lawrence Yates laments this lack of perseverance, arguing, "Given time, pacification might have worked; but time ran out."[112] It is equally valid to view the pacification effort as not being a failure to persevere long enough but rather a failure to start early enough. Komer argues that to be successful, the surge in American interest in pacification that finally gained traction in 1968–1969 would have been better started in the late 1950s or early 1960s.[113]

In the final analysis, pacification probably represented the best hope for the achievement of American and South Vietnamese victory in Vietnam, but the strategy was never fully embraced. The effort to secure the South Vietnamese rural population from VC control and to strengthen the popular legitimacy of the GVN was a mammoth undertaking that would require significant commitment. Instead, the failure of pacification is best explained by "its limited duration and scope."[114] Komer notes that "even after 1967, pacification remained a small tail to the very large conventional military dog. It was never tried on a large enough scale until too late."[115] By then the communists' skillfully executed strategy of protracted war had exhausted American perseverance. The lack of adherence to the principle of perseverance in terms of resources, emphasis, time, and effort doomed the pacification program to failure.

Conclusion

In large part, the overall failure of the U.S. effort in Vietnam stemmed from poor adherence to the principle of objective based on an under-appreciation of the population as the center of gravity. This deficiency led to pacification being labeled "the other war," and the resulting problems with unity of effort. With the creation of CORDs, the pacification program demonstrated an evolving adherence to unity of effort, but its earlier experience in this principle was seriously deficient, and even CORDs was unable to fully rectify the problem.

The pacification effort also seriously failed to adhere to the principle of security by its inability to protect the South Vietnamese peasant from the VC. Guenther Lewy attributes this failure to the initial poor adherence to objective. The various pacification efforts, he writes, "failed because of the lack of a secure environment, in which they could thrive, the result of a faulty strategic concept."[116] Securing the population would require that additional troops be diverted from "the big war," a diversion that was resisted based on the misapplication of the principle of objective. Absent these resources, the pacification effort resorted to compromising the principle of restraint through the Phoenix program in order to gain some measure of security. This trade-off proved effective, but not broad enough in scope to produce strategic results.

The misunderstanding of objective also contributed to pacification's problems with legitimacy. It was perceived as not legitimate by many American military officials who preferred the strategy of attrition, and it was perceived as not legitimate by many South Vietnamese for a variety of reasons. To some South Vietnamese elites, pacification represented a threat to their base of power. To many South Vietnamese peasants, pacification simply did not adequately meet their needs, including the most basic need of security. Army chief of staff General Harold Johnson drew a connection between the principles of legitimacy and security, arguing that "the people will support their government when it can provide some security for them."[117] As executed, pacification failed to resonate with the host nation.

Failure to convince the American population of the legitimacy of continuing the effort caused pacification, and the entire U.S. commitment to South Vietnam, to strongly fail in adhering to the principle of perseverance. In explaining "How the Weak Win Wars," Arreguin-Toft concludes, "Strong-actor military and political elites must prepare their publics for long-delayed victories against even very weak adversaries when those adversaries employ indirect defense strategies" such as guerrilla war.[118] This preparation did not occur during the Vietnam War, resulting in a loss of commitment among the American public.

This analysis suggests relationships among several of the principles, both in terms of correlation and balanced application. Like the aggressive population control measures used during the Greek Civil War, Phoenix deliberately and effectively compromised restraint in order to facilitate security. All the other relationships among the principles are less productive and illustrate the dangers of a negative "snowball effect." The failure to properly analyze the objective led to difficulties with unity of effort, legitimacy, and security. The failure to ensure domestic legitimacy led to a failure to adhere to perseverance. By not practicing the balanced application of the principles of OOTW, the pacification effort in Vietnam failed.

CHAPTER 5

Nicaragua and Honduras: Restraint Enables Perseverance

Throughout the 1980s, the United States pursued a policy designed to support the Contra resistance to the Sandinista government in Nicaragua. President Ronald Reagan was a staunch proponent of the Contras, but his efforts were subject to two key limitations: the memory of Vietnam caused public opinion to be against direct military intervention, and the vagaries of Congress caused Contra assistance to be inconsistent. One tool that was available to President Reagan, however, was the indirect application of U.S. power in a way that achieved unity of effort with a variety of diplomatic, information, military, and economic resources. The absence of direct combat involvement allowed the U.S. to effectively adhere to the principles of restraint and security. By placing the situation in Nicaragua in the context of the larger struggle of defeating the Soviet Union, President Reagan also adhered to the principle of objective. Adherence to restraint and objective enabled a decade of perseverance in an operation that faced numerous challenges to its legitimacy. As a result of this OOTW, the U.S. accomplished its objective of limiting the influence of communism in Nicaragua and Central America.

Background

The U.S. had been dispatching troops to Nicaragua since 1853, and the construction of the Panama Canal ensured American interest would not wane. The Bryan-Chamorro Treaty of 1916 granted the U.S. the exclusive right to build a second trans–Isthmian canal through Nicaragua, as well as various naval bases, in exchange for $3 million. The continuing U.S. military, economic, and infrastructure presence made Nicaragua, in effect, an American protectorate until 1925, when President Calvin Coolidge withdrew the contingent of marines that had been ensuring stability in Nicaragua for the preceding fifteen years.[1]

Trouble erupted within a month of the marines' departure when a civil war broke out between Conservative supporters of General Emiliano Chamorro and Liberals, who seized much of Nicaragua's Atlantic Coast, including the town of Bluefields where a considerable American business community was located. Marines were once again dispatched to Nicaragua, and by May 1927, the U.S. was able to compel the belligerents to sign the Peace of Tiptapa.[2]

Although Henry Stimson, the U.S. envoy who had brokered the peace, crowed, "The civil war in Nicaragua is now definitely ended," looking back with the benefit of hindsight, Max Boot concluded, "In reality it was just beginning."[3] Liberal commander Augusto Sandino refused to accept the peace and gathered a band of followers to oppose first the government of President Adolfo Diaz, and soon thereafter the Americans that supported it.[4]

Sandino proved to be an elusive prey, and while the marines launched a frustrating effort to bring him to bay, he emerged as a "hero to the left."[5] In Moscow, the Communist International (Comintern) sent "fraternal greetings to the workers and peasants of Nicaragua, and the heroic army of national emancipation of General Sandino."[6] Although Sandino welcomed the communist support and had some communists on his staff, he lacked a developed political agenda of his own. Perhaps for this reason, he had trouble rallying his countrymen to his cause, and, although he remained a problem for the marines, the election of 1928 resulted in a resounding victory for his archenemy, the Liberal candidate Jose Mariaq Moncada. The election was supervised under the watchful eye of U.S. Army Brigadier General Frank Ross McCoy and some 5,000 American servicemen, and even the defeated Conservatives conceded it was the fairest in the country's history.[7]

After the election, the U.S. presence was steadily reduced to about 1,500 marines by 1929. This small force garrisoned the large cities and provided direction for the Guardia Nacional (National Guard). Although the marine presence included the legendary Chesty Puller and the Guardia Nacional grew into a highly effective constabulary force, isolated marine contingents were regularly subjected to well-executed attacks from Sandino's men. The guerrillas made Nicaragua's Atlantic coast their primary base of operations, and the insurgency continued to fester.[8]

Liberal candidate Juan Sacasa was elected president in 1932 amid growing pressure in the Depression-racked U.S. to bring the marines home.[9] When the marines departed in early 1933, Sacasa, feeling vulnerable without the accustomed American protection, entered into negotiations with Sandino. On February 2, the government and the guerrillas agreed to a ceasefire, officially ending the long war. Tensions remained, however, between the Guardia

Nacional, which had become increasingly politicized with the departure of the marines, and Sandino's stalwarts. Sacasa became stuck in between these two forces and quickly lost effectiveness.[10]

As Sacasa floundered, Anastasio Somoza Garcia, the head of the Guardia Nacional, began to fill the void. He resolved to take matters into his own

President Somoza passes between saluting police officers after he leaves the Capitol during his 1938 tour of Washington. Photograph by Harris & Ewing. Library of Congress.

hands, and on February 21, 1934, his forces abducted and killed Sandino, his brother, and two of his generals. They also raided a guerrilla camp in the north the next day, effectively crushing what was left of Sandino's force. Somoza grew in power, and in 1936 he deposed Sacasa and became president of Nicaragua. Somoza was an autocrat whom President Franklin Delano Roosevelt famously described as "a sonofabitch, but he's our sonofabitch." He ruled until his assassination in 1956, but after that, his sons continued the family dictatorship.[11]

The Somozas's heavy-handed dynasty created a great disparity between the political and agricultural elite on the one hand and the rural population on the other. Amid the widespread belief that the government was exploitative and corrupt, an insurgency developed. The Sandinista National Liberation Front, named after Augusto Sandino, the assassinated guerrilla leader, was founded in 1961 by young members of Nicaragua's Partido Socialista Nicaraguense (FSLN), a "Moscow-line" communist party. Led by Carlos Fonseca, the Sandinistas advocated a revolutionary armed struggle against the Somoza government. "Marxism," Fonseca declared in 1968, "is now the ideology of the most ardent defenders of Latin American humanity. It is high time for all Nicaraguan revolutionaries to embrace the goal of proletarian liberation."[12]

In spite of Fonseca's bold rhetoric, in the early 1970s the movement had fewer than one hundred members and controlled no Nicaraguan territory. By 1972, divergent strategic views had divided the Sandinistas into three separate factions. Of these, the Tercerista, or "insurrectional" faction, gained control of the national directorate in 1977 after pursuing an agenda of broadening the revolution's base of support by forming alliances with non–Marxist anti–Somoza elements, including middle class professionals, disaffected businessmen, and Catholic priests who subscribed to liberation theology. The Tercerista succeeded in engineering a multi-class insurrection that was formidable enough to defeat the Nicaraguan Army in 1979, march into the capital of Managua, and install a new regime.[13]

President Jimmy Carter refused to intervene as the Sandinista revolution gained momentum. His foreign policy was designed to reduce the Cold War emphasis on containment and confrontation, and instead promote human rights — including in the notoriously repressive Somoza regime — and generate dialogue. Carter criticized America's history of imperialism in Latin America and vowed to transfer the Panama Canal, the ultimate symbol of American dominance in the region, back to Panama. He pledged that no Latin American government would be overthrown by his administration.[14]

The Sandinista revolution tested Carter's rhetoric, and some in his administration, most notably National Security Advisor Zbigniew Brzezinski, urged intervention. "A Castroite take-over in Nicaragua," Brzezinski cautioned, "would impact on US–Soviet relations and on the President's domestic political standing, particularly in the South and the West."[15] Carter refused to budge and instead adopted a policy of "conditional accommodation" and "restraint." He shipped $26.3 million in food, medicine, and other humanitarian supplies to Nicaragua and promised a long-term $75 million U.S. economic aid package if the Sandinistas respected human rights, practiced political pluralism, and did not aid Marxist revolutions in neighboring Central American countries. In September 1979, Carter hosted former Tercerista *comandante* Daniel Ortega, now the president in the new Sandinista government, and other top Nicaraguan officials to a White House visit.[16]

Carter took comfort in the Sandinistas' public announcements pledging their commitment to political pluralism and a "mixed economy." Behind the scenes, however, the party hardliners were consolidating control over the police, the state security agencies, a new "Sandinista People's Army," and other organs of armed power. The Sandinistas also concluded that they must follow the path of Cuba and, in the face of predictable hostility from the U.S., turn to Moscow for a patron and protector. In October, Ortega told a visiting Soviet KGB official he "regarded the USSR ... as a class and strategic ally, and saw the Soviet experience ... as a model to be studied and used" in Nicaragua. "Our strategy," Ortega explained, "is to tear Nicaragua from the capitalist orbit and, in time, become a member of ... Comecon" (the Soviet bloc international economic organization).[17]

Nicaragua's ties to Cuba were even closer, and Michael Grow concludes, "In many respects, the Sandinistas were Cuban clones."[18] Both Nicaragua and Cuba were ideologically anti–American nationalists who viewed many of their country's problems as being generated by the American imperialists and the self-serving local collaborators that did their bidding. Ortega vowed that the "popular revolution" had brought to an end Nicaragua's long history of "submissions and sell outs." Now, he would have to prepare to defend against direct and indirect attack from the country the Sandinistas had come to see as the "rabid enemy of all peoples who are struggling to achieve their definitive liberation."[19] He was eager to support like-minded revolutionaries, and by the mid–1980s, it was becoming increasingly apparent the Sandinistas were helping move weapons from Cuba to Marxists guerrillas in El Salvador. President Carter's hope that accommodation would produce moderation in Nicaragua was quickly losing credibility.[20]

These disappointing developments in Nicaragua were just one of several foreign policy problems plaguing Carter as the 1980 presidential election approached. The Iranian revolution and ensuing hostage crisis continued to humiliate the nation. The December 1979 Soviet invasion of Afghanistan had breathed new life into the superpower rivalry. The Organization of Petroleum

Exporting Countries doubled the price of oil and ignited a domestic energy crisis that many Americans blamed on the President. In contrast to Carter's passivity, the Republican presidential challenger Ronald Reagan condemned the "Marxist Sandinista takeover of Nicaragua" and declared his support of the Nicaraguan people in their efforts to establish a free and independent government.[21]

In the face of charges he was "weak" on foreign policy in Nicaragua and elsewhere, Carter began to reverse his accommodation of the Ortega government. He approved a "covert political-action program" that authorized the Central Intelligence Agency (CIA) to transfer $19.5 million in funds to "private business groups, organized labor, political parties, and the press" in an effort to promote opposition to the Sandinistas. To help El Salvador resist its Marxist insurgency, he renewed aid that had been suspended since 1977 as a result of El Salvador's poor record of safeguarding human rights. Ultimately, he halted the $75 million economic aid package to Nicaragua, based on "conclusive proof" of the Sandinistas' involvement in arms transfers to the El Salvadoran guerrillas. By the end of his term, Carter's attitude toward Nicaragua had decidedly shifted from restraint to confrontation.[22]

Carter's new-found vigor did little to reassure the American public, and in 1980, Reagan was elected president after capturing 50 percent of the popular vote and a staggering 90 percent of the electoral vote. The landslide empowered Reagan with a mandate to rebuild U.S. national power and prestige, and adopt a more aggressive response to challenges abroad. He announced, "Restoring both our strength and our credibility is a major objective of this administration."[23] For Reagan, a new policy toward Nicaragua would be a key part of this equation.

Analysis of the Principles

Objective

President Reagan's resolve to undermine the Soviet system exceeded that of any previous administration.[24] A specific global objective outlined in his National Security Decision Directive was "to contain and reverse the expansion of Soviet control and military presence throughout the world, and to increase the costs of Soviet support and use of proxy, terrorist and subversive forces."[25] Reagan's strategy to aid anti–Soviet insurgencies attempting to overthrow Marxist regimes in the Third World eventually became known as the Reagan Doctrine.[26] Specifically, he saw Nicaragua's increasing ties with the Soviet Union, East Germany, and Cuba, as well as Nicaragua's growing military, as a serious threat to American interests in Central America.[27] CIA Director William Casey shared Reagan's concern, and in a March 1980 meeting of the

National Security Council, Casey asked, "If we can't stop Soviet expansion in a place like Nicaragua, where the hell can we?"[28]

Casey's observation suggests that more was at stake than just Nicaragua. The Reagan Administration felt that over the past years U.S. credibility had suffered, and now Reagan "wanted to send a message to others in the world that there was new management in the White House." He argued, "American strength and American integrity must ... be taken seriously — by friends and potential foes alike." Thus, Reagan made it a foundational principle of his foreign policy "to send as powerful a message as we could to the Russians that we weren't going to stand by anymore while they armed and financed terrorists and subverted democratic governments."[29] Secretary of State Alexander Haig agreed that "only a credible show of will and strength" could convince the Soviets "it was better to accommodate to the United States and the West than to go marauding against their interests and security."[30] Haig added that U.S. standing with other nations was at stake as well. "Especially in the Third World," he noted, "deep doubts existed about the United States and its capacity to project power in defense of its own interests."[31] By tying the local outcome in Nicaragua to the broader struggle to reestablish American credibility and defeat global communism, President Reagan's objective also would encourage adherence to the principle of perseverance.

Reagan soon embarked on a campaign to change the U.S. approach to Nicaragua from one of moderation to one of confrontation. He pulled together representatives from such organizations as the CIA, the Department of Defense, the National Security Council, and the Department of State to create a secret planning body called the Restrictive Interagency Group (RIG) to develop options. There was already a small army of a few hundred Nicaraguan exiles being formed inside neighboring Honduras, and based on input from the RIG, Reagan decided the best way of challenging the Sandinistas in Nicaragua was through an insurgency.[32]

Following the collapse of the Somoza regime, small bands of Guardia Nacional had taken refuge in neighboring Honduras and Guatemala. By 1980, several anti–Sandinista leaders such as former Guardia Nacional Colonel Enrique Bermudez had begun the tedious process of organizing these disparate groups into a unified fighting force. Fearing a spillover of the revolution into their own country, members of the Honduran government assisted the effort. In the meantime, Bermudez and others travelled abroad, trying to generate support. By the time of Reagan's election, Bermudez had made contacts in the United States and begun lobbying the Republican Party for backing. He also found a sympathetic ear in Argentina, where a fanatically anticommunist military dictatorship had recently crushed a communist insurgency. Seeing the Sandinistas as the new threat to Marxist expansion in the hemisphere, the

Argentines began providing Bermudez with money, advisors, and military training.[33]

While Bermudez was in Argentina, his ally, Honduran Police Chief and Army Colonel Gustavo Alvarez, was visiting CIA Director Casey in Washington to present a proposal to transform the anti–Sandinista exiles in Honduras into a force potent enough to launch into Nicaragua to ignite a civil war. Alvarez surmised the action would likely prompt a Nicaraguan retaliatory strike into Honduras to which the U.S. could respond with a crushing invasion to solve the Nicaraguan problem once and for all.[34]

The plan seemed perfect to Casey. The U.S. would supply money and weapons, the Argentines would supervise the military operations, and the Hondurans would provide the territorial base. Casey took the plan to President Reagan, emphasizing that the Argentines were already training the Nicaraguan exiles in Honduras, and the U.S. would merely be "buying in" to an existing operation.[35] Reagan liked the idea and authorized the expansion of the heretofore small covert insurgent aid program to $19 million. With this support, the Contras, as the insurgent movement became known, eventually grew to a strength of some ten thousand.[36]

Securing Honduras as a base for the insurgency became absolutely essential to the U.S. effort, and indeed, Honduras played host both to the Contras and to a variety of U.S. military activities. Honduras's shared borders with Nicaragua, El Salvador, and Guatemala made its geopolitical importance to the United States obvious. Additionally, its status as the original "banana republic" provided a basis, no matter how controversial, of cooperation with the United States.[37] Furthermore, Honduras had reason to worry. As Honduran Ambassador to the Organization of American States Robert Martinez Ordonez said in 1983,

> It is of highest priority for the rest of the Central American countries to discuss the regional problems created by Nicaragua because of its worrisome arms buildup, its direct participation in the destabilization of other Central American governments, and its clandestine arms trafficking.... Nicaragua has upset the Central American region's military balance. In only 4 years its armed forces have grown by 1,300 percent.... The size of the Sandinista Armed Forces is much greater than the total of the military troops in the rest of the Central American countries.[38]

Honduran leaders did not hesitate to accept U.S. interest and influence. In April 1982, General Alvarez, by this time the commander-in-chief of the Honduran armed forces, declared that "Honduras is in agreement that the United States, as a friendly country, [may] intervene militarily in Central America." Such support was not unrewarded. American economic aid to Honduras rose from $50.7 million in 1980 to $139 million in 1984. Military aid grew even more dramatically, from $3.4 million in 1980 to $79.7 million in 1986. By 1985, Honduras was the eighth leading recipient of U.S. economic and military aid.[39] In June 1983, retiring army chief of staff General Edward Meyer stated, "I believe Honduras is a strength. I'd really like to anchor the defense of the region initially on Honduras."[40] In fact, one observer would go as far as to describe Honduras as "the linchpin for the administration's regional warfighting strategy."[41]

One model of strategy describes it as a three-legged stool made up of "ends, ways, and means." The "ends" are objectives, the "ways" are the concepts for accomplishing the objectives, and the "means" are the resources for supporting the concepts.[42] President Reagan had established a clear strategy along this formula of ends, ways, and means. The end was the eradication of communism in Nicaragua. The way was through insurgency. The means would be by leveraging the geographic location and cooperation of Honduras. In articulating such a clear strategic vision, Reagan strongly adhered to the principle of objective.

Legitimacy

While Reagan was completely convinced of the legitimacy of supporting the insurgency, the opinion was far from universal. "The high priority assigned the issue by the president and the intense scrutiny given the policy by Congress" would be a continual source of friction between the two branches of government.[43] The Sandinistas were well aware of the divisiveness of the issue in the U.S. and used the fickle nature of U.S. support to gauge the intensity of their activities. In fact, the inconsistency of congressional support led the Reagan administration to take extraordinary measures to keep the insurgency alive, measures that pushed the very limits of the operation's domestic legitimacy.

In March 1986, the House voted against the Reagan administration's $100 million military and humanitarian aid package for the Contras.[44] Within forty-eight hours of the House vote, Sandinista military units crossed the border into Honduras on a mission to locate and destroy Contra logistics bases, training centers, and medical centers.[45] The specific objectives were a major base of the Nicaragua Democratic Force, the main Contra group, and a smaller Contra base that included an airstrip. Both sites were in Honduras's El Paraiso province, about ten miles from the Nicaraguan border.[46]

Reports of the size of the operation varied from 800 to 2,000 Sandinista troops with Reagan administration officials estimating some 1,500. Among these forces were what the State Department described as "special counterinsurgency battalions." After the operation, Nicaragua admitted that some 2,500 men were involved.[47]

Perhaps based on the assessments of their Cuban advisors, the Sandinistas expected to find a demoralized and disorganized Contra force that would run rather than fight. Instead, the Sandinistas were met by some 7,000 Contras, including "battle-hardened units that had just been rearmed and resupplied." About half the Sandinistas were stopped near Las Vegas, and the rest launched four unsuccessful assaults on a Contra camp, which was initially defended by 700 Contras and then reinforced by another 300. When the Sandinistas broke off the attack and tried to withdraw, they were blocked by another 6,000 troops from the crack Jorge Salazar regional command, which had doubled back from its own operation into Nicaragua. With the escape route cut off, the Sandinistas scattered.[48]

The Sandinista attack into Honduras had the potential to lend much legitimacy to the Reagan administration's support for the insurgency, but instead the ambiguity and controversy of the situation produced a much more mixed result. On the night of March 24, Honduran President Jose Azcona formally requested urgent U.S. military assistance, to include airlifting Honduran troops. Initially, however, the Hondurans had denied or minimized the incident. Opponents of the Reagan's administration's Contra policy seized upon this condition to accuse the administration of exaggerating, if not fabricating, the incident. These charges would be repeated in March 1988 in debates surrounding another border clash.[49]

In actuality, the confusion can best be attributed to a diplomatic dilemma that Honduras faced. The Honduran government had repeatedly denied that Contras operated from bases within its borders, making it difficult for them to acknowledge a Sandinista raid against bases it would not publicly recognize. Additionally, while the Hondurans knew they were dependent on the United States, they were not eager to appear overly so. To a certain degree, national pride was at stake.[50] Both the American and Honduran governments were wrestling with their own issues of domestic legitimacy.

Surely there was some encouragement from Washington for the Hondurans to request aid. U.S. Charge d'Affaires Shepard Lowman reportedly demanded a meeting with Azcona and Foreign Minister Carlos Lopez Contreras and insisted the Hondurans request U.S. military aid while scolding them for their low key response. Lowman was quoted by one Honduran official as saying, "We're here trying to help you, and you're going to leave us hanging in Washington." In fact, John Ferch, the U.S. ambassador to Honduras, later admitted he had put some pressure on Azcona to request aid.[51]

But neither the American self-interest in publicizing the incident nor the Honduran awkward response alters the fact that the Nicaraguans entered Honduras in an attack that did not constitute "hot pursuit" of the Contras. In response to the Honduran request, President Reagan approved a $20 million emergency assistance package, which included air defense weapons, conventional ordnance, emergency spare parts and armament for helicopters, and essential training.[52] The aid also involved airlifting Honduran troops to the border. Fifty U.S. pilots and crew members used ten Huey and four Chinook helicopters to move 600 Honduran soldiers to within ten miles of the fighting. While the United States had begun building a military presence in Honduras in 1980, this action marked the first direct involvement of U.S. troops in a Honduran military operation.[53]

Also at stake was the legitimacy of the Contras as a fighting force. While media headlines focused on the U.S. helicopter involvement, many observers seemed to overlook the fact that the Contras won a clear victory. Sensitive to his own need to preserve legitimacy, Nicaraguan Army Chief of Staff Joaquin Cuadra Lacayo at first denied the incident, stating that "it is absolutely false the Nicaraguan troops have violated Honduran territory." Eventually, the Nicaraguan government acknowledged the attack and even admitted to 40 dead and 116 wounded. As the battle for legitimacy continued, Nicaraguan President Ortega justified the raid, explaining that "Honduras lost control of its sovereignty by having the mercenary forces [meaning the Contras] there." Thus, Ortega established that he now considered any area in Honduras where Contras were encamped to be a legitimate military target.[54]

While some considered the incident as proof "that the contras are indeed a serious resistance force, quite capable of holding their own against the Nicaraguan army if given half a chance," others feared that the use of U.S. helicopters foreshadowed Central America as "being the next stop for US combat forces." Others began to draw analogies between the current situation and Vietnam, a war in which the United States had clearly failed to build and sustain legitimacy.[55]

Amid these speculations, Nicaragua's border violation did have a profound legitimizing effect on U.S. politics, especially because it occurred the very week that the Senate was debating President Reagan's Contra aid bill. The attack seemed to validate the Reagan argument, and administration officials were delighted by the windfall, saying, "We knew what Ortega was but we never expected he'd help us prove it so badly." Pat Buchanan gloated, "Danny Ortega, you're my man." Even House Speaker Thomas O'Neil, a leading foe of Contra aid, pronounced Ortega as "a bumbling, incompetent Marxist-Leninist-communist." O'Neil described the raid as a "tremendous blunder" and warned that it could trigger wholesale changes of congressional votes.[56]

The incident did not, in fact, change any senator's vote, but it did quash attempts to further restrict the House's limits on Contra aid. On March 27, the Senate voted 53 to 47 to approve a $100 million package of military and humanitarian aid for the Contras.[57] Senate Majority Leader Robert Dole concluded, "I think Ortega gave us a boost."[58] In effect, the Nicaraguan misstep and the stout Contra response gave the Reagan administration a tenuous claim to legitimacy in what remained a see-saw battle for support.

The victory, however, was short lived. On November 21, President Reagan and Attorney General Edwin Meese made the embarrassing announcement that National Security Advisor John Poindexter and National Security Council staff member Lieutenant Colonel Oliver North had initiated a program to circumvent the sporadic congressional funding by "overcharging" Iran for weapons and diverting some of the proceeds to the Contras. Reagan dismissed Poindexter and North, but the incident haunted his presidency and cast a pall over the legitimacy of the insurgency. As Secretary of Defense Caspar Weinberger put it, "The Contras should have been funded, but there is only one way to secure legal spending by our Government, and that is by vote of the Congress."[59] For many, the Iran-Contra Scandal became the defining event in the Reagan administration's Nicaraguan policy, and it presented an enormous failure to build domestic legitimacy.

Restraint

One result of this relatively weak sense of legitimacy was that U.S. support for the insurgency would have to closely adhere to the principle of restraint. In a nation still bruised by the memory of the Vietnam War and with a military clearly still in the rebuilding process, direct action, for all of Reagan's aggressive rhetoric, was an option fraught with problems. While Secretary of State Haig proposed consideration of direct military intervention, even the Joint Chiefs of Staff were opposed to such a course.[60] Their sentiments were consistent with remarks made by General Paul Gorman, former commander of the U.S. Southern Command, who at a 1988 colloquium on low intensity conflict noted, "The United States armed forces will not be combat participants in the sorts of struggles that are at issue here. The role of US forces in low-intensity conflict will almost invariably be indirect, and that certainly pertains to the role of the United States armed forces in any kind of support for insurgencies abroad."[61] Such would be the case with regard to the Nicaraguan resistance.

According to one observer, "the Republican administration came to office with an inflexible mind-set on Nicaragua. It was dedicated to removing the Sandinistas from power by whatever means necessary."[62] President Reagan began planning the largest defense build-up in history, which would then allow him to launch a "strategic offensive" designed to "roll back" Soviet influence from the Cold War frontiers.[63] However, very practical considerations limited the direct use of force and led to restraint manifesting itself in Reagan's approach to Nicaragua through a concept Todd Greentree calls "selective engagement." The notion of selective engagement recognizes there are limits to the U.S. involvement in Third World conflicts. It is consistent with the lessons learned from Vietnam that the United States should avoid using its troops to fight protracted internal conflicts in foreign countries. Selective engagements encourage rapid action for specific short-term contingencies but try to avoid overly ambitious continuous direct involvement in protracted conflicts.[64] Throughout his two terms, President Reagan would use numerous selective engagements of his military forces to adhere to the principle of restraint as he pursued his foreign policy in Central America.

Part of this process was a series of military exercises the United States staged in Central America in an effort to influence Ortega without resorting to force. In August 1981, Assistant Secretary of State for Inter-American Affairs Thomas Enders had travelled to Managua for two days of secret talks with Ortega and other top Sandinista officials in hopes of reaching a negotiated settlement in which the Nicaraguans would agree to end their support for the El Salvadoran insurgency. Ortega issued Enders a strong rebuff, informing him the Sandinistas had already "seen the crossroads" and "decided to defend our revolution by force of arms, even if we are crushed, and to take the war to the whole of Central America if that is the consequence."[65]

As a result of this bellicose response to attempted diplomacy, the U.S. executed Exercise Halcon Vista (Falcon View) in October 1981. This relatively low-key affair was a three-day exercise designed for the immediate military purpose of evaluating the U.S.–Honduran ability to "detect and intercept hostile coastal incursions."[66] Strategically, the exercise was "designed to signal that the United States was in a position to intervene militarily if the FSLN did not acquiesce" to Ender's proposals.[67] Even one U.S. military official understood the true purpose of the maneuvers was "a deliberate attempt to stick it in their [the Sandinistas] eye."[68]

Halcon Vista was followed by Combined Movement, which began in late July 1982 and lasted two weeks. The object of these maneuvers was to "conduct combined/joint movement in support of Honduran Army forces to meet an aggressor force in a remote area of Honduras." To this end, the U.S. Air Force transported 1,000 Honduran soldiers and their equipment to an area on the Atlantic coast about twenty-five miles from Honduras's southeast border with Nicaragua. During the maneuvers, U.S. troops also began construction of a new Honduran airstrip at Durzuna, which could accommodate fighter jets and transport planes. The airstrip was just six miles from the Morocon military base, which served as the main camp for the Miskito Contras.[69]

The next major exercise was codenamed Big Pine. It lasted for eight days during February 1983 and took place in the Moroccan area near the Nicaraguan border. Big Pine involved 4,000 Honduran and 1,600 American troops practicing to repel an invasion from the imaginary country of "Corinto." Coincidentally, Nicaragua has a port of the same name. Ten U.S. C-130s, thirteen helicopters, and two U.S. Navy landing craft participated in the exercise, and U.S. Army engineers upgraded a dirt airstrip at Puerto Lempira on Honduras's Atlantic coast.

The biggest exercise, however, was the gigantic Big Pine II, which began on August 3, 1983, and lasted six months. Big Pine II involved 12,000 U.S. troops and included drills in naval interdiction, aerial bombings, airlifts, amphibious landings, and counterinsurgency techniques.[70] The exercise also included building or improving runways at Aguacate, San Lorenzo, and Trujillo. Furthermore, contracts were signed providing for construction of and access to airfields at La Ceiba, La Mesa, and Palmerola.[71] As a July 23 article in the *New York Times* explained, "The plan approved by Mr. Reagan does not envisage any immediate combat role for United States forces, but does call for making preparations so that American forces can be swiftly called into action if necessary."[72]

With the conclusion of Big Pine II, President Reagan authorized the Pentagon to "develop and implement plans for new exercises in Honduras and naval activities in waters off Central America in a manner that will maintain steady pressure on the Nicaraguans."[73] These exercises included the three-month Grenadero I in April 1984; Big Pine III, involving 4,500 troops from January to April 1985; the 6,000-man Universal Trek '85 from April to May 1985; and Solid Shield in May 1987, which involved 50,000 U.S. personnel.[74]

This almost continuous U.S. presence in the region was consistent with an inter-agency strategy paper prepared for a July 8, 1983, National Security Council meeting, which stated, "Today the situation in Central America is nearing a critical point. Nonetheless, it is still possible to accomplish US objectives without the direct use of US troops (although the credible threat of such use is needed to deter overt Soviet/Cuban intervention), provided that the US takes timely and effective action." The paper recommended that "the Secretary of Defense shall develop plans for joint exercises in the region. In particular, exercise possibilities in Honduras should be planned."[75]

Through these maneuvers, the U.S. established a presence in Central America that could not escape the notice of Nicaragua. "Presence" is a military mission option on the lesser end of the application of force spectrum.[76] However, this series of maneuvers allowed President Reagan to accomplish three objectives: providing covert support for Contra operations, waging psychological war on the Sandinistas, and building the infrastructure to make overt military intervention possible and the threat credible.[77] This approach also allowed him to meet the requirement of restraint as a principle of OOTW.

Still, the failure of Ender's diplomatic mission indicated that mere exercises would not compel a change in Ortega's behavior. On November 16, 1982, the National Security Council endorsed a plan to establish a secret U.S.–funded, CIA–directed paramilitary force of "non–Americans" to attack the "Cuban-Sandinista support infrastructure in Nicaragua and elsewhere in Central America."[78] Politically unable to deploy U.S. military forces to combat, the covert option allowed President Reagan to pursue his Central American objective "in the least violent and least controversial manner possible." By requiring "no public explanation, no public defense, and no public vote in Congress," such an alternative met Reagan's need for restraint, but would ultimately pose some problems with legitimacy.[79]

Unity of Effort

The overriding need for restraint and the continuing challenges to the legitimacy of its support for the insurgency meant that the U.S. had to get the most out of every one of its activities. The principle of unity of effort requires that every activity contribute to the achievement of a common goal, and the limited U.S. military activity certainly achieved synergy with other attempts to influence the Sandinistas' behavior. The steady stream of exercises and their associated improvements to Honduran infrastructure created a threat of intervention that played on an acute Sandinista fear of the U.S. military. This psychological pressure has been described as "perception management," and recognizes what one observer notes is the inseparability of "the military from the political from the psychological in low intensity conflict." This relationship is apparent in an American official's description of Big Pine I as a "substantial feint" designed to convince the Sandinistas "that they will be finished if they do not bend to the general line adopted by Washington."[80]

But while America's military power relative to Nicaragua's was unquestionably superior, this unrealized potential alone was not enough. To be of value, a resource must be "both mobilized in support of foreign policy objectives and made credible."[81] Recognizing this, the National Security Council stated, "No threat should be made [without] willingness to follow through [with] military force."[82]

Ortega was convinced the U.S. meant business. At the height of Big Pine II in November 1983, just days after the successful U.S. invasion of Grenada, the Nicaraguan government mobilized the population to defend the country. Thousands of Nicaraguans were pulled from their jobs to participate in emergency militia training, causing production to come to a standstill. The government ordered citizens to dig air raid shelters, and 1,000 Cuban advisors were ordered back to Cuba "to remove any pretext for an invasion."[83] Ortega was obviously worried, and these actions represented a diversion of scarce Nicaraguan resources and manpower from economic and social programs to defense.[84]

The pressure brought on by the increased U.S. presence in the region and the invasion of Grenada had a marked impact on Nicaraguan politics. The government announced an amnesty program for certain Miskito Indians that had taken up arms against the Sandinistas and a "safe conduct" program for the other members of the armed opposition. The senior Salvadoran guerrillas in the Managua area maintained a substantially lower profile, and Nicaragua cancelled plans to airdrop logistical support to guerrillas in the Olancho area of Honduras. There was a temporary relaxation of press censorship, and Bayardo Arce, coordinator for the political committee of the Sandinista Front for National Liberation, cited U.S. pressure as a reason for the scheduling of the 1984 Nicaraguan elections.[85]

According to a Georgetown University study, if the United States invaded Nicaragua, it would take two months of relatively high intensity fighting and five years of U.S. military occupation to oust the Sandinistas, eliminate their support, and pacify the countryside. This direct intervention could cost "between 2,392 and 4,783 dead with 9,300 to 18,600 wounded."[86] However, by the carefully unified effort of diplomatic threat and credible show of military force, the Reagan administration was able to disrupt the Sandinistas without firing a shot.[87]

Security

The steady buildup of military capability left the U.S. well-postured when another border clash occurred in 1988, one that bore a striking resemblance to the incident that had happened two years earlier. Again the situation was closely tied to the U.S. political scene. Again there was a Sandinista raid against Contra camps inside Honduras. Again there were charges of U.S. pressure to force Honduras to declare an emergency. And again the U.S. military became involved. Borrowing an expression from Yogi Berra, one Honduran observer said, "It's *déjà vu* all over again."[88] This time, however, the U.S. response would be much more dramatic and require a close adherence to the principle of security.

On February 3, 1988, Congress voted to terminate aid to the Contras, but before the February 29 funding cutoff, the CIA was able to fly in an estimated 300 tons of supplies to Contra depots in Honduras.[89] With little chance of additional outside help, the Contras were forced to fall back to the border areas in order to protect their scarce supplies. It was a situation similar to what the communist insurgents experienced after the withdrawal of Yugoslav support in the Greek Civil War, and it caused a deviation from the Contras' normal guerrilla tactics of dispersion. By having to consolidate to defend their supplies, the Contras became very vulnerable to the superior Sandinista firepower. In the words of the State Department, "the resistance position is difficult."[90]

Realizing the vulnerability of the Contra position and hoping to deal them a severe blow before peace negotiations resumed on March 21, Ortega began planning a raid into Honduras. On March 8, he warned that the Contra resistance "should prepare itself for another heroic drive" by the Sandinistas.[91] In fact, the United States had been monitoring a Sandinista build up in the Bocay Valley of northern Nicaragua for weeks. The State Department estimated twelve combat battalions in the area, which at full strength would represent about 6,000 troops. The battalions were supported by at least ten Soviet MI-17 helicopters, and the Sandinistas had diverted a significant amount of their scarce supply of fuel to accommodate the helicopters. A new base was built in Bonanza, about fifty miles inside Nicaragua, to provide command and control and logistical support for the operation. Obviously, this effort would be a better planned and resourced attack than the ill-fated 1986 incursion.[92]

On March 10, the Sandinistas launched a 1,500 to 2,000-man attack into Honduras. The other 4,500 Sandinistas from the State Department's 6,000-man estimate remained in the Bocay region. In addition to these troops, the Sandinista attack included Soviet-supplied AN-26 aircraft, artillery, rockets, and Soviet M-25 "flying tank" attack helicopters.[93]

The Honduran government's response to the border violation was somewhat slow in developing, as it had been in 1986. A senior administration official, however, stated that President Azcona had telephoned U.S. Ambassador Everett Briggs upon learning of the Sandinista action and asked "what the American attitude was." Briggs quickly consulted Washington and then informed Azcona that the U.S. would help Honduras in any way it could. Azcona, planning on his air force being forced into action, requested a package that included U.S. aerial surveillance, electronic targeting equipment, radar, weather-data equipment, and electronic countermeasures devices. Washington promptly approved this request but summarily rejected Azcona's additional desire for U.S. helicopters and paratroopers to assist in combat operations. Instead, Briggs suggested U.S. troops might be used in a symbolic training exercise in Honduras if Azcona were to make a formal request.[94]

On March 16, Azcona sent a letter to Washington seeking "effective and immediate assistance." The U.S. responded by deploying a task force comprised of 2,000 troops from the 82nd Airborne Division at Fort Bragg, North Carolina and 1,100 more from the 7th Infantry Division (Light) at Fort Ord, California. The deployment was codenamed Operation Golden Pheasant, and White House spokesman Marlin Fitzwater described it as "a measured response designed to show our staunch support to the democratic government of Honduras at a time when its territorial integrity is being violated by the Cuban and Soviet-supported Sandinista army." The State Department described the action as being "based on a special relationship of security existing between the United States and Honduras."[95]

According to the army's low-intensity doctrine of the era, Operation Golden Pheasant was designed to be a "show of force." Such operations focus on specific problems that require rapid and decisive solutions, and their purposes include lending credibility to the nation's promises and commitments, influencing other nations by deploying a viable military force, and reassuring a friend or ally.[96] All of these objectives were at work during Operation Golden Pheasant.

But the intention of a show of force is just as the name implies — a *display* rather than a *use* of force. The Reagan administration was very clear on this point. One senior official stated, "We're not going down there to knock the hell out of somebody."[97] Another spokesman confirmed that there was "no intention" of sending U.S. troops into combat.[98] The State Department echoed that "the brigade task force will not be deployed to any area of ongoing hostilities" and stressed that the deployment involved only light infantry, no artillery.[99] In spite of this deliberate purpose, some derision could be inferred in *Time's* comment that the troops "first pitched their tents ... more than 100 miles from the Contra sanctuaries that were the target of the incursion ... grandiloquently characterized by the Reagan Administration as an 'invasion.'"[100]

Rapid deployability is critical to the success of a show of force, and this aspect of Operation Golden Pheasant was facilitated by the army's recent fielding of light infantry divisions like the 7th Infantry Division, as well as the engineering work accomplished by previous exercises in Honduras.[101] The air movement involved simultaneous actions on both coasts of the United States and three distinct missions. On the Atlantic side, twenty-three C-141s and one C-5 aircraft picked up elements of the XVII Airborne Corps and 82nd Airborne Division and airlanded them at Palmerola. Additionally, eight C-141s conducted a strategic airborne insertion of 700 paratroopers from the 82nd at La Paz. The show of force is a specified mission for airborne forces because of their excellent deployability, and the 82nd showed its ability to execute this critical task.[102] From the Pacific coast, two battalions from the 7th Infantry Division flew on twenty-six C-141s and one C-5 to Palmerola.[103]

Paratroopers of the 82nd Airborne Division descend on the drop zone at Palmerola Air Base during Operation Golden Pheasant. Photograph by Tech Sgt. Bob Simons. Department of Defense.

The fact that Palmerola air force base was available for Operation Golden Pheasant is a good example of the unity of effort benefits reaped by the establishment of a U.S. presence in Honduras. Palmerola's construction as a military command and control facility was begun in 1983, and after Big Pine II a contingent of troops was left behind there to "aid in the operational aspects" of future maneuvers. By March 1984, 1,486 U.S. troops manned Palmerola, comprising "a self-contained combat control team fully able to direct a battle force of tens of thousands of troops."[104] Although Operation Golden Pheasant was not nearly that ambitious, the presence of the Palmerola infrastructure greatly facilitated the operation.

In order to effectively influence the developing geopolitical situation, peacetime contingency operations require a rapid response by a credible military force, and the prompt deployment of Operation Golden Pheasant met this requirement.[105] The first C-141 took off from Pope Air Force Base, North Carolina, at 7:03 A.M. Eastern Standard Time on March 17 and landed at Palmerola at 4:07 P.M., less than twenty-four hours after the alert notification. The entire deployment was completed within thirty-three hours of the launch of the first aircraft.[106] General Frederick Woerner, commander of the U.S.

Members of the 82nd Airborne Division assist Honduran jumpers from the 2nd Airborne Battalion with rigging their parachutes during Operation Golden Pheasant. Photograph by Tech Sgt. Bob Simons. Department of Defense.

Southern Command, noted that "the demonstration of our ability to react as quickly as we did is most certainly a reassuring factor for our allies, not only here in Honduras, but elsewhere."[107] Honduran Defense Minister Wilfredo Sanchez Valladares echoed these sentiments, telling the paratroopers that "the morale of the Honduran people has been reinforced by [your arrival]."[108]

FM 7-98 cites one example of a show of force as "a training exercise that coincides with a troublesome international political situation."[109] Such was the nature of Operation Golden Pheasant. A few hours after landing, most of the 1st Battalion, 504th Parachute Infantry Regiment, which had airlanded at Palmerola, was flying by Blackhawk and Chinook helicopters closer to the Nicaraguan border for the first of several combined exercises with Honduran troops. By March 20, all four infantry battalions and the support troops were conducting training at four different locations around Honduras. The Americans soldiers had positive comments about the combined training and the Honduran soldiers.[110]

As the name implies, a "show" of force must be visible. With this in mind, a media pool of eleven journalists representing television, radio, and print was involved in the operation from its early stages. Brigadier General Daniel Schroeder, the joint task force commander and chief of staff of the XVII Airborne Corps, stressed that the media "would be given full access to everything possible and that the operation was going to be entirely upfront." Television crews, reporters, and photographers were already in position at Palmerola before the first troops arrived. Each evening, the media representatives were briefed on the next day's training and told when and where to report the following morning. From March 17 to March 27, there were more than 500 media personnel on assignment in Honduras, representing some 160 news organizations and eleven foreign countries.[111] The United States wanted full coverage of Operation Golden Pheasant to send a clear message to the Sandinistas and others that American support of both the Contras and Honduras was still tangible. There was some truth in *Time*'s conclusion that Operation Golden Pheasant was "more media event than military action."[112]

Nicaragua predictably protested to the United Nations, accusing the United States of creating an "artificial crisis" in an attempt to justify and continue its "warlike policy" in Central America.[113] Ortega ridiculed President Reagan, saying, "Superman was defeated in Vietnam, and Superman will be defeated again if he disembarks in Nicaraguan territory."[114] Many news sources were likewise critical of the action, and some observers derisively labeled it "airborne diplomacy."[115]

Among those that challenged the American claim to legitimacy was an article in *US News and World Report* that argued that the Reagan administration had played "one of its last cards" in the Nicaragua conflict and might have "shattered" prospects for Central American peace in the process.[116] Others criticized the president for taking advantage of and straining U.S. relations with Honduras. Old jokes about the "USS *Honduras*" were revived.[117] *Current History* pointed to "growing tensions between the Honduran people and the United States military,"[118] and a Honduran political analyst stated, "Six years ago there was no anti–Americanism in Honduras. Now it is increasing every day."[119] In Honduras, the liberal paper *El Tiempo* asked, "Does the state of Honduras really exist?" and opposition legislator Efrain Diaz argued that Operation Golden Pheasant "proves how the government has no policy of its own."[120]

Certainly, Operation Golden Pheasant meant different things to different people, but as *US News and World Report* admitted, "Despite Ortega's tough talk, however, his troops did take notice of the American presence; [within days of the deployment] the U.S. State Department reported that the Sandinistas' offensive forays against Contra positions had all but ceased." As in 1986, this border violation was seen as "another stunning example of Ortega's masterful knack of bad timing." The attack belied Ortega's commitment to the Central American peace process and strengthened the Reagan administration's position that, without additional funding, the Contra resistance was finished.[121] Once again it appeared as if the Reagan administration had won another razor thin victory in its battle against the Sandinistas for legitimacy in the region.

Nonetheless, comparisons to Vietnam again surfaced, and there were antiwar protests in Washington, Chicago, and San Francisco.[122] House Speaker Jim Wright accused administration officials of "obviously trying to do everything in their power to keep the war going," and Senator Christopher Dodd, the most persistent Democratic critic of the administration's Central American policy, suggested the whole operation was designed to trick Congress into approving a new aid package. Following Dodd's theory, *Time* argued that by deploying troops, President Reagan sent a "clear, if unspoken, message to the U.S. public: if Congress refused to fund the contras' fight against the Marxist-oriented Sandinista regime, the American boys just might have to do the job instead." Senator Tom Harkin went one step further, accusing the administration of pursuing a "three-for-one strategy" designed to divert public attention from Independent Counsel Lawrence Walsh's criminal indictments of Poindexter and North and their accomplices in the Iran-Contra Scandal, to revive U.S. aid to the Contras, and to sabotage the Central American peace talks. Senate Majority Leader Robert Byrd added, "I hope it [Operation Golden Pheasant] does not prove to be counterproductive [and] does not derail the peace process."[123]

But, as the military was quick to point out, if it did anything, Operation

Golden Pheasant certainly did not delay the peace process. An article in *Military Review* boasted,

> If Exercise Golden Pheasant's demonstration of the rapid deployment of 3,000 soldiers provided a lesson for Americans, it was this: when the exercise began more than 2,000 Sandinistas were inside Honduras and showed no signs of leaving. After the deployment of U.S. troops, the Sandinistas not only withdrew from the country, but for the first time, began to engage in serious negotiations for peace. Golden Pheasant was a show of force that worked.[124]

The result would have certainly been different if the U.S. had suffered casualties as a result of Operation Golden Pheasant. Instead, close adherence to the principle of security allowed the U.S. to send a strong signal to the Sandinistas while at the same time protecting support for the insurgency from criticism that the U.S. was being sucked into another Vietnam. Operation Golden Pheasant was a textbook show of force that included the force structure necessary to ensure security, but the restraint necessary to maintain legitimacy.

Perseverance

Operation Golden Pheasant also was a profound demonstration that the U.S., or perhaps more precisely the Reagan administration, remained committed to the insurgency and willing to maintain the principle of perseverance. Upon assuming the presidency, Reagan had vowed to confront communism, and by placing Nicaragua in the context of this overall struggle, he was able to sustain the strategic effort in spite of its tactical and operational ebb and flow. It was a phenomenon similar to the impact the broad objective of the Truman Doctrine had on facilitating perseverance during the Greek Civil War.

While Assistant Secretary of State Elliott Abrams contended the U.S. had "no significant tangible interests in Central America," he did recognize the international perceptions that were at stake. "If people see that the Americans are not going to move against the Sandinistas in their own backyard," he asked, "what will they do ten thousand miles away?"[125] Likewise, Secretary of State Haig noted that President Reagan "knew that a failure to carry through on this challenge at the heart of our sphere of interest would result in a loss of credibility in all our dealings with the Soviets."[126] Reagan took the matter to Congress, arguing

> If Central America were to fall, what would the consequences be for our position in Asia, Europe, and for alliances such as NATO? If the United States cannot respond to a threat near our own borders, why should Europeans or Asians believe that we're seriously concerned about threats to them? If the Soviets can

assume that nothing short of an actual attack on the United States will provoke an American response, which ally, which friend will trust us then?

The National security of all the Americas is at stake in Central America. If we cannot defend ourselves there, we cannot expect to prevail elsewhere. Our credibility would collapse, our alliances would crumble, and the safety of our homeland would be in jeopardy.[127]

Against such logic, perseverance was not negotiable.

Reagan's steadfast commitment to the Contras proved tough for Nicaragua's Soviet benefactors to match. His aggressive policy threatened not just Nicaragua, but the much more important Soviet ally of Cuba. When Fidel Castro asked the Kremlin for reassurances of support, Premier Leonid Brezhnev reportedly replied, "We cannot fight in Cuba because it is 11,000 kilometers away. If we go there, we'll get our heads smashed."[128] In another similarity to Greece, the Soviets had to choose their battles, and apparently Nicaragua was expendable. By continuous pressure and perseverance, Reagan was wearing down the Sandinistas' ability to resist.

Thus, on March 23, less than a week after Operation Golden Pheasant began, the Sandinistas agreed to a cease fire. The agreement called for:

- Cessation of all hostilities beginning immediately and extending 60 days after April 1st;
- High-level negotiations April 6 in terms of a definitive cease fire;
- Arrangements for phased amnesty;
- Respect for freedom of speech in Nicaragua;
- Measures for political dialogue and full political rights; and
- Measures for verification of this agreement.[129]

In the final analysis, doubters of the wisdom of President Reagan's resolve (including his use of the military) concerning Nicaragua would have to eat at least a little crow. *Time* conceded that "The US rescue mission, for the moment, seems to have saved the rebels from what might have been near military extinction." Yet the magazine expressed doubts about the overall health of the resistance, stating that the Contras' "long-range future appears far from assured."[130]

In actuality, it was the long-range future of Daniel Ortega that was in jeopardy. Eight years of President Reagan's military, economic, and political pressure had left the Sandinistas at the helm of a desperate economy and a divided populace.[131] Furthermore, the collapse of the communist regimes in Europe deprived Ortega of any hope for Soviet aid. The Soviets simply could no longer afford to subsidize inefficient revolutions so far from their own borders.[132]

The importance of Soviet aid cannot be overemphasized. From 1980 to 1988, Nicaragua had received over $5.2 billion in economic and military aid from East-bloc sources. On the other hand, the United States had provided just $282 million to the Contras and only $6.8 billion total to Guatemala, Honduras, El Salvador, Costa Rica, and the Contras. In fact, in 1984, Nicaragua received more military aid from the Soviet Union than the United States gave to all of Central America combined.[133] The United States certainly appeared to have gotten more bang for its buck.

Ortega's only choice was to liberalize his government. The first tangible step in this process occurred on March 17, 1989, when he freed 1,894 ex–National Guardsmen who had been serving long sentences in the Tipitapa prison. All were granted unconditional amnesty except for thirty-nine former officers accused of the most serious crimes.[134]

In the following months, the Nicaraguans enjoyed political freedom unheard of in the past ten years. The anti–Sandinista press operated free of censorship, and political dissidents were allowed to protest unmolested. Amidst this reformed climate, critics of Ortega, with support from some foreign governments, challenged Ortega to cut his presidential term short and hold an early election.[135]

Remarkably, Ortega agreed, setting the date for the election at February 25, 1990, nine months earlier than the law required.[136] The results were astounding. Not only were Ortega and the Sandinistas defeated, but many of the opposition votes came from districts adjacent to the military bases, which were expected to vote almost unanimously for the regime. In the final tally, challenger Violeta Chamorro, the wife of a publisher martyred a decade before, emerged with 55 percent of the vote. The Sandinistas pulled just 42 percent.[137] This upset victory was less than two years after *Newsweek* had predicted the ultimate demise of the resistance, citing amongst other reasons the failure to accomplish "the crucial goal of creating a political infrastructure within the country."[138] In fact, while still entertaining many reservations about the conduct of the resistance, *Newsweek* later admitted that "the election result did overturn much liberal wisdom about Nicaragua."[139] It also confirmed the effects of American perseverance in pursuing its objective of removing Sandinista rule in Nicaragua.

Conclusion

In large part, the success of the U.S. intervention in Nicaragua and Honduras stemmed from President Reagan's staunch framing of the objective as extending well beyond events in Nicaragua to include U.S. credibility and the overall defeat of global communism. Because of the importance of these issues, especially within the Reagan administration itself, perseverance was ensured.

However, inconsistent domestic perceptions of legitimacy compelled Reagan to pursue an indirect approach to his objective, which dictated strong adherence to the principle of restraint. This strategy of "prolonged low-intensity conflict" was critical to perseverance and illustrates the interaction between this principle and restraint. Thomas Walker explains, "Since the human and material expense to the United States — and therefore, the political cost — were expected to remain low, it was felt that a war of this sort could be carried out indefinitely."[140]

Ironically, the American experience in Vietnam impacted both restraint and perseverance. The memory of the costs associated with direct involvement compelled Reagan to practice restraint in Nicaragua, but the damage done to U.S. credibility by its withdrawal from Vietnam encouraged Reagan to practice perseverance in Nicaragua.[141]

The indirect military approach also enhanced security in this OOTW. No direct action ground combat troops were committed to Nicaragua, and what U.S. military forces that were employed were involved only in exercise, support, and show of force roles. The regular U.S. presence in Honduras and the region enhanced security by building militarily critical infrastructure that added credibility to the U.S. threat without causing casualties that would have undercut legitimacy.

Reagan's approach to Nicaragua reflected mixed adherence to the principle of unity of effort. The U.S. achieved exceptional cooperation with Honduras and the Contras. The presence of the Contras was indispensable, given the political impossibility of a U.S. ground combat presence. However, the executive and legislative branches failed to achieve unity of effort and were often at odds. The Reagan administration's efforts to skirt the congressional obstacle resulted in the Iran-Contra Scandal and serious damage to the operation's legitimacy.

This analysis reinforces several of the observations from the Greek Civil War case study concerning relationships among the principles. In both examples, a clear presidential statement of objective that placed the specific crisis in a broader context facilitated perseverance. In both cases, restraint also facilitated both security and perseverance. Also, both cases showed the impact of external support and control of borders on the principle of security. As a point of marked contrast, however, in the case of Nicaragua, the U.S. found itself in the unfamiliar position of supporting an insurgency rather than combatting one. President Reagan adapted well to this role and showed a certain skill in waging protracted war.

Domestically, the legitimacy of Reagan's strategy was subjected to constant attacks, particularly by Congress. This weak adherence to legitimacy created some degradation of unity of effort between the legislative and executive branches. This friction was overcome by President Reagan's strong personal commitment to the objective, but not without political cost. On the other hand, unity of effort was achieved among the instruments of national power in a way that clearly demonstrated that the military role can be a supporting one. According to John Hunt, in OOTW "the military role is to create conditions in which decisive action can be taken by political means," and the American experience in Nicaragua and Honduras is an excellent example of the indirect application of military power as a contributing instrument of foreign policy.[142]

CHAPTER 6

Beirut: Unity of Effort Between Diplomacy and Force

Lebanon plays host to three major religions, and by the early 1980s, at least forty-seven different sects or political groups were vying for power and control.[1] The government of Lebanon was unable to exercise sovereignty amid such decentralization and competition. Instead, power rested in myriad "foreigners in combat boots" from Israel, Syria, the Palestine Liberation Organization, and elsewhere.[2] In 1982, the U.S. was added to this mix as a member of a Multinational Force (MNF) nebulously designed to support diplomatic efforts to restore some sense of stability and sovereignty to the country. The negotiated withdrawal of Syrian and Israeli forces turned out to be flawed, leaving a gap in unity of effort between the military and diplomatic initiatives. The inability to achieve the agreement that was intended to underpin the MNF's presence resulted in a failure to adhere to the principle of objective. As the situation declined, the MNF lost its legitimacy with the Moslem population and the violent militias that represented it. Unaware of the ramifications of this change, the MNF continued its strong adherence to restraint, based on its understanding of being a peacekeeping force. The result was a catastrophic lapse in security that made the MNF vulnerable to a terrorist attack on October 23, 1983. The tremendous loss of life forced the U.S. to come to grips with the futility of the effort, and in exasperation and without a realistic policy objective to direct the mission, perseverance failed. With the departure of the MNF, regular Syrian, Israeli, and Hezbollah violations of Lebanese sovereignty persisted. As a result of this OOTW, the U.S. failed its objective of supporting the government of Lebanon's ability to control its territory. The scope of the disaster was so great that it was investigated by both the House Armed Services Committee and a special Department of Defense Commission.[3]

Background

The United States had sent forces to Lebanon in 1958 when the country's factional tensions threatened to plunge the country into civil war. Having quieted this immediate crisis without attempting to resolve its underlying causes, the Americans withdrew after just 102 days. Lebanon maintained a precarious stability until the early 1970s, when tension along its border with Israel increased, especially after King Hussein ejected Yasir Arafat's Palestine Liberation Organization (PLO) from Jordan in 1970. The PLO relocated to south central Lebanon, which commandos used as a base to conduct operations against Israel. Israel responded to these attacks with reprisals against Palestinian bases in Lebanon and helped arm Christian militias within Lebanon to battle rival Moslem groups.[4]

The escalating regional crisis erupted into war on October 6, 1973, when Egypt and Syria attacked Israel on the Jewish holy day of Yom Kippur. Benefiting from the initial surprise, Syrian forces regained control of the Golan Heights that Israel had captured in the Six Day War of 1967, and Egypt secured a beachhead across the Suez Canal in the Sinai. Israel recovered enough to slow the Arab momentum, and then, after receiving significant military arms and supplies from the U.S., counterattacked and appeared poised to win another sweeping victory when the U.S. and the Soviet Union helped broker a United Nations ceasefire on October 22. Before then, however, the Organization of Petroleum Exporting Countries (OPEC) punished the U.S. for its support of Israel by imposing an oil embargo that caused gas prices to skyrocket and created an energy crisis in the U.S. Between October 1973 and January 1974, OPEC raised the price of petroleum to $11.56 a barrel, four times its pre-war level.[5]

The traumatic experience in Vietnam led to an American reluctance to reengage in the international arena, especially in areas that might result in a military commitment. However, the 1973 Arab-Israeli War appealed to strong American interests related to both Israel and oil.[6] Neo-isolationism began to give way to a rejuvenated containment in which observers such as Robert Tucker argued for a "countervailing power" against either Soviet or Arab threats to the oil fields that sustained the U.S. and its allies.[7] The Middle East situation was tailor-made for the personality, background, and negotiating style of Secretary of State Henry Kissinger. While Kissinger's skill seized the national imagination and beguiled Congress, it also seemed to require a specific American response to domestic turmoil in countries that many Americans regarded as outside the realm of direct and vital American interests.[8]

President Jimmy Carter would build on Kissinger's efforts in the Middle East, but while Kissinger's insistence on *Realpolitik* alienated many Americans,

Carter would restore a moral dimension to American foreign policy by advocating a strong human rights agenda. In this context, Carter was drawn to the political status of Palestinians, a Middle East issue Kissinger had avoided. Furthermore, Carter's human rights agenda would be only one of several contending national interests, with strategic, political, and economic concerns still being powerful. Indeed, America's increasing dependence on oil would ensure that the Middle East remained high on America's foreign policy agenda. In 1978, Carter worked with Egypt and Israel to reach the Camp David Accords, which ended thirty years of fighting between the two countries. The peace required an enormous amount of underwriting by the United States, both financially and militarily. It would also further tie the U.S. to military involvement in the region.[9] But while Egypt was pursuing an accommodation with Israel, the PLO stepped up its attacks, including a March 11, 1978, commando raid. Israel responded by invading Lebanon on March 14, and within a few days had occupied the entire southern part of the country except for Tyre and its surrounding area. The Lebanese government protested the Israeli invasion to the UN, arguing that it had no connection with the PLO raid. On March 19, the UN Security Council issued Resolutions 425 and 426, which called upon Israel to withdraw its forces and paved the way for the United Nations Interim Force in Lebanon (UNIFIL) to arrive in the area on March 23. The threefold purpose of UNFIL was to confirm the withdrawal of Israeli forces, restore international peace and security, and assist the government of Lebanon in ensuring the return of its effective authority in the area.[10] It consisted of some 6,000 troops from Finland, Fiji, France, Ghana, Ireland, Italy, the Netherlands, Norway, Senegal, and Sweden, but its positions were regularly infiltrated by the PLO.[11]

Thus, President's Carter's diplomatic success with Egypt and Israel did not extend to the broader Middle East, and he remained vulnerable to criticisms of foreign policy weaknesses. Soviet adventurism in Africa, the stalled Strategic Arms Limitations Talks, the Soviet invasion of Afghanistan, and the Iran hostage crisis all made Carter, and the U.S., appear weak on the international front. When Ronald Reagan became president, he brought with him a mandate to reverse that trend. However, rather than sustaining Carter's emphasis on the Middle East, Reagan devoted much of his anti-communist attention to Latin America, especially in Nicaragua.[12]

In the meantime, Lebanon continued to unravel. In 1975, the country had plunged into a savage civil war, and the beleaguered government invited Syria to restore order in June 1976. Indeed, Syrian not only arrived to help, but they stayed. By 1982, the Syrians were pressing to install a puppet Lebanese government.[13]

The PLO took full advantage of the situation and continued to use

Lebanon as a base to launch rocket attacks and raids into Israel. Hoping to end the threat once and for all, on June 6, 1982, Israel invaded Lebanon again with the initiation of Operation Peace for Galilee. The massive attack, with the equivalent of eight divisions, was intended to push the PLO fighters about twenty-five miles back into Lebanon to eliminate their ability to range Israel with rocket attacks. Advancing on three axes, the Israelis quickly brushed aside the unprepared PLO defenses and soon pushed the Syrians back to Beirut. The hapless UNIFIL force was overrun and for the next three years remained behind Israeli lines, its role limited to providing what protection and humanitarian assistance it could to the local population. While the shattered remains of the PLO huddled in the Moslem western sector of the city, the Israelis closed in to eliminate their enemy. They sealed off Beirut and cut water and electricity supplies. At the same time, the Israeli-backed Christian Phalange seized the opportunity to attack their Druze rivals in the Shuf (alternatively Shouf) Mountains to the east of Beirut.[14]

When it became apparent that Israel intended to press its attacks, the unlikely combination of pro–American Saudi Arabia and pro–Soviet Syria joined together on July 16 to ask the U.S. to help facilitate a PLO evacuation. By this time, Secretary of Defense Caspar Weinberger described the Reagan

A Swedish member of UNIFIL at an observation post in the town of Srifa, southern Lebanon, in April 1978. Courtesy United Nations.

administration as "very worried about the effect of the house-to-house fighting in Beirut that we were sure would come about if something were not done to try to halt the conflict."[15] In response to this imminent crisis, American Special Envoy Philip Habib arranged for a withdrawal of both PLO and Israeli forces from Beirut and the introduction of a peacekeeping force that included U.S. Marines.[16]

Elements of the 32nd Marine Amphibious Unit (MAU) commanded by Colonel James Mead had landed in Lebanon on June 23 to evacuate American citizens from Juniyah. As a result of Habib's negotiation, Mead's men now became part of a Multinational Force (MNF), not under United Nations control, but "simply the product of cooperation of the participating countries," which originally were the U.S., Italy, and France.[17]

In July, the MNF landed with the full consent and agreement of the Lebanese government and deployed to its agreed upon positions. The Americans and French secured the port of Beirut, and the Italians protected the roads to Damascus. The Americans made every effort to portray restraint and neutrality, carrying only personal weapons and leaving their mortars, tanks, and artillery offshore.[18]

Ambassador Habib superintended the departure of more than 8,000 PLO soldiers safely out of West Beirut by ship and some 6,000 more by land. Most went to Algeria, North Yemen, and Tunisia, where the PLO was headquartered. In spite of America being a staunch ally of Israel, U.S. Marines personally guarded Arafat as he boarded his steamer.[19]

During the operation "everything went well," and "Mead reembarked his men without incident."[20] Secretary of Defense Weinberger considered the "action to be a complete success because with virtually no losses, we had not only taken out the PLO army, one of the principal magnets for an Israeli house-to-house attack through Beirut, but we had removed a principal cause of instability in Lebanon itself." He called the MNF's arrival "not only timely, but lifesaving."[21]

There was, however, one untoward development that had occurred without notice. Sometime during the summer, some 300 to 500 Iranian revolutionaries had come to Lebanon to resist the Israeli invasion. This group formed the nucleus of what would become Hezbollah. The PLO may have been largely ousted from Lebanon, but the arrival of the Iranians merely "replaced one terrorist threat with another."[22] The October 31, 1983, suicide attack on the MNF would eventually be traced to Hezbollah, but for the time being, the fanatical group remained in the shadows. Its mission accomplished, the MNF was disbanded, and on September 10, it departed Lebanon.[23]

The departure of the MNF left Beirut with no functioning civil authority, and the respite was not to last long.[24] Four days after the MNF's departure,

Colonel James Mead leads the 22nd Marine Amphibious Unit down the bow ramp of the tank landing ship USS *Manitowoc* to begin their peacekeeping operation in Beirut on September 29, 1982. Photograph by Robert Feary Phan. Department of Defense.

Bashir Gemayel, the Maronite Christian chief of the Phalangist militia and President-elect of Lebanon was assassinated. Within days the Israeli Army moved back into Beirut, and the Phalangist militia, now led by Elie Hobeika, staged a massacre of some 700 unarmed Palestinians in the Sabra and Shatila refugee camps. The Israeli Army, commanded by Brigadier General Amos Yaron, remained on the periphery during the atrocities.[25] Ambassador Habib and President Gemayel had both promised that the Palestinian refugees would be safe after the departure of the PLO from Beirut. Now, "the Israelis were going in for the kill."[26] Fearing further instability, Bashir's brother Amin Gemayel, who had been elected as the new Lebanese president, appealed for American and European help. On September 20, President Reagan announced the U.S., France, and Italy would reconstitute an MNF to replace the Israeli Army and the Phalangists in Lebanon until the Lebanese Army could assume that responsibility. On September 29, Colonel Mead's redesignated 22nd MAU returned to Beirut.[27] Habib hopefully felt the MNF would be "a presence behind which the [government of Lebanon] could assert authority over West Beirut."[28]

Mead's second stay in Lebanon was short. On October 30, the 22nd MAU was relieved by the 24th MAU, commanded by Colonel Thomas Stokes. The 24th MAU remained until February 15, 1983, when Mead returned for a third time with the 22nd MAU. On May 30, Colonel Tim Geraghty and the 24th MAU assumed the mission again. Arriving in the midst of a "deceptively bright and optimistic" scene, Geraghty and his marines would find a completely different situation in Lebanon than the previous MNFs had encountered.[29]

Analysis of the Principles

Unity of Effort

Unity of effort problems within the executive branch and between the diplomatic and military efforts hounded the MNF from its inception. There has historically been a tension between the Department of State and the Department of Defense in most U.S. presidential administrations, but the struggle between Secretary of Defense Caspar Weinberger and Secretary of State George Shultz was particularly heated.[30] As the U.S. presence continued, tension between the president and Congress also would mount after September 8, 1983, when Congressman Clarence Long initiated a debate on the War Powers Act.[31] This challenge to presidential power may have encouraged administration reluctance to acknowledge a marine combat role,[32] but the true problem with unity of effort in Beirut began with the contending views of secretaries Shultz and Weinberger over the proper use of the military.

As secretary of state, Shultz "stressed the need to interweave diplomacy and force in a wide range of situations."[33] While he argued for the "prudent, limited, proportionate uses of our military power,"[34] he complained that "to Weinberger, as I heard him, our forces were to be constantly built up but not used: everything in our defense structure seemed geared exclusively to deter World War III against the Soviets; diplomacy was to solve all the other problems we faced around the world."[35]

For his part, Weinberger interpreted the State Department's position as being

> we should not hesitate to put a battalion or so of American forces in various places in the world where we desired to achieve particular objectives of stability, or changes of government, or support of governments or whatever else. Their feeling seemed to be that an American troop presence would add a desirable bit of pressure and leverage to diplomatic efforts, and that we should be willing to do that freely and virtually without hesitation.[36]

He considered the National Security Staff to be "even more militant" with an "eagerness to get us into a fight somewhere — anywhere — coupled with their apparent lack of concern for the safety of our troops, and with no responsibility therefor."[37]

Conversely, Weinberger believed that "we should not commit American troops to any situation unless the objectives were so important to American interests that we had to fight." Even then, the commitment of the military would be "as a last resort" to be used only after "all diplomatic efforts failed."[38] Because Weinberger did not think these conditions had been met in Lebanon, he opposed the deployment of the second MNF. The Joint Chiefs of Staff shared Weinberger's opposition to the plan, but the State Department and Deputy National Security Advisor Robert "Bud" McFarlane continued to strongly press for a second MNF. In the end, what Weinberger calls McFarlane's "petulant" demands carried the day.[39] Out of loyalty and professionalism, Weinberger "supported the President's decision fully," but Thomas Hammes argues there certainly was "no attempt to seek the effective interagency response essential to bring peace."[40]

While Weinberger maintained the MNF was more of a vulnerability than a threat,[41] Shultz pursued his theory that diplomacy could work "most effectively when force — or the threat of force — was a credible part of the equation."[42] Eight months later, Shultz's efforts produced what Weinberger called "a curious agreement" between Lebanon and Israel. "Why such an agreement was reported to us in such glowing terms by George Schultz," Weinberger said, "has always remained a mystery to me." Weinberger raised his objections with Shultz before the agreement was signed, but Shultz remained "extremely proud and protective of his agreement, and none of [Weinberger's] arguments ... made the slightest impression on him."[43]

Like Weinberger, the 24th MAU dutifully followed orders. Lieutenant Colonel H. L. Gerlach, who commanded the Battalion Landing Teram (BLT) 1/8, the ground element of the MAU, explained, "The political and diplomatic side of the house set up the parameters, and we accomplish our mission within them."[44] These parameters, however, were critical, and Weinberger insisted that the military's success "was premised on achieving a *diplomatic* success."[45] Geraghty would come to believe the failure to establish this diplomatic success was the 24th MAU's ultimate undoing. "When you have the State Department leading the way, and the politicians fixing our bayonets," he criticized, "it becomes a loser's game."[46]

The Department of Defense Commission that investigated the October 23, 1983, disaster seemed to agree with Geraghty, concluding "that there is an urgent need for reassessment of alternative means to achieve US objectives in Lebanon."[47] The military presence in Beirut had been intended to support a negotiated solution to Lebanon's crisis. The hoped-for synergy never materialized, and the U.S. diplomatic and military instruments of power failed to achieve unity of effort. The failure of the U.S. intervention in Beirut clearly showed the limits of what the military could do alone.

Objective

While Secretary of State Shultz saw the second MNF as a tool to facilitate his on-going negotiations, Secretary of Defense Weinberger objected that it did "not have any mission that could be defined. Its objectives were stated in the fuzziest possible terms."[48] The principle of objective requires a seamless connectivity between the strategic and operational levels of action. In this regard, the U.S. strategic development in Beirut represented as much of a violation of the "ends, ways, and means" model as Nicaragua and Honduras represented its successful application.[49] This critical linkage was dangerously missing in Beirut.

President Reagan wanted to communicate America's strategic interest in Lebanon, but it was unclear how this interest translated to an operational mission. In his September 29, 1982, message to Congress, Reagan said the MNF's "mission is to provide an interposition force at agreed locations and thereby provide the multinational presence requested by the Lebanese government to assist it and the Lebanese Armed Forces."[50] The September 23 JCS Alert Order used similar language, describing the U.S. forces "as part of a multinational force presence in the Beirut area to occupy and secure positions along a designated section of the line south of the Beirut International Airport to a position in the vicinity of the Presidential Palace."[51] It was clear where the MNF was supposed to be, but what it was supposed to do there and why remained vague.

Marine Corps Commandant General Paul X. Kelley identified the core of the problem as the fact that the operation described in these instructions was "not a classic military mission."[52] As the marines grappled with how to make sense of the guidance, they gravitated toward the idea of "presence."[53] Glenn Dolphin, who was a communications officer on the 24th MAU headquarters staff, recalls he "didn't envy Col. Geraghty's job in having to get a handle on this presence thing."[54] Journalist Eric Hammel, author of a detailed account of the marine experience in Beirut, contends it was "a phrase no Marine commander had ever before seen on an operations order."[55]

What Geraghty concluded was that "the mission of the MAU in Lebanon is a diplomatic mission." "It was important to me, in the interpretation of that mission," he explained, "that there was a presence mission. That means being seen."[56] Career army officer and military historian Daniel Bolger contends that Geraghty and other marine commanders "misinterpreted their assigned mission," but explains the failing as "a function of trying too hard to translate overarching political objectives into military terms, always a risk when national policy rides on the backs of tired colonels far from home."[57] Bolger argues the marines created for themselves "a self-designated nonmilitary role" when they could have concentrated on the "occupy and secure" portion of the JCS Alert Order.[58]

According to Robert Jordan, the Marine Corps public affairs officer in Beirut and later executive director of the Beirut Veterans of America, "Presence was interpreted to mean a showing of the flag, a symbol of American interest and concern for the legitimate government of Lebanon and a neutral stance toward Israel, Syria, and the various religious and political factions."[59] Later, the "mission" was defined to be the interposition of the MNF between the withdrawing Israelis and Syrians, but the problem remained, of course, that there was not an agreed-upon withdrawal.[60] "Absent this," Weinberger writes, "there was no *military* action that could succeed, unless we declared war and tried to force the occupying troops out of Lebanon." He argues that even after the "objective was 'clarified,' the newly defined objective was demonstrably unobtainable."[61] The American presence in Beirut did not adhere to the principle of objective.

Legitimacy

The imprecision of the mission would also negatively impact the MNF's legitimacy. Dolphin writes in his memoirs, "Over the years, I've heard discussions about the mission being 'fuzzy' or how the word 'presence' lacked definition in the military context." By the time the 24th MAU arrived for its tour in Lebanon, Dolphin believes "the meaning of the word presence had evolved into 'peacekeeping.'"[62] Earlier, however, Chief of Naval Operations Admiral James Watkins had told Congress, "We are not in a peacekeeping mission. Peacekeeping could well be a combat operation. This is not a combat operation."[63] The Department of Defense Commission Report was no doubt correct in concluding "that the 'presence' mission was not interpreted the same by all levels of command."[64]

As a result of imprecise terminology that led to such confusion, military doctrine writers refined their vocabulary during the 1990s. While these improvements came too late to help the MNF, they shed valuable light on how to best characterize the situation in which the marines found themselves, and its implications for legitimacy.

By 1993, FM 100–5 had described peacekeeping operations (PKO) as supporting "diplomatic efforts to maintain peace in areas of potential conflict."[65] For a PKO to "maintain peace," peace must already exist. In the wake of the assassination of the Lebanese president and the Israeli invasion that preceded the second MNF, and certainly in the case of subsequent MNFs, it is difficult to describe the situation in Lebanon as being one of peace. Instead, when Colonel Mead returned with the second MNF, the Syrians and Israelis were in direct combat with each other. A legitimate military mission would be to forcibly separate belligerents, but that is not what peacekeeping forces do.[66]

FM 100–5 also noted that PKOs "require the consent of all parties involved in the dispute."[67] The first MNF entered Lebanon with the approval of the government in Beirut and the concurrence of the various Christian and Moslem factions. President Gemayel may have requested the second MNF, but he could not speak for all the various factions.[68] The usual procedure is that diplomatic negotiations establish a mandate that "describes the scope of the peacekeeping operation."[69] The second MNF lacked the legitimacy that consent and a mandate provide.

"The Application of Peace Enforcement Operations at the Brigade and Battalion White Paper" appeared a year after FM 100–5 and noted that because "the success of the peacekeeping force depends on the consent of the former belligerents, the force must shepherd its own legitimacy by actual and apparent neutrality."[70] Of course, in the case of the second MNF there was no "consent," and the belligerents were active rather than "former," but the emphasis on neutrality remained. FM 100–5 notes that peacekeeping "demands that the peacekeeping force maintain strict neutrality," and Gunnery Sergeant Randolph Russell remembered telling many civilians in Beirut, "We're a peacekeeping force, we don't take sides."[71] In spite of these efforts, the perception arose that the Americans were aligned with the Lebanese, and the MNF became caught in the middle of several warring factions that did not acknowledge its legitimacy. By these measures, interpreting the MNF mission as "peacekeeping" was a flawed concept.

However, these problems remained deceptively beneath the surface when Mead's 22nd MAU first arrived in Beirut. According to the Department of Defense Commission Report, the MNF was "warmly welcomed by the local populace" and "the environment was essentially benign."[72] That generally peaceful condition continued, in spite of "the deterioration of the political/military situation in Lebanon," until April 18, 1983, when a terrorist attack on the U.S. Embassy killed sixty-three people, including seventeen Americans.[73] Still, as Mead departed and passed the mission to Geraghty, Mead felt the MNF was on good terms with the various factions in Lebanon. He called the LAF "our friends," while also claiming, "The Shia Moslem populations in our area treated us with the same courtesy and respect we had showed them."[74] He was proud that the MNF had helped Lebanon move "a few inches closer to peace and sovereignty" and felt enough progress had been made that the LAF would be able to exert governmental control throughout the country within a year.[75]

Geraghty considered neutrality to have been critical to Mead's success, and the new MNF commander "was very adamant to maintain that neutrality

Colonel James Mead talks with a Lebanese Armed Forces general in Lebanon on October 1, 1982. During Mead's tour, he reported having a comfortable relationship with the LAF. Photograph by Mark Dietrich. Department of Defense.

that I think we had built up — and goodwill — for over a year." He endeavored to walk "a razor's edge to maintain our neutrality" and treat "all Lebanese factions alike, showing no favoritism toward one group or another." Whatever successes had been made, Geraghty attributed to this approach.[76]

Unfortunately for Geraghty, what the Department of Defense Commission Report would describe as "a series of circumstances beyond the control" of the commander would bankrupt his predilection for neutrality.[77] What would ultimately pass for a withdrawal agreement was finally brokered on May 17, 1983, eighteen months after the second MNF returned to Lebanon and just weeks before the arrival of Geraghty's 24th MAU. Departing 22nd MAU commander Mead had high hopes for the negotiation, praising it as the work of diplomats who "had been able through patience and persistence to bring about a compromise in a highly complex and emotionally volatile situation."[78]

Mead's high hopes notwithstanding, in reality, the agreement was a seriously incomplete settlement, signed only by Lebanon and Israel, not Syria. Accompanying the deal was a secret side letter, accepted by Secretary of State Schultz but unknown to Lebanese President Gemayel, that Israel would not withdraw if Syria did not withdraw simultaneously. Israel also required information about all Israeli soldiers missing in action and the return of all Israelis being held prisoner of war and the remains of dead Israeli soldiers before Israel would withdraw. Secretary of Defense Weinberger considered this side letter to amount to giving "President [Hafiz] Assad of Syria veto power over any withdrawal and thus over Israel's ability to establish better relations with a key Arab neighbor, Lebanon." "Assad promptly exercised this [power]," Weinberger continues, "by not withdrawing." He declared "the May 17 'agreement' was not only absurd, but was nullified from the start" by Syria's veto power.[79] Similarly, diplomatic historian John Boykin labels the agreement "stillborn" and a "charade."[80] Weinberger describes it as "a losing proposition from the get-go" and considers it "a wonder anyone could have been naïve enough to believe it would work."[81] Such assessments did not bode well for the MNF.

The day of the agreement, President Reagan also announced at a televised news conference, "The MNF went there to help the new [sic] government of Lebanon maintain order until it can organize its military and its police to assume control of its borders and its own internal security." Hammel considers this a significant expansion of the original MNF presence as "merely a symbolic act of solidarity with a reemergent Lebanese national entity" to now taking "an active role in policing borders and *providing for internal security* ... [that] positively identified American servicemen with the besieged Gemayel government."[82]

The situation was further agitated on May 20, when President Reagan notified Congress he had removed his ban on the sale of seventy-five F-16 fighter aircraft to Israel. Syria responded by stepping up its activities in the Bekaa Valley, and Libyan military contingents were also reported to have entered the area.[83] On July 6, Syria formally rejected the withdrawal plan, but seemingly expected the Israelis to withdraw unilaterally. Syria's Moslem Druze allies began a major effort to eject the Christian Phalange from the Shuf Mountains, and the Druze and Amal Shiites prepared to fill the gap left by the anticipated Israeli departure. The Lebanese Army readied itself to do the same thing. The Department of Defense Commission Report noted the MNF's "initial conditions had dramatically changed,"[84] and Bolger describes the mission as having now "reached a crossroads." Neutrality was no longer an option.[85]

The marines had been training the LAF for six months in hopes that the more professional the LAF became, the less need there would be for the MNF or the Israelis to remain in Lebanon. Although the LAF was officially the non-partisan representative of all of Lebanon, it was traditionally dominated by the Maronite Christians, which caused it to lack legitimacy with the Druze and Moslem groups. Boykin explains, "Since the Marines were supporting the LAF, the Druze reasoned, then they too were enemies. As that perception increased, so did fire at the Marines from Druze and other factions."[86] The perception was reinforced from July 19 to July 23, as President Gemayel traveled to the U.S., where President Reagan described him as "our friend."[87] In Beirut, daily bombardments protested Gemayel's visit, and the MNF rapidly found itself "caught in the middle of the conflict erupting around them."[88]

While Gemayel was in the U.S., President Reagan announced his July 15 appointment of Robert McFarlane, a retired marine lieutenant colonel, to replace Habib as his Middle East Ambassador. McFarlane took a more confrontational approach than Habib had attempted.[89] In an effort to buttress Gemayel, McFarlane severed all U.S. contacts with the Druze. While Gemayel's defense advisor Wadia Haddad crowed, "We have the United States in our pocket," Druze leader Walid Jumblatt turned to Syria for more support.[90]

On July 20, the Israeli cabinet authorized a partial withdrawal of its forces to the Awali River, less than twenty miles south of Beirut. The U.S. was able to persuade Israel to delay the order twice to give additional time for the LAF to prepare, but on August 28, the initial troop movements began.[91] Druze and Amal fighters rushed to fill the vacuum left in the northern Shuf range and Christian East Beirut. The LAF was unprepared for this challenge, and marine Lieutenant Gregory Blazer recalls they "began using our lines as protection for movement up and down the coast road, which put us in direct fire of forces hostile to the Lebanese Armed Forces, trying to control the positions that the IDF [Israeli Defense Forces] withdrew from."[92]

Every time the marines fired back in self-defense, the Moslems saw them as being in league with the Christian-dominated Lebanese Army. Even Moslem troops within the LAF debated with their Christian officers about returning fire on their coreligionists.[93] Captain Morgan France, who as commander of Amphibious Squadron 8 was the overall commander in Lebanon, and Geraghty struggled to develop "a postured response," which advanced incrementally from pointing weapons and launching Cobra attack helicopters to popping illumination flares over active hostile positions to finally opening fire. Some junior marines felt such restrained tactics as responding with nonlethal illumination flares to mortar and rocket attacks that had killed their comrades made the Marines "sitting ducks." More seasoned ones understood Geraghty was "in a tough political position."[94] From the command perspective, more was at stake than politics. France explained, "We were very concerned with remaining neutral. That was the linchpin of our mission and the linchpin of Tim's [Geraghty's] survival."[95] Geraghty had to carefully weigh short-term military expediency against the potential long-term benefits of neutrality.[96] By this point, however, neutrality and the legitimacy that it was hoped to engender, had become impossible. Now, declares Hammel, "There was a full-blown war in The Root [marine slang for Beirut], and the MAU was part of it."[97]

On September 4, when the Israelis withdrew their main forces from Khalde, the marines were trapped in a similar situation. Without coordination, two Lebanese armored columns advanced through the marine positions in an effort to replace the departing IDF. In fighting that exceeded the August incident, the maneuver gave the impression the marines were laying down a base of fire in support of the Lebanese advance.[98] Dolphin assesses that "with the LAF operating dozens of armored vehicles so close to our positions ... the Druze militia would see [the Marines'] defensive fires as being in direct support of an LAF offensive."[99] In such a situation, "perceptions are everything."[100] At first Geraghty authorized only illumination rounds be fired, but by this time the strategy "was beginning to lose its punch."[101] When Druze batteries continued to shell the marines, the USS *Eisenhower* launched F-14A Tomacat fighters that located the position which was then destroyed by naval gunfire from the USS *Bowen*.[102]

In spite of this necessary deviation from neutrality, Geraghty still resisted Ambassador McFarlane's request to launch carrier air strikes in support of LAF forces in danger of being overwhelmed by an assortment of militia fighters at Suq-al-Gharb, the critical high ground overlooking the Beirut International Airport. Only when U.S. Special Forces personnel with the LAF reported Syrian tanks were closing in on their position on the morning of September 19, did Geraghty consent to supporting fires from the USS *Virginia* and the USS *John Rodgers*. Bolstered by this support, the LAF line stiffened and held.[103] A ceasefire was arranged for September 26, leading Jordan to surmise, "It appeared that *presence* and a good salvo or more of naval gunfire had indeed made peace a possibility."[104] Perhaps the measured use of added firepower was moving the MNF in the direction of the combination of security and restraint that had proved successful for Operation Bluebat and Operation Power Pack. Instead, Jordan concludes, "Hindsight shows that the optimism was misplaced."[105]

Indeed, many would later point to Suq-al-Gharb as a "turning point" in America's role in Beirut.[106] Boykin argues that "with the Americans now shelling Druze positions in the Shouf in support of the LAF, the Marines lost their only real asset, their neutrality. They were now seen as full partisan participants in the civil war, and the attacks on them by various factions increased even more."[107] Michael Petit agrees that with this new development "the nature of the Marines' role in Lebanon changed dramatically."[108] Whatever tenuous claim to legitimacy the MNF once may have had was now gone.

Restraint

However, it was based on this assumption of legitimacy that the MNF placed its high premium on the principle of restraint. In his September 23, 1982, message to Congress, President Reagan had emphasized, "In carrying out this mission, the American force will not engage in combat. It may, however, exercise the right of self-defense and will be equipped accordingly." He also expected the mission would last "only for a limited period."[109] Because there was never any intention of the MNF engaging in combat, it was only lightly armed. Moreover, Secretary of Defense Weinberger describes the MNF as being "quite insufficient in numbers or configuration to deal militarily with either the Israelis or the Syrians, and certainly not with all the factional militias of Christians and Moslems who fought each other with great ferocity and had been doing so for many years. Indeed, the second MNF was not designed or intended to deal militarily with *any* other forces."[110]

The apparent calm that Mead found when he returned to Beirut "hardly necessitated a bona fide defense," and he understandably focused on establishing a presence.[111] Indeed at that time, Secretary of Defense Weinberger argues, Mead "had no mission other than to 'establish a presence.'"[112] At this point "the operation was intended to be of short duration," so little attention was paid to much beyond that.[113]

When the second MNF deployed, the Joint Chiefs of Staff instructed it to follow the standard "peacetime rules of engagement" and fire only in self-defense and defense of collocated LAF units.[114] One of Stokes's initial acts as commander of the MNF was to refine these ROE in an effort to keep "an innocuous exchange of fire" from erupting into mayhem.[115] Stokes's ROE stated:

- In every possible case, local civil/military authority will be used.
- Marines will use only the degree of military force necessary to accomplish the mission or reduce the threat.
- Wherever possible, avoid injury to noncombatants or damage to civilian property.
- Response to hostile fire will be directed only at the source.
- Marines will act in self-defense only.[116]

Stokes's ROE "clearly imposed commonsense restrictions that he felt had to be stated in simple, unheroic terms to attack-minded combat infantrymen who had been told every day of their careers, beginning from training-day one, that they were thoroughbreds."[117] It was the same challenge Lieutenant General Bruce Palmer had faced in the Dominican Republic of "ratcheting-down" the aggression of soldiers in a non-traditional role. Geraghty noted the same difficulty in adjusting to a mission that was "not solely military, an offensive mission, more Marine-oriented" like the MAU was used to.[118]

Stokes went to great lengths to signal the MNF's impartiality. He began jeep patrols into the Phalange strongholds of Christian East Beirut, a move which no doubt impressed many Moslems. He dealt decisively with Israelis who seemingly "expected special treatment by the Marines," and his actions garnered extensive and favorable coverage in the Moslem press.[119] The difficulties with the Israelis came as somewhat of a surprise given the positive diplomatic relationship between Israel and the U.S., but Israel had come to resent the Americans as the protectors of the PLO that Operation Peace for Galilee had intended to crush.[120] The MNF had few friends in Beirut, but Stokes did his best not to take sides.

Where Stokes unintentionally deviated from his policy of neutrality was in his dealings with the Lebanese Army. In his September 29, 1982, address to Congress, President Reagan had stated the MNF "will operate in close coordination with the Lebanese Armed Forces."[121] In December, the 24th MAU began training the LAF in coordination with the Office of Military Cooperation. The goal was to raise LAF readiness to a level where it could help the government of Lebanon ensure the sovereignty of the country. However, by training the Christian-dominated LAF, the marines "inadvertently compromised the neutral image they had tried so hard to build."[122] Hammel declares it "was in its way among the most crucial decisions taken during the entire Marine experience in Beirut, for it inextricably linked the intentionally visible Marines to the fate of the LAF and, by extension, identified the Marines and their government completely with the fate of the Gemayel government."[123]

When Mead returned to Beirut for his third time on February 15, 1983, and replaced Stokes's 24th MAU, the 22nd MAU soon felt the effects of Moslem perceptions that the MNF had moved too close to the LAF. On March 15, an Italian squad hit a minefield and took sniper fire. The next day, someone dropped a grenade off a rooftop onto a marine patrol in West Beirut. During the same week, two grenade attacks occurred against French patrols. In the midst of these increased threats to the MNF, Mead reports that cross training with the LAF increased.[124]

The growing violence peaked on April 18, when a van carrying the equivalent of a 2,000-pound explosive charge crashed into the U.S. Embassy, killing sixty-three people. Hezbollah later claimed responsibility for the attack, boasting it was part of a "promise not to allow a single American to remain on Lebanese soil. When we say Lebanese soil we mean every inch of Lebanese territory."[125] Mead quickly upgraded security measures, increasing patrols, improving positions, and placing his Amphibious Assault Vehicles (amtracs) to provide protection. Special Envoy Habib agreed with the actions, noting that "policymakers at the civilian level don't make the rules of engagement."[126]

Mead's strong precautions appeared to have worked, and the 22nd MAU

President and Mrs. Reagan pay their respects to the victims of the U.S. Embassy bombing in Beirut at Andrews Air Force Base, Maryland on April 23, 1983. Ronald Reagan Library.

completed its tour without further serious incident, although on May 7 the marines received indirect fire from an unknown source and location.[127] When Geraghty's 24th MAU arrived, the commander picked up on the emphasis his predecessors had placed on restraint. In explaining the impact of the interpretation of the "presence" mission, Geraghty says, "It was a mission where we were not to build up any permanent-type structures because to emphasize the temporary nature of our mission, which is my understanding as to why the Marine Corps went in and not the Army to start with, and that is why we maintained ships offshore."[128] Staff Sergeant Todd Frederick agreed with Geraghty's assessment, explaining, "If you start digging tank ditches and setting up hard barriers, it completely counteracts what you're telling everybody else, that you're not really in a combat situation."[129]

When the level of violence increased dramatically after the Israelis began their withdrawal, Geraghty tried to respond with as much restraint as possible. The MNF fought back in self-defense but refused to contribute to the escalation. Geraghty explained, "I think a lot of the shelling and the casualties that we took there over the months were really directed to–as bait to force us to have a large response into the village and we didn't do that."[130] FM 100–5 would later assert, "Peacekeeping often involves ambiguous situations requiring the peacekeeping force to deal with extreme tension and violence without becoming a participant."[131] Geraghty refused to violate this charge.

Hoping to gain legitimacy by restraint, Geraghty claimed the MNF "earned the respect of the people."[132] His strategy was not without precedent. Such restraint had served Operation Bluebat forces well during the 1958 U.S. intervention in Lebanon. Likewise, discipline had been a key to the success of Operation Power Pack forces in the Dominican Republic in 1965–1966. In fact, "The Application of Peace Enforcement Operations at the Brigade and Battalion White Paper" would insist, "Only well-disciplined soldiers will be successful in peacekeeping operations."[133] In Lebanon, however, Secretary of Defense Weinberger argues that the militias interpreted American restraint as weakness and continued "their season of rising threats" that had begun with the April 1983 embassy bombing.[134] The difference was that the restraint exercised by Bluebat and Power Pack forces was backed up by strong adherence to the principle of security. Moreover, by the time of Geraghty's tour in Beirut, the MNF was clearly no longer in a traditional peacekeeping situation. Restraint would not work in the absence of security or legitimacy.

Security

The MNF's problems with security began with its failure to adhere to the principle of objective. "Without a clearly defined objective," Weinberger argues, "determining the proper size and armament and rules of engagement for such a force is difficult at best."[135] This initial problem was exacerbated when legitimacy became an issue. Assuming it had legitimacy that it did not, the MNF relied on restraint rather than security.

After the U.S. intervened on behalf of the LAF at Suq-el-Gharb on September 19, the USS *New Jersey* arrived in the eastern Mediterranean to give the MNF a significant firepower advantage. The *New Jersey's* sixteen-inch guns ensured the MNF was able to win any large-scale artillery duels. Understanding this reality, the anti–American forces adjusted their tactics and increasingly practiced asymmetric warfare. Corporal Michael Petit, a member of the 24th MAU, recalls, "The heavy fighting was over, but the sniping and terrorist attacks had just begun."[136] Jordan agrees, describing the MNF as now being "targeted for terrorist and sniper attacks."[137] Geraghty himself barely escaped a roadside car bombing on October 19.[138]

General indications of this new approach were legion. The Department of Defense Commission Report notes that "from August 1983 to the 23 October attack, the USMNF was virtually flooded with terrorist attack warnings." However, "those warnings provided little specific information on how and when a threat might be carried out."[139] There was a worldwide paucity of human intelligence sources available to confirm or deny the threats, and in an effort to prevent casualties from the increased militia violence, Geraghty had curtailed all but a few local security patrols on August 31. Without these focused resources, the vague reports from national intelligence services provided little in the way of timely, tailored, and "actionable" information.[140] Certainly, none of the reports matched the vehicle actually used in the attack.[141]

If the reports lacked specificity, they did paint a picture of security conditions that had "continued to deteriorate as progress toward a diplomatic solution slowed." The MNF, however, did not keep up with this new reality.[142] Geraghty complained, "The whole nature of the mission changed, but not our [combat size or area of operations]." Without those adjustments, Geraghty believes, "We never should have been there."[143] Secretary Weinberger seemingly agreed, and he put forward a proposal that would immediately withdraw the MNF from Beirut and place it in readiness aboard relatively safe ships offshore. According to Hammel, when the National Security Council met to consider the idea on October 18, "others attending the meeting prevailed upon Weinberger during a break to drop the proposal."[144] Weinberger implies this pressure came from the State Department, stating their claims that the U.S. could not appear to "cut and run ... carried the day."[145] This opportunity missed, the marines were left in what Weinberger called "the 'bull's-eye' of a large target at Beirut Airport."[146]

It would not be long before this vulnerability was exploited. At about

5:00 A.M. on October 23, a large truck was seen slowly circling the southern parking lot outside the BLT headquarters building. Such cargo trucks were "nothing out of the ordinary," and this one attracted little special notice. About an hour later, the same truck or a similar one reappeared and began to circle again. This time, however, the driver gunned the engine and blasted through the ineffective obstacles and past the sentry booth. The guards had no time to react, and within seconds the driver detonated the explosive equivalent of over 12,000 pounds of TNT into the enclosed atrium of the BLT building.[147] It was the largest conventional blast ever seen by the Federal Bureau of Investigation's forensic experts.[148]

In analyzing the implications of the attack on the principle of security, three main arguments present themselves. The first is Weinberger's consistent claim that security was impossible given the flawed diplomatic arrangement. "We did not and could not, under the basic terms of the MNF agreement," he explains, "equip or authorize our Marines to take the kind of normal responsive actions Marines are trained to do to protect themselves in combat. That would include seizing and holding the high ground around their basic position and patrolling aggressively to insure that the airport was not only occupied but fully secured." He felt "we could not either guarantee their safety, nor give them the means to provide for their own security, under the arrangements and conditions then prevailing in Lebanon." The best, if not only way, to achieve security in such a predicament would be to "dissolve the MNF and leave."[149]

The second way of coping with the security implications of the attack was to describe it as "an unconventional bolt out of the blue, unanticipated by rational men who had done their best to prepare themselves for more ordinary direct and indirect fire threats."[150] Reflecting this logic, the Department of Defense Commission Report labeled the attack "unprecedented," and Marine Corps Commandant General Kelley testified, "No one that I talked to in Lebanon or anywhere else could ever show me a thread of evidence that would show this kind of massive assault where you were actually penetrating a position with a five-ton truck going sixty miles an hour. This had just never been conceived of before."[151] Even if the attack had been anticipated, Secretary Weinberger argued the impossibility of the security challenge in lamenting, "Nothing can work against a suicide attack like that, any more than you could do anything about a kamikaze flight diving into a carrier in World War II."[152] In fact, the explosion was of such a magnitude that the Department of Defense Commission Report concluded, "Significant casualties probably would have resulted even if the terrorist truck had not penetrated the USMNF defensive perimeter but detonated in the roadway some 300 feet from the building."[153]

The final approach is a critical review of the security procedures and decisions made by the chain of command. This analysis focuses on the billeting of such a large number of personnel in a single structure, the ineffective rules of engagement, and a lax security posture. For these omissions, the Department of Defense Commission Report found the BLT and MAU commanders had failed "to take the security measures necessary to preclude the catastrophic loss of life in the attack on 23 October 1983."[154]

When Mead arrived with the second MNF, he opted to use a cluster of buildings at the Beirut International Airport (BIA) to house his headquarters and service units. Assuming there to be little risk of artillery or ground attack, Mead made his decision based largely on convenience. "It was simply logistics," he said.[155]

After the rocket attacks on July 22 and August 8, Gerlach and Geraghty agreed to move the remainder of the BLT support personnel and a reaction force of 150 men into the BLT headquarters building. No one questioned the fateful decision at the time. Petit notes, "The BLT was one of the safest buildings in the compound. It had endured earlier fighting and survived Israeli artillery barrages without being harmed. Even a minor earthquake in June had caused no structural damage."[156] Jordan says the building was "considered to be a fortress."[157] After intense shelling in September and increased sniper and terrorist attacks in October, messing facilities also were moved to the BLT headquarters building.[158] By the time of the October 23 attack, one quarter of the BLT, approximately 350 personnel, were concentrated in what the Department of Defense Commission Report termed "a lucrative target for attack." After the attack occurred, the Commission concluded that the billeting decision had "contributed to the catastrophic loss of life."[159] Ironically, Jordan notes, "many of the same Congressmen who later reviewed Marine security and use of the building posed for pictures and were briefed atop its roof just weeks before it was destroyed."[160]

The ROE also came under close scrutiny. By the time Geraghty assumed command, the ROE had evolved from the peacetime ROE under which Mead deployed, to Stokes's four rules, to a list of ten:

- When on post, mobile or foot, keep a loaded magazine in the weapon, bolt closed, weapon on safe, no round in a chamber.
- Do not chamber a round unless told to do so by a commissioned officer unless you must act in immediate self-defense where deadly force is authorized.
- Keep ammo for crew-served weapons readily available but not loaded. Weapon is on safe.
- Call local forces [LAF] to assist in self-defense effort. Notify headquarters.

- Use only minimum degree of force to accomplish any mission.
- Stop the use of force when it is no longer needed to accomplish the mission.
- If you receive effective hostile fire, direct your fire at the source. If possible, use friendly snipers.
- Respect civilian property; Do not attack it unless absolutely necessary to protect friendly forces.
- Protect innocent civilians from harm.
- Respect and protect recognized medical agencies such as the Red Cross, Red Crescent, etc.[161]

Geraghty spent a considerable amount of time briefing his men on the rules, and each marine was given a ROE card to carry.[162] Additionally, four alert conditions were established, ranging from Condition IV, which constituted normal operations and the lowest state of readiness, to Condition I, which meant an attack against U.S. positions was imminent or in progress.[163]

The Department of Defense Commission Report noted that conspicuously absent from this set of ROE was "specific guidance for countering the type of vehicular terrorist attacks that destroyed the US Embassy on 18 April 1983 and the BLT Headquarters Building on 23 October 1983."[164] However, after the April 18 attack, the U.S. Embassy was relocated to the Duraffourd Building and the British Embassy, and a permanent unit from the MNF was assigned as guard. The MNF's theater headquarters, U.S. Commander in Chief Europe (USCINCEUR) issued an expanded set of ROE for the embassy guard mission. This new ROE was more complicated in that it directed that magazines would be inserted in weapons, weapons on safe, with no round in the chamber for some posts, while other posts required a round in the chamber.[165] However, the more robust ROE better prepared the embassy guards to respond to terrorist type acts, such as car bombings, by allowing a marine "to fire if he perceived hostile intent." The result was that the marines in Beirut now had two sets of ROE, one based on hostile act and the other on hostile intent. The "hostile intent" ROE for the Embassy became codified as the "Blue Card," and the "hostile act" ROE at the airport became the "White Card."[166] Noting a cumulative effect, the Department of Defense Commission Report concluded, "The mission statement, the original ROE, and the implementation in May 1983 of dual 'Blue Card-White Card' ROE contributed to a mind-set that detracted from the readiness of the USMNF to respond to the terrorist threat which materialized on 23 October 1983."[167]

Lulled into a false sense of security by the "presence" mission, the sturdiness of the BLT building, and the desire to not display a combative presence, the MAU had done little to harden its position. The concertina wire, eighteen-inch sewer pipe, and sandbags proved no match for a five-ton truck. In fact, they were never intended to stop such an attack. Jordan recalls, "It [never] occurred to anyone that someone would try to charge through here."[168] Indeed, on the eve of the attack, Jordan reports a fairly relaxed, business-as-usual attitude prevailed among throughout the MNF.[169] As a result, even though the compound was supposed to be at Condition II readiness, in reality it was not even at Condition III.[170]

The security failure of the MNF was not the result of a single critical defect. Rather it was "the culmination of a series of understandable small decisions that aggregated to engender a tragedy."[171] Perhaps Jordan offers the best summation of the enduring lessons relating to the principle of security in Beirut: "The attacks illustrate the vulnerability of conventional forces to such suicide strikes and the problem faced by any military organization that must surrender the initiative to its opponents."[172] One of the objections to the term "operations other than war" was that it connoted a certain security that, as in Beirut, was not always the case. Instead, Lieutenant Colonel, later General, John Abizaid would caution, "Any American force committed to peacekeeping must keep in mind the Marine barracks bombing in Lebanon."[173]

Perseverance

The October 23 attack claimed the lives of 241 service members, but remarkably there was no immediate call for a U.S. withdrawal. Certainly, the marines showed no signs of quitting. Instead, "a grim determination set in to see the mission through regardless of their loss — to make sure that their fellow servicemen had not died in vain."[174] The media coverage reflected this attitude, and the American public responded with an impressive show of support. Over 60,000 letters, most addressed simply to "A Marine. Beirut, Lebanon" poured in, encouraging the survivors. Schoolchildren sent poems and cards, and "Operation Cookie" kept the Marines well-supplied with home-baked goods.[175] Previous intelligence reports had suggested the terrorists believed that by killing or wounding one or two soldiers or marines a day, they could generate enough public pressure within the MNF countries that they would withdraw their forces. According to Jordan, "Without a doubt, the antigovernment terrorists had underrated the American people."[176]

President Reagan responded to the bombing by declaring, "We cannot and will not dishonor them now, and the sacrifices they made, by failing to remain as faithful to the cause of freedom and the pursuit of peace as they have been."[177] He added, "These deeds make so evident the bestial nature of those who would assume power if they could have their way and drive us out of [Lebanon]. We must be more determined than ever that they cannot take over that vital and strategic area of the earth or for that matter any other part of the earth." Even, Reagan's usual rival, Speaker of the House Tip O'Neill, agreed: "This is not the time to cut and run."[178] In fact, on November 18, the 22nd MAU arrived to relieve the battered 24th and assume the MNF mission.[179]

A former Lebanese cabinet official argued that America's stake in Lebanon was now even greater than before. "The Americans have over 200 dead. That earns you the right to speak up," he said. "The US has paid the price of admission."[180] America did, in fact, increase its involvement in the region. In December, the U.S. launched an air strike and then naval gunfire at Syrian targets in an effort to quiet Syrian "belligerence." Although some politicians condemned this action as "the use of excessive force in a peacekeeping mission," Secretary of Defense Weinberger notes that there were also some who called for additional military pressure against Syria.[181]

For over three months, the Reagan administration struggled unsuccessfully to translate this resolve into policy. A wave of popularity brought on by the successful invasion of Grenada gave President Reagan the opportunity to make "a graceful exit" from Beirut, and on February 8, he announced the 22nd MAU would be withdrawn.[182] Hammel credits a variety of factors for this decision: congressional disapproval of continuing the mission, the Reagan administration's failure to articulate a clear policy or objective in continuing the effort, a desire to calm the public in the upcoming election year, and the combat ineffectiveness of the LAF.[183] Weinberger hones in on the most important of the group, declaring that administration officials finally reached the conclusion "some had for so long refused to recognize; namely that we were engaging in fruitless tactics in pursuit of unreachable goals."[184]

The casualty aversion that would plague perseverance in later OOTWs was not the operative issue in Beirut. Hammel argues "the heavily battered ... single Marine infantry battalion ... could be, and was, immediately replaced."[185] It was not the losses. It was their seeming lack of purpose. This time the American failure of perseverance was a function of its original poor adherence to the principle of objective.

Weinberger drew sharp lessons from this experience, and he developed what became known as the "Weinberger Doctrine"—strategic criteria to help guide "the painful decision that the use of military force is necessary to protect our interests or to carry out our national policy."[186] The overarching concern of the criteria was that the objective, commitment, and other conditions would be strong enough to ensure perseverance. The Weinberger criteria required the following:

- The United States should not commit forces to combat unless the vital national interests of the United States or its allies are involved.
- U.S. troops should only be committed wholeheartedly and with the clear intention of winning. Otherwise, troops should not be committed.
- U.S. combat troops should be committed only with clearly defined political and military objectives and with the capacity to accomplish those objectives.
- The relationship between the objectives and the size and composition of the forces committed should be continually reassessed and adjusted if necessary.
- U.S. troops should not be committed to battle without a "reasonable assurance" of the support of U.S. public opinion and Congress.
- The commitment of U.S. troops should be considered only as a last resort.[187]

Weinberger's philosophy was aimed at "the gray area conflicts" like Beirut and other OOTWs. He found these to be "the most difficult challenges to which a nation must respond," and, as he had for Beirut, he advocated a "flexible response" that did not necessarily include military force. If, however, the decision to use force was made in pursuit of some clear purpose, then the government must "continue to carry out that decision until the purpose has been achieved."[188] When troops were committed to combat, it had to be "with the sole object of winning."[189] He admitted that in the past, this perseverance had "been difficult to accomplish."[190]

Weinberger, however, did not advocate blind perseverance. He understood that "conditions and objectives invariably change during the course of a conflict." Therefore, the U.S. commitment must be "continually reassessed and adjusted if necessary."[191] He specifically references Lebanon as being an intervention in which "conditions deteriorated" to a degree that withdrawal was required.[192]

The Weinberger Doctrine required forces be committed only in cases "deemed vital to our national interest or that of our allies."[193] This emphatic requirement worked well during the remainder of the Cold War but came under scrutiny when the demise of the Soviet Union afforded the U.S. the opportunity to pursue less critical interests.[194] As America drifted further into these "gray-areas challenges," it also became more difficult to achieve Weinberger's insistence on "clearly defined political and military objectives."[195] This departure from strict adherence to the Weinberger Doctrine would profoundly affect perseverance in post–Cold War OOTWs such as Somalia.

Conclusion

Operations other than war are generally political in nature, and this was certainly the case in Beirut. It is accepted that the military operates in support of diplomatic objectives, and Operation Power Pack had clearly demonstrated the military's ability to subordinate operational decisions to political considerations. However, in Beirut no unity of effort was established between the military and diplomatic instruments of power. The discrepancy began at the cabinet level with Secretary of Defense Weinberger and Secretary of State Shultz disagreeing over the proper sequencing, cooperation, and efficacy of the military and diplomatic efforts. Because the political agreement the MNF was intended to support never materialized, unity of effort between the two instruments of national power was fractured.

This failure to achieve unity of effort unleashed a host of other problems with the remaining principles. As Weinberger forcefully argues, without the diplomatic agreement, there was no objective for the MNF. Instead, the MNF pursued an unclear mission associated with vague notions of "peacekeeping" and "presence." Such activities emphasize neutrality and assume a legitimacy that in reality was not present in Lebanon. This inappropriate characterization of the environment led to a strong adherence to the principle of restraint at the expense of security. Earlier OOTWs, such as in the Dominican Republic, had demonstrated that restraint can be effective when it is supported by the security represented by the potential application of force, but the lightly armed MNF lacked this capability and credibility. Geraghty's use of illumination rounds as "a painstakingly conceived response aimed at showing the power of the United States in a benign fashion" is a case in point. To the American mind, such a restrained tactic would facilitate legitimacy. In the reality of Lebanon, however, it had the opposite effect when directed at people who believed that "force met with less than equal force was no force at all; a weak response was a sign of weakness, and the weak were put on the earth to be beaten."[196] The MNF's decision to emphasize restraint in the absence of security led to a loss of credibility with its challengers.[197]

The failure to adhere to the principle of security resulted in the loss of 241 servicemen on October 23, 1983. Throughout the duration of all the MNFs, some twenty more were killed.[198] Casualty aversion would later emerge as a leading threat to the principle of perseverance in other OOTWs, but in Beirut, the lack of a clearly articulated objective to justify the losses seems more to blame.

This analysis reinforces several of the observations from other case studies concerning relationships among the principles. In both Vietnam and Beirut, a lack of unity of effort negatively impacted on objective, and the problem with objective unleashed other failures. Successful OOTWs, like Operations Bluebat and Power Pack and the decade-long effort in Nicaragua and Honduras, shared the MNF's adherence to restraint, but the American experience in Beirut suggests that restraint alone does not result in success.

CHAPTER 7

Somalia: Weak Objective
Leads to Weak Perseverance

The U.S. involvement in Somalia came as a response to the anarchy, drought, civil war, and banditry that had reduced Somalia, a country encompassing approximately 637,540 square kilometers on the Horn of Africa, to a virtual wasteland. The failure of a United Nations relief effort resulted in a U.S.–led peace enforcement operation that alleviated much of the humanitarian crisis. This success was followed by another UN operation with a more expansive mandate that included nation-building. The U.S. involvement in Somalia came at a time when America was struggling with its leadership role in the post–Cold War era, and this OOTW was plagued by a weak analysis and articulation of the objective. As the mission broadened over time, additional risks developed that violated the principle of security and eventually led to the disastrous Battle of Mogadishu. The intervention was perceived as not being legitimate by various Somali warlords who had a vested interest in maintaining the existing anarchy. In an effort to shore up that weak legitimacy, the UN mandate and the U.S. rules of engagement exercised the principle of restraint, but not in a way that produced the desired results. The U.S. also suffered from unity of effort issues, both internationally and between American conventional and special operations forces, which impacted security. The costly commitment to an area outside traditional U.S. national interests suffered from weak domestic legitimacy that was unsustainable in the wake of mounting casualties, and the operation experienced a strong failure to adhere to the principle of perseverance. As a result of this OOTW, the U.S. failed to accomplish its objective of bringing order and stability to Somalia.

Background

Some 300,000 Somalis had died between November 1991 and March 1993, and another 1.5 million lives were at immediate risk because of famine.

Nearly 4.5 million of Somalia's 6 million people were threatened by severe malnutrition and related diseases. Another 700,000 had sought refuge in neighboring countries. To help relieve the mass starvation, the United Nations Security Council approved Resolution 751, which established a humanitarian aid mission known as United Nations Operation in Somalia (UNOSOM I) in April 1992. UNOSOM I's success was severely limited because Somali warlords, most notably Mohamed Farah Aideed of the Habr Gidr subclan and Ali Mahdi Mohamed of the Abgal subclan, refused full cooperation, and the limited mandate was not strong enough to compel compliance. The warlords, whom Kimberly Martin noted "maintain their authority only by preventing the emergence of a functioning state,"[1] kept the UNOSOM I troops from leaving Mogadishu Airport, and only 500 of the authorized 3,500 troops deployed.[2]

The failure of UNOSOM I quickly became apparent, and the U.S. found itself under increasing pressure to act. Responding to a variety of motivations, the U.S. won United Nations Security Council approval in December 1992 of Resolution 794, which established Unified Task Force (UNITAF), a large, U.S.–led peace enforcement operation known as Operation Restore Hope. UNITAF made great progress, and humanitarian agencies soon declared an end to the food emergency. By January 1993, food was getting to all areas of the country, leading 10th Mountain Division commander Major General S. L. Arnold to soon declare, "We have come very close to establishing the right environment to enable the Somalis to arrive at a '*Somali solution*.'"[3] In light of these improvements, U.S. forces began withdrawing in mid–February, and on May 4, UNOSOM II, armed with a much broader mandate that included nation-building activities, took over operations from UNITAF. With the benefit of hindsight, Colonel Kenneth Allard notes that at this point "the underlying causes of conflict in Somalia had only been postponed," and it was during UNOSOM II that they resurfaced and "exploded."[4] Indeed, the disastrous October 3–4, 1993, Battle of Mogadishu brought an end to the international effort to bring order to Somalia.

Analysis of the Principles

Objective

Somalia's problems with the principle of objective can be traced to the decision-making process that led to the intervention. After the disaster of Beirut, the Weinberger Doctrine had emerged as the definitive yardstick for measuring the application of military force, but by the time of Somalia, the success of Operation Desert Storm and the collapse of the Soviet empire were changing both America's perception of its military and the nature of the threat. To many, Weinberger's strict criteria for the use of force seemed to require revision.[5]

The decision to intervene in Somalia reflected these changing thoughts on the commitment of force. In the case of Somalia, vital interests were not at stake. In their place were the peripheral interests of promoting American values and a favorable world order. While such interests did not meet Weinberger's high bar, it appeared that the application of military power was likely the only option that had a reasonable prospect of producing favorable results in Somalia at an acceptable cost.[6]

Thus, rather than being the result of deliberate and methodical exposure to a criteria such as Weinberger's, the decision to intervene in Somalia was based on a series of domestic and international influences. The most conspicuous factor was an onslaught of media coverage that portrayed starvation conditions in Somalia and created the impression that only U.S. intervention could save the country. Michael Mandelbaum concludes that "televised pictures of starving people created a political clamor to feed them, which propelled the US military into action."[7] White House Press Secretary Marlin Fitzwater acknowledges this impact of the press coverage, saying, "After the election [of November 1992], the media had free time and that was when the pressure started building up.... We heard it from every corner, that something had to be done. Finally the pressure was too great ... TV tipped us over the top.... I could not stand to eat my dinner watching TV at night. It made me sick."[8] Perhaps most telling is Craig Hines's report of the media coverage's impact on President George H. W. Bush. Hines writes,

> Bush said that as he and his wife, Barbara, watched television at the White House and saw "those starving kids ... in quest of a little pitiful cup of rice," he phoned Defense Secretary Dick Cheney and Gen. Colin Powell, Chairman of the JCoS [Joint Chiefs of Staff]: "Please come over to the White House." Bush recalled telling the military leaders: "I — we — can't watch this anymore. You've got to do something."[9]

Although the true situation was pockets of hunger rather than widespread starvation, the media created a popular perception of universal life-threatening conditions that demanded action.[10] As President Bill Clinton's National Security Advisor Anthony Lake explained, "We know that when the all-seeing eye of CNN finds real suffering abroad, Americans want their government to act — as they should and we should."[11] However, these public demands for action based on media coverage can negatively affect policy decision making. Former Secretary of State Lawrence Eagleburger lamented, "The public hears of an event now in real time, before the State Department has had time to think about it. Consequently, we find ourselves reacting before we've had time to think. This is now the way we determine foreign policy — it's driven more by the daily events reported on TV than it used to be."[12]

In addition to the media coverage, there were other influences impacting American decision making concerning Somalia. In the aftermath of the end of the Cold War and the victory in Operation Desert Storm, there was tremendous pressure on the U.S. to use its status as the world's only superpower to create a favorable new world order. Indeed in 1990, President Bush had declared,

> We stand today at a unique and extraordinary moment. The crisis in the Persian Gulf, as grave as it is, also offers a rare opportunity to move toward an historic period of cooperation. Out of these troubled times, our fifth objective — a new world order — can emerge: a new era — freer from the threat of terror, stronger in the pursuit of justice, and more secure in the quest for peace. An era in which the nations of the world, East and West, North and South, can prosper and live in harmony.... A hundred generations have searched for this elusive path to peace, while a thousand wars raged across the span of human endeavor. Today that new world is struggling to be born, a world quite different from the one we've known. A world where the rule of law supplants the rule of the jungle. A world in which nations recognize the shared responsibility for freedom and justice. A world where the strong respect the rights of the weak.[13]

Somalia was just one of many crises demanding U.S. attention as Bush and others sought to forge this new world order. Bosnia was another, but the seemingly open-ended nature of an intervention there served to fracture American will and popular interest in becoming involved. Somalia, on the other hand, seemed a much less complicated way of dealing with the pressure for U.S. action and a way of buying time for America to come to grips with what its role in Bosnia should be.[14]

The end result was that the American decision to intervene in Somalia was not based on the traditional rational actor model. Indeed, one contemporary observer described it as "more generous impulse than thought-out policy."[15] It certainly gave the appearance of being a "largely tactical decision reached to solve a current, concrete problem with little apparent concern for the longer term strategic implications."[16] Absent this clearly articulated objective and end state, the 10th Mountain Division, which provided the bulk of the forces for UNITAF, lamented in its After Action Review (AAR), "The first question that was difficult to answer was, 'what is the mission?'"[17] The AAR explains that this uncertainty was due to a lack of focus, definition, and end state provided by higher headquarters.[18] Even National Security Advisor Brent Scowcroft seemed to share the 10th Mountain's frustration, telling President Bush, "Sure, we can get in.... But how do we get out?"[19]

As a result of this ambiguity, the 10th Mountain was vulnerable to the accumulation of additional missions and tasks through the phenomenon of "mission creep."[20] While these added responsibilities strained the American forces at the tactical level, the most damaging example occurred at the strategic level when UNOSOM II, armed with a more robust mandate, embarked on a nation-building operation aimed at restoring order to Somalia, disarming Somalis, and rebuilding the country's economic and political institutions.

The transition from UNITAF to UNISOM II reflected a tremendous difference of opinion between the Bush administration (and continued by the Clinton administration) and the UN over the issue of disarmament. The UN demanded a comprehensive program throughout the entire country while the U.S. favored selective arms control only in the area of southern Somalia controlled by UNITAF. Neither of the two sides would budge. As late as April, just a few weeks before the announced transition date of May 4, 1993, UN Secretary General Boutros Boutros-Ghali was still refusing to allow detailed planning for the handoff until UNITAF changed its position of disarmament, something Lieutenant General Robert Johnston, the commander of Joint Task Force Somalia, with his limited mission and forces, simply refused to do.[21]

Lieutenant General Civik Bir of Turkey (second from left), Force Commander of UNOSOM II, and Lieutenant General Robert Johnston (third from left) of the US Marine Corps, Commander, Joint Task Force on Somalia, inspecting troops at a ceremony held on May 4, 1993 in Mogadishu to mark the transfer of operational authority from the UNITAF to UNOSOM II. Courtesy United Nations.

The result was an "incomplete and at times acrimonious and incoherent transition, [that left] the new UN–led coalition ... vulnerable, at least as it struggled to get started, and ill-prepared and poorly resourced to assume its broad mission."[22]

The UNOSOM II mandate, stated in Resolution 814, included eight broad tasks:

- Monitoring the factions to maintain peace;
- Preventing and responding to outbreaks in fighting;
- Controlling heavy weapons;
- Confiscating small arms from those who are unauthorized to possess them;
- Securing all ports and lines of communication;
- Protecting UN personnel and installations;
- Continuing mine-clearing efforts;
- Repatriating refugees and displaced persons.[23]

UNOSOM II's mission was to "conduct military operations to consolidate, expand, and maintain a secure environment for the advancement of humanitarian aid, economic assistance, and political reconciliation."[24] It was an ambitious undertaking.

The differences in scope between UNITAF and UNOSOM II were striking. While UNITAF focused on the southern parts of Somalia, UNOSOM II covered the entire country. While UNITAF strictly limited its activities to securing humanitarian assistance, UNOSOM II took on the much more dangerous task of disarmament. While UNITAF had no role in nation-building, UNOSOM II was mandated to assist Somalia in rehabilitating its political institutions, rebuilding its economy, and promoting national reconciliation and political settlement.[25]

This expanding mission drew political criticism in some circles, but few immediate protests. One of the earliest opponents was Senator Robert Byrd, who called for a withdrawal of U.S. forces, stating that while he supported the initial short-term humanitarian assistance, he did not have "nation-building in mind."[26] Nonetheless, the operation muddled along with little real effort to transform Somalia into a state but with increasing confrontation and problems.[27] It was not until the U.S. suffered unacceptable casualties that President Bill Clinton announced, "It is not our job to rebuild Somalia's society."[28] From its very inception, the international effort in Somalia had suffered from poor adherence to the principle of objective. The ensuing tension had built to this catastrophic climax, and international forces soon began withdrawing. In many ways, the overall failure in Somalia can be attributed to a variety of failures all stemming from a failure to follow the principle of objective.

Restraint

From the very beginning, operations in Somalia were characterized by strong consideration of the principle of restraint. Because there was no central government from which to obtain consent for the deployment of an international force, the UN adopted a limited neutral mandate for UNOSOM I, restricting the use of force and avoiding provocative actions. UNITAF was more aggressive than UNOSOM I, challenging and disarming some clans thought to be a threat to security, but, like UNOSOM I, it generally avoided provocative actions. For example, UNITAF did not attempt to disarm all civilians on the street, instead establishing a policy of "no visible weapons."[29] When Aideed moved some of his armed "technical" vehicles from Mogadishu toward Galacio to avoid confiscation by UNITAF, Robert Oakley, whom President George H. W. Bush had appointed special envoy to Somalia, explained, "There was no perceived need to confront Aideed over the disappearance of weapons as long as they posed no threat to UNITAF forces or humanitarian operations."[30] Such accommodations contributed to UNITAF being largely

Congressmen Curt Weldon (left), and John Murtha (right) with Ambassador Robert Oakley (second from left) and Lieutenant General Robert Johnston (second from right) on the tarmac of Mogadishu Airport during a congressional visit to Somalia. Photograph by Tech Sgt. Perry Heimer. Department of Defense.

tolerated by Somali warlords because it did not threaten the political balance in the country.[31]

UNITAF indeed made great progress, and in mid–February 1993, U.S. forces began withdrawing. On May 4, UNOSOM II took over operations from UNITAF, but this successor operation was severely flawed in its misapplication of the principle of restraint. UNOSOM II attempted to take on a more ambitious mandate than UNITAF despite having fewer and lower quality troops. UNITAF had ultimately involved more than 38,000 troops from twenty-one coalition nations, including 28,000 Americans. UNOSOM II was authorized a strength of just 28,000, of which only 4,500 were from American forces.

In both UNITAF and UNOSOM II, U.S. forces operated under rules of engagement (ROE) that granted "the right to use force to defend yourself against attacks or threats of an attack." Such wording allowed soldiers and marines to use deadly force not only against "hostile acts" but also against perceived "hostile intent."[32] While the U.S. forces had a fairly flexible and robust ROE, they also faced several non-traditional situations that challenged the principle of restraint. The most obvious situation was the congested and rickety urban area that created a tremendous possibility for collateral damage, resulting in such ROE restrictions as strict limitations on the use of AC-130 aircraft.[33]

Even more troublesome were the presence and behavior of noncombatants. UNITAF and UNOSOM II troops reported that many Somali males, to include children, "would try to steal almost any item that was not firmly secured."[34] Soldiers of 10th Mountain found that fixing bayonets proved an ineffective deterrent given the risk young Somalis were willing to take to obtain any piece of American equipment that might have significant resale value, as well as the thieves' quick realization that the Americans had no intention of actually using their bayonets. Some marines countered by carrying whipping sticks, but the idea of beating Somali children proved problematic as well. A solution that worked with some effect was found in hiring Somali elders, in whose hands the stick was a traditional symbol of authority and acceptable discipline, to keep the children at bay.[35] Cayenne pepper spray also proved to be "an effective means of proportionate force against low-level threats."[36]

American soldiers also faced the challenge of conducting combat operations in and amongst the civilian population. One company commander explained, "There are so many civilians around that when you go crashing through doors there's a potential to massacre innocent civilians."[37] Somali militiamen exploited this situation by frequently seeking cover behind noncombatants or in a humanitarian facility such as a hospital.[38] In fact, Allard goes as far as to say that "women and children [were] considered part of the clan's order of battle."[39] One instance where this dastardly technique was used was during the June 5, 1993, attack on a Pakistani platoon guarding a food distribution station at National Street in Mogadishu. Unarmed Somalis descended on the Pakistanis, blocking their view and grabbing at their weapons. Then, as the UN's account of the incident records, "from positions behind the women and children in the crowd, weapons were fired at the troops."[40] Likewise, during the October 3–4 Battle of Mogadishu, Staff Sergeant Edward Yurek of B Company, 3rd Battalion, 75th Ranger Regiment reported that militiamen hid behind unarmed women and fired from in between their legs and armpits.[41]

Nonetheless, ROE cards reiterated to soldiers that "the United States is not at war,"[42] and Brigadier General Anthony Zinni, UNITAF's J3, advised, "always consider negotiations as a great alternative to violence."[43] One manifestation of these notions was the technique of "graduated response," which was used routinely in cordon and search operations. Such operations began by the open and peaceful formation of the cordon around the area to be searched, followed by loudspeaker announcements of the operation's intent and specific instructions for compliance. This step allowed inhabitants to peacefully exit the buildings before combat soldiers entered. If this measure failed, the area was saturated with CS (tear gas). If resistance continued, soldiers entered the objective using a cutting charge to create a hole in the wall and lobbed concussion grenades to seize control of the inhabitants "with as little violence as possible." Major General Thomas Montgomery, the deputy commander of UNOSOM II, reports that fifteen, ten, and five-minute warnings were normally given before attacking any target.[44] Of course, the trade-off for this graduated response was the extra time afforded the inhabitants to develop a defense or call for outside assistance.[45]

As a result of extraordinarily measured actions such as these, the 10th Mountain AAR boasted, "Our soldiers displayed tremendous restraint in the use of force throughout [Operation Restore Hope]."[46] Likewise, Special Envoy Oakley notes, "Compared with the numerous incidents in which UNITAF forces encountered sporadic shooting or mass stone-throwing, the low casualty rate among Somalis shows how hard and how successfully UNITAF commanders worked to instill restraint and discipline into the behavior of troops from all nationalities and at all levels."[47]

Such well-intended efforts notwithstanding, adherence to the principle of restraint also negatively affected the mission. The limited U.S. presence in UNOSOM II can at least be attributed to considerations of restraint as a means of building legitimacy. In spite of a "changed security situation" and "the slower than anticipated arrival of coalition forces and contributor support," the U.S. chose "to modify the composition of our force to meet these new needs without significantly raising its total size." Central Command (CENTCOM) commander-in-chief General Joseph Hoar explained, "Raising the profile of the Armed Forces in Somalia would undermine the perception of UN military forces as truly international and capable of meeting the task at hand. A highly visible American presence is not in the best interests of the United States or the United Nations."[48] Hoar's comments appeared in the Autumn 1993 issue of *Joint Forces Quarterly*, just weeks before the Battle of Mogadishu. Much of the criticism of that disaster centered on the seemingly misplaced emphasis on the principle of restraint at the expense of security.

Legitimacy

Legitimacy was also a problematic issue in Somalia. The first challenge to this principle was that UN Resolution 794, which led to the creation of UNITAF, and UN Resolution 814, which authorized UNOSOM II, were written under Chapter VII of the UN Charter. UN Resolution 794 represented the first time this chapter had been invoked. Its use would make operations in Somalia peace enforcement rather than peacekeeping, an important distinction regarding legitimacy.

Chapter VI of the UN Charter is titled "The Pacific Settlement of Disputes." It specifies non-military solutions to international conflicts, advocating disputants seek solutions through negotiation, inquiry, mediation, conciliation, arbitration, judicial settlement, resort to regional agencies or arrangements, and other peaceful means of their own choice. It also allows the Security Council to recommend peaceful solutions to international disputes.[49] The broad clauses in Articles 33–38 that refer to action taken though "other peaceful means" have been offered as justification for UN observation and traditional peacekeeping missions. Others have argued that Chapter VI is limited to diplomatic efforts, leading former Secretary General Dag Hammarskjold to refer to the UN's limited military operations as "Chapter VI and a Half."[50]

Chapter VII of the UN Charter is titled "Action with Respect to Threats to the Peace, Breaches of the Peace, and Acts of Aggression." It allows the Security Council to mandate solutions to international conflict, to include military action through "air, sea, or land forces as may be necessary to maintain or restore international peace and security." As such, Chapter VII operations move beyond peacekeeping into the realm of peace enforcement.[51] UNOSOM II represented the first time U.S. forces had been committed to a UN–led peace enforcement operation.[52]

The 1993 edition of FM 100-5 stated, "Peacekeeping operations support diplomatic efforts to maintain peace in areas of potential conflict. They stabilize conflict between two belligerent nations and, as such, require the consent of all parties involved in the dispute." Peace enforcement operations, on the other hand, "are military intervention operations in support of diplomatic efforts to restore peace or to establish the conditions for a peacekeeping force between hostile factions that may not be consenting to intervention and may be engaged in combat activities." They imply "the use of force or its threat to coerce hostile factions to cease and desist from violent actions." Under such circumstances, peace enforcement forces "cannot maintain their objective neutrality in every instance."[53] The ensuing perceptions of bias naturally affect the operation's legitimacy in the eyes of those threatened by the peace enforcement force's actions.

In his highly regarded volume on lessons learned in Somalia, Allard warns of "bright lines" that when crossed indicate the "limits to the commitment of American military power" are being reached. He notes that one of these lines "is any action in a peace operation that effectively takes sides between factions engaged in internal civil strife."[54] Although such actions are expected in peace enforcement, by forfeiting its neutrality among the various Somali clans, the U.S. damaged its legitimacy. In many ways the U.S. found itself in an untenable situation. As Jonathan Stevenson explains, "Each Somali political leader, notably Aideed, insisted on the UN's neutrality but sought US support for its own clan — which was distinctly incompatible with equilibrium among clans. Most Somalis in positions of power still could not stomach the idea of a clan-neutral, egalitarian policy arching over the network of regional clans."[55]

The legitimacy of United Nations' activities in Somalia was further plagued by the preexisting mistrust Aideed had for Secretary General Boutros-Ghali. The situation dated back at least to January 27, 1991, when opposition forces, including those led by Aideed, toppled Mahammad Siad Barre's Somali government. As then deputy foreign minister of Egypt, Boutros-Ghali had supported Siad Barre, a fact that Aideed did not forget. Special Envoy Oakley recalled, "Certainly in my talks with Aideed he made it clear he did not trust Boutros-Ghali in particular and the United Nations in general."[56] To make matters worse in Aideed's eyes, the deposed Siad Barre had found refuge in Nigeria. This association made Nigerian forces in UNITAF a specified target for Aideed's attacks.[57] The legitimacy of the Italian contingent was also questioned, based on Italy's colonial experience in the region and its leanings toward Mohamed Ali Mahdi, Aideed's chief competition for control of Mogadishu. Italy's presence was especially confrontational to younger, anti-imperialist Somalis.[58]

Another challenge to legitimacy was the American cultural misunderstanding of Somalia. Even the culturally aware Brigadier General Zinni admitted that when he deployed, "I didn't know Somalis from salamis."[59] He noted the U.S. military's traditional mindset often prevented it from gaining a nuanced "understanding of what makes people tick, what their structure is, where authority lies, what is different about their values, and their way of doing business."[60] Perhaps as a reflection of this inability to relate, it was not long before many UNITAF members began referring to Somalis as "skinnies" and other derogatory terms.[61]

One thing Zinni and other members of UNITAF did understand was the importance of weapons in Somali culture. Special Envoy Oakley noted, "If you think the National Rifle Association has a fixation with weapons, it's nothing compared to the Somalis. It's part of their manhood." To surrender his weapon meant a Somali male was not just sacrificing the security of himself and his family, he was also losing some of his masculinity.[62] This realization led the U.S. to proceed slowly with regard to weapons control, in seeming acknowledgement of Allard's observation that "forcible disarmament is the 'bright line' of peace operations: when you cross it, you have entered a de facto state of war."[63] Rather than a wholesale disarmament policy, the 10th Mountain adopted the much more nuanced "four NOs"— no technical vehicles, no checkpoints, no visible weapons, and no banditry.[64] The result according to CENTCOM's General Hoar was a deliberate program of "selective 'disarming as necessary.'"[65]

UNITAF was less adept in its understanding of the importance of clans in Somali society. Even as seemingly

A row of small arms to include a World War II .30 caliber machine gun, Soviet made AK-47s, Soviet made 7.62mm RPD Light Machine Gun, U.S. made M-16 rifle, World War II era Bazooka, and a Soviet made 7.62mm Simonov self-loading rifle with bayonet attached seized during a raid of the weapons cantonment area of Mohamed Farah Aideed. Photograph by Terry Mitchell. Department of Defense.

innocent an operation as providing humanitarian assistance can threaten legitimacy because of its inescapable political and military consequences. This risk is especially prevalent in an environment where no government exists.[66] In a clan-ridden society such as Somalia, aid was not seen as neutral or impartial if it was provided to a rival group. Strengthening any of the warring factions altered the balance of power and created a perception of peacekeeper bias.[67] UNITAF experienced this phenomenon when its bottom-up efforts to empower traditional local and regional leaders were seen by Aideed's lieutenants as threatening to their own base of power.[68] As nation-building expert James Dobbins explains, "The very act of intervention alters, often radically, the power balance and social dynamic in the subject nation and its region. By virtue of an intervention, losers suddenly become winners, and winners become losers."[69]

Norman Cooling argues that UNOSOM II continued this error. He claims, "Disregarding the long-established Somali cultural order, the UN felt that, in the interest of creating a representative, democratic Somali government, they would be better served by excluding the clan leadership. The policy reeked of arrogance coupled with cultural ignorance."[70] The problem was that since 1988, more than fourteen Somali clans and factions had fought a civil war for control of their own territory.[71] In its expanded mission, UNOSOM II directly threatened these warlords' hold on power. UNOSOM II deputy commander Major General Montgomery observes, "That [to build a nation] was not in the best interest of the warlords, who wanted, each of them, to control, and of course Aideed was the strongest of the warlords."[72] Nonetheless, 10th Mountain Division commander Major General Arnold argued equally correctly that in his view, "the center of gravity of the operation in Somalia is the erosion of the independent power of the warlords.... It must take place if Somalia is ever to return to normalcy and attempt to rule itself."[73] But by concentrating on Aideed and Ali Mahdi, Somalia's two main warlords, William Wunderle argues that the UN created the unintended consequence of actually increasing "the warlord's degree of power and authority, which was desirable to the warlords but led to the marginalization of other clans, thereby upsetting the traditional balance of the Somali kinship system."[74] Moreover, the action that Arnold noted as critical to mission accomplishment, was the same one that Montgomery explained would render the effort illegitimate in the eyes of the Somali base of power.

Some observers explained the phenomenon in terms of cultural understanding; this time in the context of the military's growing pains associated with operations in a "nontraditional environment." Lawrence Yates cautions that in situations like Somalia "where there is no hostile force, there may be a tendency on the part of conventionally oriented officers and policy makers to create one." Yates cites an unidentified marine corps general as seeing this "need to have an enemy" as a fatal flaw in the military's approach to Somalia.[75] While such conclusions seem to dismiss the complexities of the situation in Somalia and the fact that the expanded mission was a UN rather than a U.S. military initiative, they do address the difficulty of maintaining legitimacy once the operation moved beyond its initial attempt to maintain neutrality.[76] One thing is sure, the targeting of Aideed certainly coalesced Somali unity in an unprecedented way. As Special Envoy Oakley explains, "Because [Somalis] are very xenophobic, and they reacted very strongly and would not allow foreigners to come in and single out one of their people [Aideed] even though they didn't like him, those who didn't like him began to rally to his defense, not just politically but he gained a lot of recruits and fighting against the United Nations in Mogadishu came in from other clans."[77] Allard echoes this sentiment, saying that Somali culture stresses the idea of "me and my clan against all outsiders."[78]

The result of this breakdown of legitimacy was that by June, UNOSOM II was at war with various Somali parties and was suffering high casualties, including twenty-five Pakistanis killed in an ambush on June 5. United Nations Security Council Resolution 837 was passed the next day and called for the immediate apprehension of those responsible. The result was that U.S. soldiers became involved in a highly personalized manhunt for Aideed. In October, a U.S. effort to capture him ended in eighteen American deaths in the Battle of Mogadishu.

Security

Even in its humanitarian capacity, the principle of security was essential to UNITAF's success. Much of the earlier attempts to provide relief to Somalia were siphoned off by the warring factions, because, as Dennis Jett explains, "Soldiers ... will always eat before civilians. No armed group is going to go hungry while unarmed relief workers distribute food aid to noncombatants in areas under its control." Food not only sustains the individual soldier, it also can be sold for cash that the warring faction can use to buy arms, ammunition, and other essentials of violence that enhance its power. To offset this phenomenon, relief officials in Somalia switched from providing high value, saleable foodstuffs to items that had less value in relation to their bulk. They also tried to saturate the country with food in order to reduce its value.[79]

Using more traditional methods to counter the threats, the 10th Mountain Division provided security for distribution sites, convoy operations, humanitarian agency activities, ports, airfields, and other key installations. Soldiers established checkpoints, dismantled the roadblocks that had served as militia toll collection points, and disarmed bandits.[80] On the average, UNITAF forces escorted 70 convoys carrying 9,000 metric tons of supplies from Mogadishu inland each month. These efforts "ensured that relief reached those who needed it and was not looted."[81] Analysts such as James Dobbins identify security as the priority task in any nation-building operation.[82] Somalis on the ground made the same observation. For example, Omar Faiki, a 60-year old former policeman, commented, "If there's no security, there is no food."[83]

However, the security of UNITAF was impacted by a predetermined "force cap." The 10th Mountain Division AAR noted that "while the ARFOR [Army Forces] developed courses of action for deployment that considered various methods of employment of forces, it seemed as though the crisis action planning accomplished at the strategic level was based on an artificial force cap of 10,200, not based on a mission analysis."[84] Some of these courses of action called for as many as 17,000 personnel, over half again as many as the ultimate 10,200 limit.[85] The 10th Mountain lamented that once the cap was announced, it "took on a life of its own,"[86] remaining completely independent of any mission analysis. As an example of the artificiality created by such restrictions, force caps caused a lift company of the 10th Aviation Brigade to deploy without any battalion command and control.[87] The implications for security are obvious.

Concluding that such arrangements "placed a great deal of strain on commanders"[88] and that "our forces were stretched very thin,"[89] the 10th Mountain recommended that, in the future, "the missions and tasks need to be assigned to the commander to conduct and then allow him to conduct mission analysis. There may be a need to place a ceiling on forces based on lift availability or political reasons, but the commander must have the flexibility to design the force required to accomplish the mission he is assigned.... Once tasks are received, mission analysis and the staff planning process should drive the number of personnel to deploy, not the other way around."[90] When such procedures are violated, security is bound to suffer.

UNITAF forces were assisted in security operations by a revived Somali police organization that became known as the Auxiliary Security Force (ASF). The project was controversial for several reasons. Some saw UNITAF's role in its creation as mission creep. The ASF had to contend with legal prohibitions on using funds for the U.S. military to train, advise, and support foreign law enforcement agencies. Other critics noted the difficulties in vetting a national police force that would be free from disruptive clan political influences. In the end, the principle of security trumped these considerations, with Special Envoy Oakley arguing that without Somali policemen, UNITAF was "going to get people killed patrolling in dark alleys."[91] The ASF "proved adept at controlling crowds and traffic, patrolling, securing key facilities such as ports and airfields and arresting criminals," as well as freeing UNITAF personnel to perform other mission-essential tasks.[92]

In addition to mere numbers, improper force types plagued the U.S. security effort in Somalia. Concerned with his "inability to get to US or UN forces in extremis," Montgomery had requested armored reinforcement, including a full mechanized battalion and an air cavalry squadron, in July 1993. Secretary of Defense Les Aspin denied the request, in Montgomery's mind "because the United States wanted out of Somalia, wanted to lower our troop presence, rather than increasing it."[93] As things would turn out, the October 3–4 disaster which ultimately forced a U.S. withdrawal was at least partially attributable to this subordination of the principle of security to those of restraint and legitimacy.

Another cause was the failure to understand the impact of the changed objective on security. Colonel Tim Geraghty, commander of the ill-fated 24th MAU in Beirut, had personal experience with such an omission and now wondered, "How did the mission ever evolve from feeding a starving nation, into going after a rinky-dink warlord?" Once the change did occur, Geraghty believes the outcome should have been anticipated. "If there's any lesson we learned out of Beirut, it was that we never should have been there after the initial mission changed," he commented. "It's very dangerous to put US forces in a hostile environment where there's no peace to keep. You essentially become a target for fanatics."[94] Geraghty was joined by many others who saw Somalia as "almost déjà vu" from the Beirut experience.[95]

The October 3 operation, part of a larger endeavor to capture Aideed known as Operation Gothic Serpent, had begun favorably with a force of army rangers and Delta commandos conducting a daylight raid on a suspected location of Aideed and his lieutenants at the Olympic Hotel. The Americans captured twenty of Aideed's men, but the mission quickly unraveled when Somalis shot down three U.S. helicopters. The Americans soon became surrounded by thousands of Somalis, and the relief column was ambushed on its way to rescue the beleaguered soldiers. It was more than nine hours before help, primarily from the 10th Mountain Division, finally arrived.

Only after the tragedy did President Clinton announce, "Today I have ordered 1,700 additional Army troops and 104 additional armored vehicles to Somalia to protect our troops and complete our mission. I've also ordered an aircraft carrier and two amphibious groups with 3,600 combat Marines to be stationed off-shore."[96] By then it was too late. In Somalia, a failure to adjust the force structure to the expanded mission and accompanying threat had created a strong violation of the principle of security.

Even after the disaster, there remained a reluctance among some U.S. officials to commit to a strong adherence to the principle of security. When asked, "Does Somalia prove Colin Powell's doctrine that American military power, if used, should be used with overwhelming force?" Secretary of State Warren Christopher responded,

> The concept is most applicable when our vital national interests are involved, rather than a situation such as this, where President Bush decided to go into Somalia for humanitarian reasons only. When U.S. troops are involved absent a vital national interest, then some hard questions have to be asked, including "Will our forces be fully protected?" But I wouldn't say that every time U.S. forces are involved anyplace, you have to have 500,000 troops.[97]

Even the 10th Mountain AAR, after making its case for mission analysis, realized that "With all that said, commanders and their planners must remember that this [force caps] will probably be the norm."[98] Such assessments do not bode well for security in future OOTWs.

Unity of Effort

Unity of effort proved a continuing challenge in Somalia, with initial concerns centering around activities between the military and the humanitarian relief agencies. Once the humanitarian crisis subsided, new unity of effort problems emerged within the coalition itself. On a broader front, Somalia revealed the inherent problems with the UN's ability to control such an operation. The entire experience epitomized the difficulty of obtaining cooperation among a variety of stakeholders in a complex and ambiguous OOTW environment.

When the 10th Mountain arrived in Somalia, there were some forty-nine non-governmental organizations (NGOs) conducting activities.[99] While clan theft of relief supplies was one of the primary reasons a military force was needed, many NGOs remained wary of too closely associating with the military, fearing that such activity would damage the NGO's claim to neutrality and peaceful purpose. Indeed, Andrew Natsios argues that "NGOs, some of which have developed philosophical approaches to relief and development, guard their autonomy with such energy that they sometimes seem to be suggesting that autonomy is a form of strategy."[100]

In many cases, a certain mistrust bordering on animosity affected relations between the military and the NGOs. For many soldiers, the humanitarian organizations were "left-wing, anti-military, disorganized, self-righteous 'do-gooders.'" Although senior leaders like Major General Arnold considered the NGOs "the real heroes of this operation,"[101] one observer opined that "officers simply did not see women in their late twenties with Berkenstock sandals and 'Save the Whales' T-shirts as experts worthy of consultation."[102] Reciprocating, many relief workers saw the military as "right-wing, insensitive, inflexible, 'balls-to-the-wall' control freaks who demonstrated little under-standing of the situation in Somalia or what was required of them to alleviate the widespread suffering."[103]

Any lack of unity among the military and relief agencies would allow warring factions, in Somalia and elsewhere, to "manipulate the outside stake-holders working in the crisis, playing one off against another, to achieve their political and military objectives."[104] Although this "cultural gap" was never bridged completely, it was mitigated in Somalia by the creation of the Civil-Military Operations Center (CMOC) and the collocated Humanitarian Oper-ations Center, which served as liaison and coordination centers for issues involving convoy escorts, general security, and weapons policy.[105] The CMOC was set up jointly by Ambassador Oakley and Philip Johnson, head of CARE. Daily coordination meetings were held among the lead state for the particular sector, NGOs, and the military, and governance was by committee. James Fearon and David Laitin consider the CMOC in Somalia as an example of how "ad hoc committees can arise to spontaneously solve at least part of the coordination problem" inherent in such complex operations.[106]

In other cases, unity of effort in Somalia was affected by the lack of com-mand structure inherent in the traditional principle of unity of command. During UNITAF, the 10th Mountain Division had operational control of coalition forces including the Canadian Airborne Battle Group, 1st Battalion Royal Australian Regiment, 1st Belgian Para Battalion, and Royal Moroccan Forces Somalia. The 10th Mountain AAR states that "coalition operations worked well during Restore Hope," but while the division was especially appreciative of the firepower and ground mobility provided by coalition forces, the AAR also identifies several challenges to achieving unity of effort.[107]

The 10th Mountain noted clear distinctions between what coalition forces were capable of doing and what they are willing to do, as a function of "the political agendas by which coalition military commanders are constrained."[108] Indeed, the 10th Mountain felt "a coalition commander may accept a mission or turn a mission down, based on national pride or political agenda rather than a pure military reason."[109] As operations in Somali became increasingly dangerous and controversial, some national contingencies had to seek guidance from their respective capitals before carrying out even routine tactical orders.[110] To achieve unity of effort under such circumstances, the 10th Mountain stressed the necessity of "meeting shared expectations among partners." This result can be best achieved by "open and frank discussions ... to eliminate or at least limit the ... differences in understanding" and by "experimentation and patience."[111] In such situations, creating the conditions necessary for unity of effort is a continual process.

These unity of effort considerations in UNITAF were exacerbated during

UNOSOM II when the UN expanded its objectives well beyond humanitarian relief. While supporting the broader mission, Secretary General Boutros-Ghali stated he was also "conscious of the feeling in some quarters that UNO-SOM is deviating from its primary task of ensuring the safe distribution of humanitarian assistance" and was "concentrating disproportionate efforts and resources in military operations."[112] In Mogadishu, Jonathan Howe, a retired admiral who President Clinton put forward in March 1993, at Secretary General Boutros-Ghali's request, to be the special representative to the UN Secretary General for Somalia, appealed for unity among coalition members. Understanding that "there are bound to be growing pains," Howe also lamented, "I regret ... there have been differences in approach."[113]

Part of these "growing pains" was the relief of Italian General Bruno Loi, who had held unilateral talks with Somali elders allegedly linked to Aideed and reportedly agreed to delay weapons searches in hopes of reducing escalating violence. Other reports alleged Italians had warned Aideed when operations against him were about to take place.[114] Howe explained Loi's dismissal, saying, "We have to have unity of command, we have to have confidence among commanders. We have to have one policy and unity to carry it out."[115] One UN official said the Italians should "either get on the team or get off,"[116] and in spite of Howe's efforts to restore cooperation, *Newsweek* decried "the mess in Mogadishu ... [as] the result of a team effort in mismanagement that would be comical if lives weren't at stake."[117]

Another unity of effort problem occurred when American soldiers found themselves working more closely with non–Western partners, which is perhaps reflective of Samuel Huntington's assertion that "by and large, single civilization organizations do more things and are more successful than multicultural organizations." Specifically, Huntington believes, "military alliances ... require cooperation among their members, cooperation depends on trust, and trust more easily springs from common values and culture."[118] Instead of this trust, UNOSOM II was plagued by a certain amount of mutual suspicion. One Pakistani complained, "The US is quick to stir up trouble with air strikes, but it is my men and other Third World soldiers who always draw the tough assignments on the ground."[119] The result, according to *Time's* Marguerite Michaels, was that "fear and resentment are fraying cohesion."[120]

The presence of non–Western forces in Somalia was part of a growing trend during the era of expanded peacekeeping in the 1990s when fully two-thirds of countries contributing forces to peacekeeping operations were from the developing world. These soldiers were typically less well fed, well led, and well equipped than their Western counterparts, creating a differential in capabilities among the force. Nonetheless, developing countries may be motivated to supply forces because the UN typically provides contributing countries about a thousand dollars a month per man. Many developing countries actually make money from UN peacekeeping operations, in part because it is up to the government to determine how much of the UN-provided money goes to the individual soldier. Pakistan, for instance, retains the entire amount and gives nothing extra to the soldier. The impact of such a policy on soldier motivation and morale is predictably negative.[121]

The degradation of unity of effort among the coalition was dangerously apparent when logistical delays and poor coordination with Pakistani and Malaysian troops slowed the rescue of Task Force Ranger soldiers at the Battle of Mogadishu. An ad hoc rescue team had been formed primarily from 10th Mountain assets, but which also included fourteen to sixteen Malaysian armored personnel carriers (APCs) and four Pakistani T-55 tanks. The 10th Mountain is a light infantry division with only light-skinned wheeled vehicles for ground transportation. Therefore, the Malaysian and Pakistani assets were critical to the operation's success. The plan was for the 10th Mountain soldiers to ride on the APCs, attacking mounted as far as possible, and break through to Task Force Ranger. Once at the helicopter crash site, the casualties would be loaded on the APCs, and the convoy would fight its way back to the UN compound.[122]

In addition to language problems, Captain Charles Ferry, who as an infantry company executive officer participated in the rescue, reports experiencing the same problems with the differences between capabilities and willingness that the 10th Mountain noted in UNITAF. Ferry writes that "it seemed that the [Pakistani] tank commander had been ordered to go only about halfway to the objective, and that did not support the plan."[123] Although American liaison officers were with both Malaysians and Pakistani units, they were unable to convince their coalition partners to cooperate. Ferry reports that only after "a sharp exchange" was the issue seemingly resolved.[124]

As the rescue column advanced, it came under heavy fire, and the original Malaysian and Pakistani reluctance quickly reappeared. The Pakistani tanks had, in fact, been ordered to go only so far on National Street and then stop. Ferry reports, "I didn't see them again until the next morning."[125] The two lead Malaysian APCs did move forward but did not make the correct turn north and "continued out of sight" down National Street, not to be heard from again until the next morning.[126] The American company commander reported "he was having a hard time getting the [other] Malaysian APCs to move under fire." At one point, the lead APC stopped and refused to move, effectively blocking the company's progress.[127] Only after much prodding were stalwart Americans like Ferry able to get a few APCs to the crash site to evacuate the dead and wounded.[128] As the column made its way back to safety, Ferry reports, "several times, other leaders and I had to run into the street to get the Malaysian APCs moving again."[129] Once the Malaysians did get moving back to safety, there was no stopping them. Ferry reports seeing "six or seven soldiers ... running as fast as they could under fire to catch the vehicles. But the APCs did not stop."[130]

Ferry was not alone in his identification of problems with unity of effort. Captain J. B. Burton identified problems with a lack of UN doctrine at the tactical level; no common tactics, techniques, and procedures; and language barriers. Burton's conclusion was that unity of effort was so difficult to achieve that multinational forces should not be combined at the tactical level.[131] Other observers focused on the discrepancy in capability between the American forces and the Pakistani and Malaysian forces, the latter two simply being untrained in quick reaction search and rescue operations. Combined with the fact that most coalition operations required clearance from the respective countries' defense ministries, there certainly was "not a recipe for fast action."[132] Nonetheless, Major David Stockwell concluded, "By international standards, [the Pakistani and Malaysian response] was speedy," indicating the inherent difficulties of multinational operations.[133] Making no allowances for such excuses, Lieutenant General Bernard Trainor complained, "There's no unity of command, and no good command and control system."[134]

Trainor's assessment of unity of command problems was not confined to coalition forces. There were serious breakdowns within the U.S. military structure as well, leading Allard to conclude that "there should be no mistaking the fact that the greatest obstacles to unity of command during UNOSOM II were imposed by the United States on itself."[135] In keeping with a long-standing reluctance to place American soldiers under foreign command, Major General Montgomery did double duty as deputy to UNOSOM II commander Lieutenant General Cevik Bir (a Turk) as well as serving as the commander of U.S. Forces Somalia. However, when Task Force Ranger arrived in August 1993, its commander, Major General William Garrison, reported directly to CENTCOM. The result was "essentially three parallel chains of command."[136]

Garrison was obligated merely to consult with Montgomery, and Montgomery learned of the exact nature of the October 3 raid only hours before its initiation. At the tactical level within U.S. Forces Somalia, awareness of Task Force Ranger operations was even less, with many officers in the 10th Mountain's quick reaction force (QRF) feeling completely ignorant of the special operations. Compartmentalization and extreme secrecy are obviously normal in special operations, but in Somalia there emerged a psychological distance between the 10th Mountain and Task Force Ranger that further hampered cooperation.[137] The end result of all these factors was that the QRF made few specific preparations to assist Task Force Ranger if necessary.

In the final analysis, most observers agree that a situation as complex as the one in Somalia was beyond the UN's ability to directly control. The UN is best suited to deal with consensual, traditional peacekeeping scenarios rather than peace enforcement operations like Somalia. These operations "simply [run] too much against the grain of what the organization and its members can or are willing to support administratively, financially, and politically."[138] In future such situations, analysts recommend unity of effort will best be facilitated by "military coalitions that have the blessing of the UN but are not under direct UN control."[139] In UNOSOM II, the absence of such an arrangement plagued unity of effort.

Perseverance

Perseverance is perhaps the most difficult principle to achieve in an OOTW, and Somalia certainly proved to be no exception. Jett identifies outright failure, indefinite extension, and a declaration of success as the three possible outcomes of peacekeeping operations. He contends that Somalia contained elements of all three of these possibilities. "When continuation (the second outcome) proved unsustainable and something that could be called victory (the third outcome) proved unobtainable," Jett explains that "failure (the first outcome) became inevitable."[140] Edward Luttwak offers a similar analysis, concluding that "outside intervention would make sense only if it were prolonged indefinitely, in effect turning Somalia into a colony again, this time under UN control. Otherwise, all the costs and risks of intervention can achieve only ephemeral results at best."[141]

Although it is estimated that the Americans inflicted up to two thousand casualties on the Somalis during the Battle of Mogadishu, the American losses and the chaotic nature of the operation created a domestic outcry in the United States.[142] As a peripheral interest, Somalia had never evoked a deep U.S. commitment, and the October fiasco led to the Clinton administration's decision to withdraw U.S. troops by March 1994. David Rieff explains this loss of perseverance in the context of objective and legitimacy. He argues,

> The American public came to think of the hunt for Aideed, even though they knew it was being carried out by U.S. Army Rangers, not as war but as police work. Casualties in war are understood to be inevitable. Soldiers are not only supposed to be ready to kill, they are supposed to be able to die. But casualties in police work are a different matter entirely. There, it is only criminals who are supposed to get hurt or, if necessary, killed, not the cops. Again, the fundamental problem has not been some peculiar American aversion to military casualties. Rather, there has been an essential mistake in the way such operations are presented to the public, and, perhaps, even in the way they are conceived of by policymakers. Under the circumstances, it should hardly be surprising that public pressure on Congress and the president to withdraw U.S. troops predictably arises at the first moment an operation cannot be presented in simple moral terms, or when casualties or even the costs start to mount.[143]

Other analysts argue that if these losses had been used as a rallying cry, public resolve might have been steeled. Max Boot cites the work of two political scientists who contend, "Had the administration chosen instead to galvanize public opposition to ... Aideed, our research suggests that Americans would have tolerated an expanded effort to catch and punish him."[144] By this point, however, the Clinton administration had begun rethinking its policy of "assertive multilateralism" and was eager to cut its losses.

The U.S. withdrawal compelled the UN to terminate UNOSOM II and withdraw all peacekeepers by March 1995. Some observers, including Montgomery, saw this development as the result of a calculated strategy on behalf of Aideed.[145] Walter Clarke, the deputy chief of mission at the U.S. Embassy from March through July 1993 agreed, explaining, "I think he [Aideed] tended to look at the UNITAF period as a period of putting his force together, restoring some of his units, but certainly in preparation for events after UNITAF had gone.... If he was going to get the UN out of there, which I think was clearly one of his objectives, he was going to have to take some actions."[146] In Somalia, as is often the case, time was on the side of the belligerents rather than the peacekeepers.

Other analysts believe Somalia failed, not because of a lack of perseverance, but because of the presence of it. Michael Maren argues,

> The UN's peacekeeping machine was cursed with a built-in flaw: it desperately needed to succeed. When the only way to bring peace to Somalia might have been to walk away, the bureaucracy was compelled to stay and find a peace for which it could take credit. As the UN stayed in Somalia it continued to supply the raw material of the conflict — loot.[147]

Jett sympathizes, arguing that "while designed to save lives, humanitarian aid can, if it fuels the conflict and prolongs the war, ultimately cost more lives than it saves."[148] Such arguments suggest that in some cases it may be better to let nature take its course than to cling to a stubborn perseverance that maintains an artificial and untenable situation.

The end result was that perseverance in Somalia suffered from both internal and external challenges. In many ways, nation-building activities of the size and scope required by Somalia are doomed because of the immense amount of time necessary to build trust among the warring parties. While this time passes, the international community's enthusiasm is dampened by increasing expenses and few visible improvements. Indeed, as in Somalia, the warring parties themselves are often interested in an early withdrawal because such a presence interferes with their own internal agendas and will be tolerated for the shortest time possible.[149] While the size of the work to be done is immense, the time to do it is limited. The situation is almost mutually exclusive.

Francis Fukuyama notes that the problem of long-term capacity-building goes well beyond the instance of Somalia. By taking over responsibility for providing services directly, external agencies may please donors by delivering immediate aid, but they do nothing to strengthen local bureaucracies and prepare them for the international community's departure.[150] In Somalia, "there was no sustained effort to help Somalia reestablish national and regional institutions or civil administration" and "there was no attempt ... to build civil or political institutions."[151] Absent this domestic capacity, what little progress that had been made in Somalia rapidly evaporated.

Whatever the exact cause, the failure of the UN effort in Somalia marked a watershed in peacekeeping operations. Jett contends that with the eighteen American soldiers who were killed on October 3–4, "the expectations that had been so high in late 1988 [when the UN was awarded a Nobel Peace Prize for peacekeeping] also died."[152] Indeed, the UN reported that at the end of 1995, it had some 60,000 personnel serving as peacekeepers at an annual cost of about $3.5 billion. A year later it had just 26,000 peacekeepers at an annual cost of about $1.6 billion. The report admitted, "Clearly, the pendulum has swung away from the heady days of what some have referred to as peacekeeping overstretch."[153] The most serious example of the impact of the Somalia disaster was the world's failure to provide a meaningful response to the genocide in Rwanda, but its effects would also be felt in Haiti.

Indeed, the international community's commitment to humanitarian interventions seemed to crumble in the aftermath of crisis. National Security Advisor Anthony Lake offered to resign, but President Clinton would not allow it, instead blaming the failure on the UN. He entered into "a recurring war of wills" with Boutros-Ghali that ended in the U.S. using its diplomatic influence to oust the secretary general in 1996.[154] While the UN continued to conduct a number of peacekeeping operations after Somalia, most were the longstanding operations in places like Cyprus and the Western Sahara. New initiatives were generally small in scale and short in duration, such as the fifteen monitors sent to verify the Libyan withdrawal from the Aouzou strip. Only two major undertakings were attempted over the next six years, and both involved situations in which the chief sponsors were receiving large numbers of refugees from the countries to which the peacekeepers were sent (Haiti, whose refugees were reaching the U.S., and Albania, whose refugees were reaching Italy).[155]

With the departure of the international presence, Somalia quickly returned to the chaotic state it had been in during mid–1992 and continues to be a trouble spot. The rise of the Council of Islamic Courts (CIC)—a loose coalition of clerics, business leaders, and Islamic court militias — in 2006 led to an intervention by Ethiopian forces concerned about CIC ties to al Qaeda. The intervention resulted in the collapse of the CIC, but Somalia remains plagued by violence from extremist groups, including al Shabaab, which has confirmed its cooperation with al Qaeda insurgents in the region.[156]

Amidst challenges from rivals like al Shabaab, "the current government [of Somalia] barely exists beyond the tiny pocket of the capital it controls." The country is again plagued by a humanitarian crisis with the Food Security and Nutrition Analysis Unit estimating more than 40 percent of the population is in need of emergency humanitarian assistance. International donors, however, are reluctant to contribute amidst concerns that shipments are being diverted to al Shabaab and other militant groups, another similarity to the situation in the early 1990s.[157]

Another of the major problems with Somalia is that it is "a pirate's paradise."[158] In 2008, Somali pirates had "a banner year," attacking 111 ships and enjoying success 44 times.[159] Somali piracy is basically a kidnapping/ransom business, receiving as much as $3 million in ransom for the release of the *Sirius Star* in January 2009.[160] Analyst James Wombwell notes that the problem of "piracy emanating from Somalia can only be resolved ashore," but concedes that "in light of the US experience in Somali in the early 1990s, it is understandable that American policymakers are reluctant to take on that task."[161]

With its lack of central authority, violence, lawlessness, and humanitarian crisis, Somalia remains a failed state that has shown distressingly little progress in spite of international efforts to bring stability to the region. Returning normalcy to Somalia appears to be a task well beyond the limits of the perseverance of the U.S., or for that matter, the international community as a whole.

Conclusion

Much of the failure of the U.S. intervention in Somalia can be traced to the haphazard analysis of the objective and the failure to make security adjustments as the mission changed. Because the objective of nation-building in Somalia was not broadly accepted by the American people or important to U.S. national interests, perseverance could not be sustained in the wake of growing numbers of casualties. The U.S. experience in Somalia shows a clear connection between the domestic legitimacy of the objective and the public's willingness to exhibit perseverance when the OOTW undergoes difficulty.

Somalia also serves as a caution that OOTWs with nation-building as an objective are likely to be inherently problematic. 10th Mountain Division commander Major General Arnold recognized from the beginning that when it came to making a nation out of the chaotic situation in Somalia, "history was not on our side." "For centuries," Arnold explains, "the Somali warrior had been fiercely independent, uniting with extended family and other sub-clans only when challenged from external forces; showing some limited loyalties to the clan and demonstrating little, if any, sense of national unity. Even with a common language and religion, homogeneity in Somalia was a myth."[162] Arnold's observation is consistent with Francis Fukuyama's assertion that "nation-building in the sense of the creation of a community bound together by shared history and culture is well beyond the ability of any outside power to achieve.... Only states can be deliberately constructed. If a nation arises from this, it is more a matter of luck than design."[163]

In addition to the general challenges posed by nation-building, Somalia demonstrates the limitations of the military's capabilities in this area. Allard argues that "while military power may well set the stage for such action, the real responsibility for nation-building must be carried out by the civilian agencies of the government better able to specialize in such long-term humanitarian efforts."[164] He warns that "an institution built around can-do attitudes and the expectation of success" may be tempted to try to do too much and instead needs to focus on tasks derived from mission analysis and clearly defined objectives.[165] Rather than the overreliance on the military instrument of power that epitomized the Somalia operation, Allard recommends a more balanced application of military, diplomatic, and humanitarian efforts.[166]

Fukuyama sees the need for unity and synergy between these different efforts throughout what he identifies as three "distinct aspects or phases of nation-building." These are post-conflict reconstruction, creation of self-sustaining state institutions, and the strengthening of weak states.[167] It is in this first phase that the military must play a specific role.

During the post-conflict reconstruction phase, Fukuyama acknowledges the need for outside powers to provide "short-term provision of stability through infusions of security forces, police, humanitarian relief, and technical assistance to restore electricity, water, banking and payment systems, and so on."[168] Obviously, the provision of security and restoration of basic physical life-sustaining infrastructure is within the military's capability and should be a specific role for the military to play. Fukuyama's definition of nation-building also requires an occupational authority in order to provide the direct leverage that an external position cannot.[169] Obviously, a military presence provides such leverage.

The problem lies in the transition from phase one to phase two. The military must not just establish security; it must be able to transition the ongoing responsibility for maintenance of that security to someone else. An international peacekeeping force, a retrained police force, and a newly formed apolitical and civilian-controlled host nation military are all candidates to assume the security function, but have all proved elusive to realize. Unfortunately, while such organizations may have the perception of legitimacy needed to allow nation-building to take root, they all too often lack the capability that the U.S. military, though perhaps perceived as less legitimate, clearly has.

In Somalia, this transition was envisioned as occurring between UNITAF and UNOSOM II. However, misunderstandings of the principle of objective led to a lack of unity of effort between the U.S. and the UN during the transition and left UNOSOM II overly committed to the principle of restraint and ill-prepared to adhere to the principle of security. This condition was compounded by the fracturing of legitimacy associated with the expanded mandate. These failures doomed the effort, which had begun with such good intentions and shown initial promise, to catastrophic failure.

CHAPTER 8

Haiti: Restraint Needs Either Security or Legitimacy

The declining situation in Haiti was another of the many crises confronting the U.S. in the post–Cold War era. While Haiti appealed primarily to America's humanitarian and special interest group considerations, its proximity to Florida and the potentially disruptive effects of an influx of refugees also posed some security concerns. Pursuant to these combined interests, the U.S. deployed a joint task force under the auspices of the United Nations Mission in Haiti with the objective of preparing a peaceful transition of the Haitian government from its ruling military junta to its exiled democratically elected president. Because the UN and U.S. were operating under the faulty assumption that the junta accepted the legitimacy of the peacekeeping mission, the joint task force relied on the principle of restraint rather than security. In reality, the junta rejected the agreement, and a small group of protesters was able to repel the landing of the U.S. ship that carried the lead elements of the joint task force. Unity of effort difficulties abounded within the hastily thrown together task force, but the most serious failure regarding this principle existed between the diplomatic negotiators of the agreement and the military officials that would be charged with executing it. The incident occurred on the heels of the Battle of Mogadishu in Somalia, and the U.S. was little interested in practicing perseverance in another potentially dangerous environment. This intervention highlights the OOTW principle of perseverance by suggesting either legitimacy or security is a prerequisite for perseverance. It also demonstrates the inappropriate application of the principle of restraint and the mixed application of the principles of objective and unity of effort. As a result of this OOTW, the U.S. failed to accomplish its objective of facilitating the peaceful transition of power in Haiti in 1993.

Background

François "Papa Doc" Duvalier maintained an authoritarian rule of Haiti from his election as president in 1957 until his death in 1971. He ensured the loyalty of the army, formed an even larger militia group called the Tonton Macoute, which "operated as hired political thugs," and skillfully manipulated American anticommunism to secure support. Before he died, he engineered a referendum, which by the suspicious tally of 2,391,916 to 0 ensured the direct succession of his son Jean-Claude or "Baby Doc." Baby Doc showed little interest in the responsibilities of government, and Haiti soon devolved into a den of corruption, disorder, and squalor. With his regime on the verge of collapse, Duvalier resigned in 1986 and went into exile.[1]

A rapid succession of leaders followed Duvalier until Jean-Bertrand Aristide was elected president in 1990. Aristide was a Catholic priest who had risen to prominence in 1986 as a vocal critic of Duvalier. His popularity with the poor and his advocacy of his own loosely defined version of socialism alienated him from the Haitian elites, who viewed him as a threat to their status quo power. On September 30, 1991, Aristide was ousted from office in a military coup led by Lieutenant General Raoul Cedras, Aristide's erstwhile hand-picked chief of staff.[2]

As a result of the series of coups between the rules of Baby Doc Duvalier and Aristide, large amounts of international aid to Haiti had been suspended. With the government unable to pay its rank and file troops, many soldiers began resorting to armed bank robberies and home invasions as a source of income. Seeing the crime wave as a preferable option to a mutiny within the unpaid ranks, junta leaders did little to suppress the activity. The marauders were given the folkloric term *zenglendo*, which connoted "at a time when the Haitian people needed to trust state authority the most, the army had transgressed the public confidence ... and had turned on the populace in new and treacherous fashion." By the time of the Cedras junta, the army had become the "main obstacle to law and order," with the *zenglendo* often carrying out their crimes in loosely organized gangs behind the special protection of the military. Amid such chaos, thousands of Haitian "boat people" fled across the Caribbean for Florida.[3]

Haiti's plight soon attracted international attention, but in February 1993, Cedras deflected the attempt of United Nations negotiator Dante Caputo to arrange for the deployment of international human rights observers to monitor conditions in the country. Amid rising pressure from the Congressional Black Caucus, President Bill Clinton in March declared his intention to restore Aristide to power and help rebuild Haiti's economy. The next month Cedras acquiesced to resign in exchange for amnesty for himself, his family, and his staff. Aristide agreed to the conditions, and Caputo returned to Haiti to begin facilitating the process.[4]

Upon his arrival, however, Caputo was met by renewed resistance from Cedras. Seemingly unconvinced that the international community was prepared to act forcefully, Cedras began "playing a game, attempting to deflect increased economic sanctions by agreeing to vacate power. When pressured to leave, however, he would renege on any agreement."[5] Only after the UN Security Council took the drastic measure on June 16, 1993, of voting to impose a ban on petroleum sales to Haiti and freeze financial assets of key Haitian authorities did Cedras seem to take notice. Just four days after this United Nations Security Council Resolution (UNSCR) 841 went into effect, Cedras and Aristide met separately with mediators at Governor's Island, New York to work out a plan to return Aristide to power.[6]

The resulting Governor's Island Accord was signed on July 3 and contained provisions for amnesty for those Haitians who had participated in the 1991 coup, the lifting of sanctions imposed by UNSCR 841, Cedras's retirement, and Aristide's return to Haiti on October 30, 1993. It was a deeply flawed document, which according to one Haiti expert left the Haitian military with "so much to lose and so little to gain."[7] Shortly after the agreement was signed, Haiti plunged into its worst period of violence since the coup. Pro-Aristide activists were routinely beaten, intimidated, or arrested. Corpses were deposited on the doorsteps of hotels where UN observers lived. Gunfire became a regular sound, and thousands of Haitians were killed or disappeared. Rather than preparing for a departure, Cedras appeared to be consolidating his power.[8]

Analysis of the Principles

Objective

The Governor's Island Accord closed by stating the pledge of Aristide and Cedras to "the peaceful transition to a stable and lasting democratic society in which all Haitians will be able to live in a climate of freedom, justice, security, and respect for human rights." Part of the implementation of this process was for the international community to provide "assistance for modernizing the armed forces of Haiti and establishing a new police force with the presence of United Nations personnel in these fields."[9] Pursuant to this provision, on September 23, 1993, UNSCR 867 was passed, authorizing "the establishment and immediate dispatch of the United Nations Mission in Haiti (UNMIH)" to Haiti. The mission would be "comprised of up to 567 United Nations police monitors (UNPMS) and a military construction unit with a strength of approximately 700, including 60 military trainers."[10]

In August 1993, after the signing of the Governor's Island Accord, the Joint Chiefs of Staff directed the creation of Joint Task Force Haiti Assistance Group (JTF HAG). Colonel J. G. Pulley, commanding the 7th Special Forces Group at Fort Bragg, North Carolina was designated the commander. The JTF's mission was to "deploy to Haiti under United Nations operational control and conduct military training and humanitarian/civic action programs in support of Haitian democratization." Pulley describes the mission as fitting "the classic Foreign Internal Defense profile, undertaking civic-action programs designed to help a friendly government solidify its position, protect itself from subversion and lawlessness and mobilize popular support by improving conditions for its people."[11] Lieutenant Colonel Phil Baker, who was the JTF's officer in charge of developing the plan to professionalize and train the Haitian Army staff, described the mission more informally: "We were supposed to do the high vis[isbility] things, the medical and construction and humanitarian things, with the intention of showing the Haitians that Aristide was returning, and look at the money he's bringing back; hey, this is a good deal."[12] Baker saw his task as being to "do good things as representative of the United States Army."[13]

Aerial view of the port facility at Port-au-Prince, where the USS _Harlan County_ intended to dock. Photograph by Sergeant R. J. Pixler. Department of Defense.

The ambiguity of the mission may have been intentional. Former Ambassador to El Salvador Robert White surmises that the ongoing uncertainty in Somalia convinced negotiators at Governor's Island to avoid being too specific about military details for fear of attracting congressional attention and suspicion. White criticizes this approach, arguing, "What the Clinton administration should have done is to go precisely the other way. They should have been more aggressive in defining the peace mission instead of less."[14]

With the authorizing of UNSCR 867 in September, two U.S. tank landing ships (LSTs) were prepared to transport JTF HAG to Haiti. The USS *Harlan County,* under Commander Marvin Butcher, left first, arriving at Port-au-Prince on October 11 with 225 UN observers. The USS *Fairfax County* was scheduled to follow later. Butcher's mission was to transport JTF HAG to Haiti and then provide berthing and life support to the embarked troops until they moved on to the dock. Once the landing was complete, the troops would come under the command of Colonel Pulley, who had flown to Haiti earlier and would meet the ship at Port-au-Prince.[15] Joint Task Force Haiti Assistance Group was a reality, but, according to one State Department official, "The Department of Defense had major concerns about the mission."[16]

Unity of Effort

The deteriorating situation in Haiti had not escaped the notice of the Pentagon, and in September 1991, the 82nd Airborne Division at Fort Bragg, North Carolina began dusting off contingency plans in case a non-combatant evacuation operation was required. Eventually the urgency of the situation diminished, but staff officers continued to monitor developments.[17] Still, the implications of the Governor's Island Accord seemed to catch planners off guard. Baker was ordered to report to U.S. Atlantic Command (USACOM) in Norfolk, Virginia within twenty-four hours from his erstwhile posting at Fort Leavenworth, Kansas as a military history instructor. When he arrived, he went to the JTF HAG planning cell where he found that

> everything was in chaos. Planners from all services were thrown together trying to figure out what they were doing without much organization. Lots of people were just doing what they thought they needed to do; what they were comfortable with whether or not it had anything to do with the plan. Everybody at least looked busy. In the middle of the chaos was a Marine lieutenant colonel under a lot of pressure trying to produce an operations order. I remember that chairs were scarce; if you left yours for even a second, someone stole it.[18]

The result was that JTF HAG was a hastily assembled group that lacked unity of effort. Walter Kretchik describes it as "an ad hoc organization whose personnel ranged from various subject-matter experts on Haiti to officers who knew nothing about the country and its problems." "Many assigned to the JTF," according to Kretchik, "had little idea of what they were expected to do."[19]

Aside from the water-land division of labor between Butcher and Pulley, few other responsibilities were clearly defined. With USACOM providing only minimal instructions for embarkation and departure, for example, boarding was conducted in a piecemeal and inefficient fashion. Baker recalls standing around with other personnel waiting to board when the *Harlan County's* executive officer came up to the group and asked who was in charge. Baker said, "Everyone looked around or at their feet. I noticed that I was the senior officer so I said I guess I was. The executive officer then asked for a manifest, a list of equipment, copies of orders, and other administrative stuff."[20] Baker then rounded up the senior noncommissioned officer and an army captain, appointed them his first sergeant and executive officer, and began the painstaking work of getting things organized. In the meantime, marine warrant officer "Gunner" Hayes superintended the loading of equipment. As the *Harlan County* prepared to depart the next day, the last arrival of JTG HAG, a navy doctor, ran up the gangway and leaped aboard.[21] It was an inauspicious beginning to say the least.

A starboard bow view of the tank landing ship USS *Harlan County* underway during maritime interdiction operations in 1991. Photograph by Charles Stover. Department of Defense.

Perhaps more significant was the lack of synchronization between the diplomatic and military efforts. Pulley noted that JTF HAG had been deployed into an environment that had not "been well-prepared diplomatically."[22] Instead, he felt that "diplomats hoped the presence of a UN military force would somehow drag the diplomatic process forward and create a more secure environment. Instead, diplomatic progress remained stalled, and the environment became even more dangerous."[23] It was a situation reminiscent of Beirut in 1982–1983.

The fissures between the Pentagon and the State Department had developed during the Governor's Island meetings. As the plans emerged, French-speaking UN member nations such as France and Canada were assigned the task of establishing the new police force while the military training fell primarily to the U.S. According to Kate Doyle, "The problem was that while the Defense Department had served as the architect for the training package, it did not have a central role in designing the mission itself."[24] Pulley had little opportunity to direct the JTF HAG staff, instead finding himself consumed by demands from higher headquarters and "inundated with insubstantial guidance from all quarters."[25] The military appears not to have been afforded much opportunity to exercise its own mission analysis procedures.[26]

For his part, Pulley tried to establish some unity of effort by deploying to Haiti ahead of the *Harlan County* and meeting with American diplomats there. He brought with him five liaison officers who were especially appreciated by the overloaded staff at the U.S. Embassy, the office of the UN's Deputy for Peacekeeping Operations, and elsewhere. Pulley found the liaison officers of immense value, declaring that even though they "had only begun to develop their relationships when the UN mission unraveled, their roles were validated during their brief period of operation."[27] Pulley met with his liaison officers daily, as well as personally interacting with his own diplomatic counterparts. For example, he was with U.S. charge d'affaires Nikki Huddleston to observe the *Harlan County*'s arrival at Port-au-Prince and was able to provide liaison during that crisis, but by that point it was largely too late.[28]

In fact, Pulley was in no position to provide anything more than liaison at this point in the operation. He had no command authority over JTF HAG while it was still aboard the *Harlan County*. While still in the transportation phase, the *Harlan County* was not "subordinate to JTF HAG or a part of it."[29] Although Pulley was the nominal JTF commander, he found himself caught in a no-man's land "with essentially no assets at his immediate disposal."[30] Whatever decisions would be made while JTF HAG was still aboard the *Harlan County* in Port-au-Prince would be the prerogative of Commander Butcher.

Legitimacy

The U.S. intervention in Haiti suffered from weak legitimacy, both domestically and in Haiti itself. Like Somalia, U.S. involvement in Haiti was based on values rather than interests, and the Clinton administration failed to articulate to the domestic audience the importance of risking American lives and treasure for such an ill-defined pursuit. Within Haiti, the Governor's Island Accord also had little legitimacy, being perceived by Cedras and his followers as a violation of Haitian sovereignty that had been forced upon them by a meddling U.S. Thus, in Haiti the agreement could be easily resisted, and in the U.S. there was little support for exercising any more than a token effort to enforce its provisions.

Like Somalia, the situation in Haiti was another international event that caught the U.S. at an awkward policy transition between the Bush and Clinton administrations while it struggled to define its role in the post–Cold War world. Both Presidents Bush and Clinton faced pressure from domestic constituencies as they grappled with the increasing numbers of refugees fleeing Haiti by boat for Florida. The result was another deviation from the rational actor decision-making model.

The Bush administration's initial policy in dealing with the mounting refugee crisis following the ouster of Aristide was to have the coast guard intercept the boats and take the Haitians to a makeshift camp at the U.S. Navy Base at Guantanamo Bay in Cuba. There extensive asylum interviews were conducted to determine those whose claims were based on human rights and political issues versus purely economic ones. By the end of February 1992, almost 33 percent of the Haitians who reached the base at Guantanamo were permitted to apply for asylum. In May, however, the Bush administration responded to domestic concerns about illegal immigration and decided to close the Guantanamo camp and begin escorting detained boats back to Haiti without any asylum review at all. In explaining the new policy, Richard Boucher of the State Department stated, "It was increasingly clear that [the Guantanamo camp] was acting as a magnet and causing more Haitians to get on boats in the hopes of getting there."[31] By June, the policy change had effectively curtailed the exodus.[32]

As a presidential candidate, Clinton decried Bush's "cruel policy of returning Haitian refugees to a brutal dictatorship without an asylum hearing," and as president-elect he insisted the U.S. "should have a process in which these Haitians get a chance to make their case." However, coming to fear such pronouncements might unleash a new wave of refugees, Clinton announced in early January 1993 that he would reverse his position and maintain the Bush policy. "The practice of returning those who flee Haiti by boat will continue, for the time being, after I become President," he explained in a broadcast to Haiti and to Haitians in the United States. "Leaving by boat is not the route to freedom."[33] Such a stance no doubt pleased Democratic Governor of Florida Lawton Chiles, who was facing a tough reelection challenge in 1994.[34]

Influencing Clinton's thinking was his experience with the "Mariel Boatlift," a six-month period in 1980 when Fidel Castro temporarily lifted restrictions that had prevented his people from leaving Cuba. More than 125,000 people left Cuba from Mariel Harbor, including those from the country's prisons and mental institutions who were deemed "undesirables." At the time, Clinton was governor of Arkansas, and his support of President Jimmy Carter's decision to house some of the refugees at Fort Chaffee, Arkansas contributed to Clinton's failed bid for reelection, losing to Frank White, only the second Republican to be elected governor of Arkansas since Reconstruction.[35] By June, Fort Chaffee housed more than 20,000 Cubans, and in October, White aired a political commercial that included footage of a thousand Cuban detainees attempting to leave Fort Chaffee on May 29 and suggested that as governor, Clinton had failed to protect the citizens of Arkansas.[36] Advisors recalled that, as president, Clinton's guiding mottos in formulating policies to deal with refugees from both Haiti and Cuba were "No More Mariels" and "Remember Fort Chaffee."[37]

President Clinton might have been able to maintain such a policy during the Cold War era of national security consensus, but by the time of his presidency, "foreign affairs agendas — that is, sets of issues relevant to foreign policy with which governments are concerned — [had] become larger and more diverse."[38] The rational actor method of decision making, which assumes a unitary state "viewed as calculating and responding to external events as if it were a single entity" was also under increasing challenge from other models.[39] Among the alternatives was the elite theory, which "is vitally concerned with the identity of those individuals making foreign policy and the underlying dynamics of national power, social myth, and class interests." Under this construct, "foreign policy is formulated as a response to demands generated from the economic and political system. But not all demands receive equal attention, and those that receive the most attention serve the interests of only a small sector of society."[40] In the case of decision making about Haiti, this "small sector of society" was the Congressional Black Caucus (CBC).

Unlike President Bush, President Clinton could not keep his distance from this powerful interest group, needing its members' votes for his domestic agenda. In late 1992, the CBC had urged the incoming Clinton administration "to focus its intention, not only on the refugee issue, but to attack its cause by demonstrating its unequivocal support for the restoration of democratic government in Haiti" and the return of Aristide. The CBC also asked Clinton to implement a policy of "equitable treatment of refugees regardless of color."[41] As predicted by elite theory, the CBC was able to determine what issues received attention and therefore direct the government to respond.[42] The result was that Clinton ultimately became "whipsawed by competing domestic pressures" that left "the administration's credibility [on Haiti] ... at stake."[43] An article in *Newsweek* would later describe Clinton's policy toward Haiti as having "had the consistency of a Nerf ball."[44] Any significant intervention, especially a risky military one, lacked legitimacy with the American public.

One of the reasons for the scant popular support was that, as Bush administration officials repeatedly emphasized, there was no vital American interest at stake in Haiti.[45] However, as the world moved further from the Cold War era, proponents of a foreign policy that supported not just U.S. interests, but also U.S. values, began gaining credence.[46] Michael Mandelbaum believes President Clinton moved too far in this direction, citing Somalia, Bosnia, and Haiti as examples.[47] Mandelbaum derides Clinton for practicing "foreign policy as social work," but admits that of these three cases, Haiti was the "one place where an appeal to values might have generated support." According to Mandelbaum, because Haiti was "nearby, poor, weak, had once been occupied by the United States, and was populated by descendants of African slaves, the United States had reason to be concerned about its fate." He believes the provision of political and economic development to Haiti "could have been presented as a good deed in the neighborhood at manageable cost and justified by the fact that America is a rich, powerful, and generous country."[48]

Yet the matter was not so clear that the American public would naturally reach such a conclusion. Proponents of an active American involvement in Haiti would have to convince the domestic audience that the U.S. had a legitimate role to play. In fact, as Glenn Hastedt explains the dynamic of the elite decision-making theory, "public reactions are often 'orchestrated' by the elite rather than being expressions of independent thinking on policy matters."[49] Mandelbaum criticizes the Clinton administration for not trying to make this case and forfeiting the chance to establish legitimacy and support for the intervention in the eyes of the American people.[50]

Nor was the case made in Haiti, where there were problems with the legitimacy of the Governor's Island Accord from its inception. Because Cedras and Aristide refused to meet together, the accord could have hardly been described as a "negotiated" one. Instead, it was shaped and constructed by UN and Organization of American States (OAS) officials in consultation with the governments of Canada, France, the United States, and Venezuela, which had been deemed "Friends of the Secretary General" for Haiti. The U.S. was able to use its military dominance to provide heavy pressure on both sides to accept the accord, but neither side fully cooperated with its implementation. Aristide was particularly reluctant to endorse the provisions, and his continued heated rhetoric served to unite the factions opposed to his regime. At the same time, backers of Cedras showed no inclination to surrender their power and profit and had genuine fears for their safety should Aristide return.[51]

Another reason the Governor's Island Accord lacked legitimacy with Cedras is because it had no enforcement mechanism. He was not self-motivated to provide such security because it was not in his own interest to relinquish power, and the international community provided him no incentive to comply. To make the intent of the agreement work would require "a message of unambiguous determination to be conveyed to the [Haitian] military in words and deeds, particularly by the United States."[52] No such message was forthcoming.

American officials received early indications that there were serious discrepancies between their understanding of the Governor's Island Accords and that of Cedras. The State Department had envisioned the recreated Haitian military as being one whose "new mission would be oriented toward civic action, engineering, disaster assistance, and coastal patrol instead of maintaining public order."[53] Pulley saw his mission as producing "an army respected for its ability to serve and protect Haitian society instead of one feared for its ability to terrorize that society at gunpoint." He prepared to embark on "a conspicuous professionalization program" that would teach "the role of a soldier in a democracy."[54]

On September 16, however, Lieutenant Colonel Michael Jones, the commander of the site survey team in Haiti, reported that the Haitian Army believed they already were "professional" and had no interest in receiving training along the lines of the American plan.[55] Pulley found the Haitian Army's interpretation of the word "modernization" in UNSCR 867 to mean that they "should be given more and better lethal weapons systems." His attempts to schedule professionalization training "were repeatedly countered by requests for tanks, self-propelled artillery, attack helicopters, and fighter-bombers."[56] Clearly, Cedras and his cronies did not perceive JTF HAG's mission as a legitimate one. It soon "became clear [to Pulley] that the JTF was operating in a political climate that the diplomatic strategists had neither predicted nor prepared for."[57]

Just as Mandelbaum faults the Clinton administration for failing to make the case for Haiti with the American people, Pulley laments the missed opportunity to have used psychological operations (PSYOPS) teams to convince the Haitians of JTF HAG's legitimacy. Deployment of these assets was delayed for fear of bad connotations that might be drawn from the terms *PSYOPS* and *propaganda*. Because of the delay, the first four soldiers of what became known as a "public-awareness team" did not deploy until the day before the *Harlan County* attempted to dock at Port-au-Prince. "By then," Pulley remembers, "the opponents of President Aristide were firmly in control of the flow of information, and the US and the UN simply did not compete."[58] The Haitian media had routinely depicted the proposed UN force "as armed interventionists, portrayed alongside damning reporting about the UN/US operation in Somali." Thus, "Haitians hostile to the operation were able to link it, however unjustifiably, with scenes of violence in Mogadishu."[59] What Pulley calls "the truth" of the U.S. intentions, which may have been JTF HAG's "best advertisement[,] ... was never communicated."[60]

After the failure of JTF HAG, Pulley hypothesized that "a Joint Task Force Haiti II may be possible" if the situation in Haiti were to "reach a point where all parties genuinely desire an accord."[61] Instead, when the *Harlan County* arrived at Port-au-Prince, it did so without the mandate of legitimacy many U.S. and UN officials naively assumed it had. As a result of this miscalculation, all planning efforts had assumed a "permissive environment" in Haiti, and UNSCR 867 made no provisions for the forced entry of the *Harlan County*, instead merely calling "upon the Government of Haiti to take all appropriate steps to ensure the safety of United Nations personnel."[62]

Security

Because of this failure to ensure the legitimacy of the *Harlan County's* arrival with Haitian authorities, Commander Butcher would quickly have reason to question the security conditions that planners had assumed. When the ship arrived in Port-au-Prince at 2:00 A.M. on October 11, Butcher had to carefully navigate his way through a maze of vessels that were anchored around the harbor approaches in what appeared to be a deliberate attempt to impede his access to the port. Butcher finally dropped anchor at 5:00 A.M. but could not berth his ship because an old Cuban tanker was occupying his mooring. Instead, he launched a small landing craft to survey the situation and found little activity other than a group of Haitian policemen on the pier. A U.S. Coast Guard commander who was serving as an attaché at the U.S. Embassy arrived at the pier only to report he was leaving due to gunfire. Butcher could hear shots as well, but they were not directed at him.[63]

Returning to the *Harlan County*, Butcher reported the situation to his headquarters in Norfolk and directed all JTF HAG personnel to go to their rooms and wait. Several Haitian boats of assorted descriptions, some flying the Duvalier-era Tonton Macoute flag, were now circling the ship, but they dispersed when Butcher ordered crew members to man the *Harlan Country's* .50 caliber machine guns.[64]

From his vantage point on-shore, Pulley could also sense the mounting tension. At 7:00 A.M. he had seen a bus full of about forty Haitians arrive at the dock. Fueled by freely dispensed liquor, the crowd worked itself into a frenzy, firing weapons in the air and chanting anti–American slogans. Pulley saw two corpses dragged off the bus and thrown into the mob, but he took some comfort in the fact that a fourteen-foot high fence and a two-and-a-half-foot thick masonry wall separated the demonstrators from the pier. The mob was loud and unruly, but without access to the pier, Pulley felt it posed little immediate threat to the *Harlan County*.[65]

By this time several Americans, including Charge d' Affaires Huddleston, Pulley, and Dr. Bryant Freeman, an expert on Haiti from the University of Kansas, had gathered on the balcony of the Montana Hotel to observe the scene. Against Pulley's warnings, Huddleston decided to drive to the dock area in an attempt to calm the situation. Upon her arrival, she found the gate to the port locked, and her armored car was quickly surrounded by a mob of drunken Haitians who were chanting "Remember Somalia." The protestors began beating on the car with ax handles, compelling Huddleston to reluctantly retreat. A live CNN video of the event gave the world a startling impression of the chaotic situation unfolding at Port-au-Prince.[66]

In a three-way conversation, Butcher, Pulley, and a USACOM official discussed the situation. Pulley considered the environment tense but still permissive, while Butcher, noting the sounds of gunfire, disagreed. Various options were considered, but all had drawbacks, and in the end it was agreed the *Harlan County* would maintain only passive security measures from a position about one nautical mile off the pier.[67]

Later in the day, Haitian boats circled the *Harlan County* but kept their distance when they saw the machine guns were manned. Butcher also used his LCPLs (Landing Craft Personnel Large) to establish a floating security ring around his vessel. At one point after darkness fell, Haitians lined up some cars on the shore and shined their lights on the ship. Using night vision devices, ship personnel saw what they believed to be two V-150 armored personnel carriers with 90-mm guns hidden behind the pier. It was a tense but quiet night.[68]

The next morning, discussions continued about how to proceed. An embassy official called to request Butcher recover his LCPLs, but Butcher refused, citing his security concerns. A few minutes later, a representative from headquarters in Norfolk called to ask Butcher to at least contract his security ring closer to the ship. While Butcher was having this discussion, two Haitian twenty-five-foot Montauk gunboats, armed with .50 caliber machine guns and carrying Haitian Police and Haitian Army and Navy personnel, emerged from Admiral Killick Naval Base to the south and raced toward the *Harlan County*. Butcher ordered all guns manned and positioned snipers along the deck, instructing his men to open fire if the Haitians so much as put their hands on the triggers of their machine guns.[69]

Butcher assumed the Haitians were monitoring his unsecure radio communications, and he decided to use that situation to his advantage. He placed an open call to the U.S. Embassy, advising it that his top priority was to protect his ship, and he intended to destroy any gunboat that got within a thousand yards of the *Harlan County*. The Haitian vessels soon left. They reappeared about two hours later, but this time they kept their distance at a respectable 2,500 yards.[70]

Butcher concluded his position was untenable, and especially with the threat posed by the Haitian gunboats, he was unwilling to risk another night in the harbor. Pulley later mused that an operation designed after JTF HAG could succeed only "in a truly permissive environment," and Butcher determined now that the current environment was not permissive.[71] He notified his headquarters in Norfolk that he was pulling out. The watch officer asked Butcher if he would wait long enough for him to obtain concurrence from Admiral Henry Mauz, the Commander-in-Chief, U.S. Atlantic Fleet, but Butcher advised him that regardless of what was going on in Norfolk, he was leaving Port-au-Prince. About thirty-five minutes later, Butcher received word that headquarters would support his decision. Within days, Pulley and his JTF HAG advance party were ordered out of Haiti. The remaining UN and OAS personnel soon followed.[72] In the words of Richard Millet, the Haitian "military and their supporters had, at little apparent cost, called the Clinton administration's bluff and won."[73]

Restraint

From JTF HAG's inception, the principle of restraint was a controversial issue. Secretary of Defense Les Aspin argued that no U.S. military force should deploy without a self-defense capability. The State Department and National Security Advisor Anthony Lake, however, were against a U.S. assistance mission going ashore in a way that might be interpreted as an overbearing show of force.[74] A fairly ridiculous compromise resulted in which JTF HAG members were allowed to ship but not carry sidearms.[75] Ian Martin describes the sidearm controversy as being "too much for some Haitians, while it would prove too little for the Pentagon."[76] Even when the security situation deteriorated after the Governor's Island Accords, Pulley lamented that "it was too late to reconfigure the force package and impossible to clear a politically sensitive increase in defensive-weapons capability with the diplomats of the US country team, the United Nations, and the de facto government of Haiti."[77]

Butcher considered landing a contingent of marines on October 11 to intimidate the crowd, but the available troops and their vehicles had already been emblazoned with "UN" insignia. Thus they would be acting under UN auspices and "violence was the one thing that the UN wanted to avoid." Similarly, a USACOM representative, well aware of the recent events in Somalia, relayed to Pulley that casualties would be unacceptable.[78] Aside from manning its battle stations in self-defense, the closest the *Harlan County* got to deviating from the principle of restraint was to play "a loud and rousing national anthem for morning colors" on October 12.[79]

The American willingness to emphasize restraint over security was tied to a naïve confidence in the Governor's Island Accords. Even after the ignominious withdrawal of the *Harlan County*, President Clinton stated, "I have no intention of sending our people there until the agreement is honored.... The Department of Defense and our military leaders are convinced that the relatively light arms that our people were supposed to carry as advisors are more than adequate to protect themselves as long as the Governor's Island agreement is being honored." However, even President Clinton seemed to understand the imprudence of taking such a risk, and he added, "But I'm not about to let them land to test it."[80] In the case of the *Harlan County*, restraint and reliance on the likes of Raoul Cedras to guarantee one's security proved to be a poor substitute for an adequately armed and organized force.[81]

Perseverance

Given the haste of the withdrawal of the *Harlan County*, JTF HAG obviously failed to adhere to the principle of perseverance. Even Cedras said, "I'm surprised that you didn't persist."[82] Lambasting the decision, *New York Times* columnist Anthony Lewis claimed, "President Clinton could have ordered an immediate strike. A small invasion force, entirely adequate to round up the military leaders and their thugs, could have been quickly assembled. Congress and the public would have supported that response to the deliberate insulting of the United States. But Mr. Clinton did not act."[83] Surely the situation was more complicated than Lewis assumes, but Peter Riehm is correct in his observation that "the departure of one warship precipitated the hasty exit of the entire international presence."[84] Loss aversion, a nebulous foreign policy, and a reluctance to commit to yet another long-term nation-building exercise all conspired against perseverance in Haiti.

What most impacted the principle of perseverance is the fact that the *Harlan County* incident occurred just days after the disastrous Battle of Mogadishu in Somalia. Americans were in no mood to suffer casualties in pursuit of uncertain ventures. Senator Robert Dole captured the sentiments of many when he asserted, "The return of Aristide to Haiti is not worth even one American life." Dole then proposed a resolution to cut off funds for U.S. military forces sent to Haiti unless Congress voted to authorize the action, an emergency evacuation of Americans was required, or the "national interest" was at stake and there was not time to obtain congressional approval.[85]

Prospect theory does much to explain the lack of American perseverance after the rebuff of the *Harlan County*. The theory holds that decision makers do not always seek to maximize objective outcomes. Instead they tend to overvalue losses compared to equivalent gains, and become risk-averse in the domain of gains and risk acceptant in the domain of losses.[86] Thus, especially on the heels of the recent casualties in Somalia, both American political and military leaders were motivated more by the negative interest of avoiding losses rather than any positive outcome that perseverance in Haiti may have promised. On the other hand, the side that fears significant losses due to inaction, as did Cedras and his supporters, will be willing to act in a less restrained manner and assume more risks.[87] The return of Aristide to power "was fundamentally unacceptable to the [Haitian] army."[88] In such a situation, regardless of relative combat power, the junta's willingness to persevere far exceeded that of the U.S. This willingness was buoyed by observations of the American response to the Battle of Mogadishu.

Many observers found the ramifications of this lack of perseverance to stretch far beyond the *Harlan County* affair. Kate Doyle argues, "US policy toward Haiti has consisted of a torrent of good intentions unmatched by courage or political will. The result is a hollow diplomacy, with unsettling implications." Doyle cautions that such failures do not just "threaten to corrode the reputation of the United States abroad and undermine its ability to influence conflicts to come." Much more dangerously, she contends, the failure of the United States to act decisively in Haiti "touches the heart of the future of international affairs: the role of the United Nations, the needs of evolving democracies, the interplay of force and suasion."[89]

By the time of the *Harlan County* debacle, America was already stretched thin with nation-building activities. Even as the once hopeful situation in Somalia was turning to disaster, there was mounting pressure on the United States to do something to stop the violent civil war that was ravaging Bosnia. In Haiti, "all federal agencies acknowledg[ed] that even if military action succeeded in toppling the junta, the subsequent chore of nation-building would be fraught with uncertainty and too burdensome for the hemisphere's dominant power."[90] When the Governor's Island Accord proved to be empty, the repulse of the *Harlan County* was a convenient excuse not to press matters in Haiti.

But the United States remained interested in Haiti, by one explanation, simply because President Clinton had made it an issue.[91] Redoubled pressure from the Congressional Black Causus, the persistent refugee problem, an effort to restore American credibility, and a genuine humanitarian concern all combined to bring a force of over 20,000 troops to the brink of invading Haiti in September 1994. Backed by this credible threat of force, a last minute diplomatic effort by former President Jimmy Carter, Senator Sam Nunn, and General Colin Powell succeeded in convincing Cedras to transfer power, and the planned invasion became a peaceful entry.

Still, problems of perseverance plagued the U.S. involvement in Haiti. To make the country a self-sustaining democracy would require the establishment of a stable political system, the rule of law, and a freely functioning market economy. As Mandelbaum notes, because of the seriousness of these tasks, the transformation "could not be accomplished overnight" and would require "a substantial American commitment." He laments, "This the Clinton administration was not able to give."[92] Indeed, the American and UN presence ended in February 1996, and the Haiti of today shows little progress for their efforts.

Conclusion

Other examples such as the Greek Civil War, Nicaragua, and Honduras have suggested that perseverance is sustainable when directed toward an objective that is clearly stated and perceived as being important to broad U.S. interests. Like Somalia, the U.S. intervention in Haiti in 1993 lacked that strong adherence to objective, and perseverance could not be maintained when casualties became an issue. Haiti supports previous cases that have suggested a strong connection between the principles of objective and perseverance.

Also like Somalia, the U.S. intervention in Haiti lacked legitimacy with the host nation, and the U.S. forces did not offset the physical threat posed by this condition by increased attention to the principle of security. The UNITAF experience in Somalia had shown the futility of exercising restraint in the absence of legitimacy or security. Both Operations Bluebat and Power Pack had demonstrated the value of mitigating uncertainty by strong security. It was this overwhelming show of force that made restraint possible in Lebanon and the Dominican Republic. In Haiti, planners forfeited security by their misplaced reliance on legitimacy and then attempted to exercise restraint without the underpinning of either security or legitimacy. The result, especially considering the *Harlan County* incident's close proximity in time to the Battle of Mogadishu, was a strong failure to adhere to perseverance.

Operation Bluebat also showed the importance of unity of effort between the diplomatic and military actors as well as between the U.S. and a host nation's military. The intervention in Haiti failed to establish unity of effort on both these fronts. In the first case, the failure bears a striking resemblance to Beirut where the military was committed to a peacekeeping situation that had not been properly structured by the diplomatic effort. In the second case, it is directly attributable to the failure to establish legitimacy in the eyes of the junta.

This analysis reinforces several of the observations from other failed OOTWs. Vietnam, Beirut, Somalia, and Haiti all have had unsatisfactory adherence to objective, legitimacy, and security. In all cases, these shortcomings led to strong failures to adhere to perseverance.

CHAPTER 9

Conclusion: The Usefulness of the Principles

Operations other than war — now called support and stability operations — will remain the U.S. military's most common missions in the foreseeable future. The current nation assistance operations in Afghanistan and Iraq are OOTWs. The evacuation of U.S. citizens from and the bombing campaign against Libya are OOTWs. The disaster relief support to Japan after the tsunami is an OOTW. The raid to kill Usama bin Laden was an OOTW. The principles of OOTW serve as a reliable tool for planning, analyzing, and study such operations.

While success comes from the "balanced application" of all the principles, the examples in this book suggest that perseverance, objective, and security form one group of "critical principles," and unity of effort, legitimacy, and restraint comprise a "second tier."

The importance of perseverance rests in the argument that, given the American military and economic advantage, the country could meet its objective in most situations if American willingness to stay the course could be maintained. In order to maintain this perseverance, the principles of objective and security are required. Carl von Clausewitz famously wrote in *On War*, "No one starts a war — or rather, no one in his senses ought to do so — without first being clear in his mind what he intends to achieve by that war and how he intends to conduct it."[1] Based on this logic, objective is the starting point and foundation of all the principles of OOTW. Various OOTWs support this theory, including the Greek Civil War and Nicaragua/Honduras as positive examples, and Vietnam and Somalia as negative ones. However, because vital national interests are often not at stake in most OOTWs, perseverance can be as much a function of costs as it is objective. To this end, security is critical because perseverance is highly dependent on keeping U.S. casualties low. Casualties or the fear of casualties was critical to the lack of perseverance in Somalia and Haiti.

The main importance of the "second tier" principles is not such much in their inherent value but in their ability to contribute to other principles. Because of the political nature of OOTW, unity of effort is critical between the military and a host of other organizations. This unity of effort must be directed toward a common objective. The cases of Vietnam and Beirut showed the threat a lack of unity of effort poses to the critical principle of objective. Unity of effort, such as with an international coalition, also can enhance legitimacy. The transition of the American intervention in the Dominican Republic from a unilateral to an Organization of American States action is an example. However, if a coalition arrangement weakens security, as it did in Somalia, the added risk must be carefully considered.

Legitimacy includes the "willing acceptance" of the U.S. action by the host government and people.[2] As such, this principle contributes to security. The cases of Beirut and Somalia demonstrate the relationship between a lack of legitimacy in the eyes of the host nation and the threat to the security of the U.S. force. A violation of restraint can threaten legitimacy.[3]

However, excessive restraint can negatively impact security, as was most notably demonstrated in Beirut. If, for whatever reason, a violation of restraint does not negatively impact legitimacy, such as in the Greek Civil War, then restraint is not a significant factor. The actual significant factor is legitimacy, however it is achieved. If, on the other hand, excessive restraint negatively impacts security, perseverance is also jeopardized. Lebanon and the Dominican Republic showed restraint can be effective in the presence of strong security. Beirut and Somalia demonstrated the inverse. Haiti suggested for restraint to be effective, either legitimacy or security must be present. Nicaragua and Honduras showed restraint can contribute to perseverance by keeping economic and human costs low. Because restraint appears to have no inherently decisive value and is so dependent on context, it is arguably the least important principle.

The type of restraint that contributes to successful OOTWs is the type of restraint backed by and enabled by a strong security presence. The type of restraint present in failed OOTWs is the restraint engendered by weakness. This finding is important, because throughout the Cold War, the Scandinavian countries of Denmark, Finland, Sweden, and Norway had gained a reputation for peacekeeping expertise. Many observers saw this "Nordic model" as providing a blueprint for OOTW in the post–Cold War environment. However, the emphasis on lightly armed forces operating behind a shield of legitimacy and consent did not survive the more complicated and less permissive changed situation. As this reality became painfully clear with experiences like Somalia, security considerations gained ascendancy.[4] The results of OOTWs examined here should serve as a warning that restraint's utility is highly dependent on a credible capability, threat, and willingness to use force. For this reason, force planners and commanders should ensure a strong adherence to the principle of security.

Chapter Notes

Preface

1. Michael Gurley, "Operation Ernest Will" (paper, U.S. Naval War College, 1995), 17. "MOOTW" is an alternative term for OOTW. The M stands for "military."

2. See Bernardo Negrete, "Grenada, A Case Study in Military Operations Other Than War" (paper, Army War College, 1996); John Cowan, "Operation Provide Comfort: Operational Analysis for Operations Other Than War" (paper, Naval War College, 1995); Richard Brasel, "Operation Joint Endeavor: Operational Guidance from the Principles of Operations Other Than War" (paper, Naval War College, 1996).

3. Bruce Berg, *Qualitative Research Methods for the Social Sciences* (Boston, MA: Allyn and Bacon, 2001), 231.

4. FM 3-0, *Operations* (Washington, DC: Headquarters, Department of the Army, 2001), 4-11–4-12.

5. FM 3-07, *Stability Operations and Support Operations* (Washington, DC: Headquarters, Dept. of the Army, 2003), 1–19.

6. David Fastabend, "The Categorization of Conflict," *Parameters* (Summer 1997), 81; FM 3-0, 9-14 and 10-13.

Introduction

1. J. Mohan Malik, "The Evolution of Strategic Thought," in *Contemporary Security and Strategy*, ed. Craig Snyder (New York: Routledge, 1999), 18; Michael Howard, *The Theory and Practice of War* (Bloomington, IN: University of Indiana Press, 1975), 5.

2. Antoine-Henri de Jomini, *Summary of the Art of War or A New Analytical Compend of the Principal Combinations of Strategy, of Grand Tactics and of Military Policy* (New York: G. P. Putnam & Co., 1854), 18.

3. FM 100-5, 2-4.

4. Ibid., vi.

5. Taw, frontpiece, ix–x.

6. FM 100-5, 2–0, 13-3–13-4.

7. Ibid., 13-0.

8. To reflect this overlapping between the traditional principles of war and the principles of MOOTW, the 2006 rewrite of JP 3-0, now titled *Joint Operations*, included a list of 12 "principles of joint operations" comprised of the nine traditional ones and the three additions, which JP 3-0 calls "other principles." The JP also eliminated the use of the expression "military operations other than war."

9. FM 100-5, 13-3.

10. Ibid.

11. JP 3-07, *Joint Doctrine for Military Operations Other Than War* (Washington, DC, Joint Chiefs of Staff, 1995), II-2.

12. FM 100-5, 13-4.

13. FM 3-07, 1-21.

14. FM 100-5, 13-4.

15. Ibid.

16. Ibid.

17. Ibid.

18. JP 3-07, II-5.

19. FM 100-5, 13-4.

20. JP 3-07, II-5.

21. Daniel Bolger, *Savage Peace: Americans at War in the 1990s* (Novato, CA: Presidio, 1995), 397–399.

Chapter 1

1. Edward Wainhouse, "Guerrilla War in Greece, 1946–49: A Case Study," *Military Review* (June 1957): 16.

2. Edgar O'Ballance, *The Greek Civil War: 1944–1949* (New York: Praeger, 1966), 89.

3. Ibid., 88.

4. Ibid., 91.

5. Ibid., 91.

6. Ibid., 95–99.

7. Ibid., 105, 108; C. M. Woodhouse, *The*

Struggle for Greece, 1941–1949 (London: Hart-Davis, MacGibbon, 1976), 133–138.

8. O'Ballance, 112–113, 121. Some sources refer to the DAS as the "DAG" (Democratic Army of Greece).

9. Rinn Shinn, *Greece: A Country Study* (Washington, DC: American University, 1986), 52–53.

10. Stephanos Zotos, *Greece: The Struggle for Freedom* (New York: Thomas Crowell, 1967), 169–170; Woodhouse, 249.

11. Thomas Paterson et al., *American Foreign Policy: A History Since 1900* (Lexington, MA: DC Heath, 1991), 449–451; O'Ballance, 137.

12. Forrest Pogue, *George C. Marshall: Statesman, 1945–1959* (New York: Viking Penguin, 1987), 164–165.

13. Howard Jones, *"A New Kind of War": America's Global Strategy and the Truman Doctrine in Greece* (New York: Oxford University Press, 1989), 135.

14. Woodhouse, 236–237.

15. Ibid., 238.

16. Robert Mages, "Without the Need of a Single American Rifleman: James Van Fleet and His Lessons Learned as Commander of the Joint United States Military Advisory and Planning Group during the Greek Civil War, 1948–1949," in *The U.S. Army and Irregular Warfare, 1775–2007*, ed. Richard Davis (Washington, DC: Center of Military History, 2007), 195.

17. Woodhouse, 260–261.

18. "War Risks in Greek-aid Plans," *US News & World Report*, March 5, 1948, 31. In spite of this concern, the same article reported on page 30 that "Plans for actually moving units of the American Army into Greece are far advanced.... At present, in readiness is a combat force of American ground troops, about one and a third undersized Army divisions and a division of Marines. The total is about 25,000 men."

19. James Van Fleet, "How We Won in Greece" (speech to the Institute for Research in the Humanities and University Extension, University of Wisconsin, Madison, Wisc, April 11, 1967).

20. Andrew Birtle, *U.S. Army Counterinsurgency and Counterinsurgency Operations Doctrine, 1942–1976* (Washington, DC: Center of Military History, 2006), 50.

21. Woodhouse, 233.

22. Ibid., 245.

23. Abbott, 30–31.

24. Steven Rauch, "Southern (Dis)Comfort: British Phase IV Operations in South Carolina and Georgia, May–September 1780," in *The U.S. Army and Irregular Warfare, 1775–2007*, ed. Richard Davis (Washington, DC: Center of Military History, 2007), 38.

25. Ibid., 43.

26. Abbott, 31–32.

27. Ibid., 42.

28. Woodhouse, 234.

29. Lawrence Wittner, *American Intervention in Greece* (New York: Columbia University Press, 1982), 136. For additional discussion of Marshall's views on the subject, see Woodhouse, 239–245.

30. Rpt, Maj Gen S. J. Chamberlin to Chief of Staff, Army (CSA), 20 Oct 47, sub: The Greek Situation, pt. 2, p. 3, 868.00/10–2047, RG 59, NARA.

31. Interviews, Bruce Williams with General James A. Van Fleet, U.S. Army Military History Institute, Senior Officer Debriefing Program, Carlisle Barracks, Pa. (hereafter cited as Van Fleet Interv) vol. 3, 33.

32. Karl Th. Birgisson, "United Nations Special Commission on the Balkans," in *The Evolution of UN Peacekeeping: Case Studies and Comparative Analysis*, ed. William Durch (NY: St. Martin's Press, 1993), 78.

33. Jones, 238.

34. C. E. Black, "Greece and the United Nations," *Political Science Quarterly* 63, no. 4 (Dec., 1948): 553.

35. Charles Shrader, *The Withered Vine: Logistics and the Communist Insurgency in Greece, 1945–1949* (New York: Praeger, 1999), 202.

36. See also Woodhouse, 248–250.

37. "The Nations: Captain of the Crags," *Time*, April 5, 1948, 26.

38. Woodhouse, 235.

39. Jones, 108 and 110.

40. Woodhouse, 235.

41. Abbott, 9–10.

42. Joint U.S. Military Advisory and Planning Group, Greece, *History of the JUSMAPG, 1949*, Headquarters, JUSMAPG (hereafter cited as *JUSMAPG History*), 2.

43. Pogue, 400.

44. Mages, 199.

45. Van Fleet Interv, vol 3, 16.

46. Birtle, 49.

47. Ibid., 48–49.

48. Dave R. Palmer, *Summons of the Trumpet* (San Rafael, CA: Presidio, 1978), 12.

49. Stephen Hosmer and George Tanham, "Countering Covert Aggression" (Santa Monica, CA: RAND, January 1986), 17.

50. Birtle, 52.

51. *US News & World Report*, October 29, 1948, 24.

52. Woodhouse, 236.

53. "Senate Passes Iraq withdraw bill; veto threat looms," April 26, 2007, CNN.com. http://www.cnn.com/2007/POLITICS/04/26/congress.iraq/index.html?eref=rss_topstories (accessed March 30, 2010).

54. William, McCaffrey, "Gen. Van Fleet:

One of the Last the Stars Fell On," *Army* (Dec 1992): 10.

55. "War Risks in Greek-aid Plans," *US News & World Report*, March 5 1948, 31.

56. L. S. Stavrianos, *Greece: American Dilemma and Opportunity* (Chicago: Henry Regnery, 1952), 203.

57. Shrader, 228; Condit, 228.

58. Woodhouse, 236.

59. O'Ballance, 166, 187.

60. Abbott, 10.

61. "Greece: With Will to Win," *Time*, May 23, 1949, 27.

62. O'Ballance, 187–188.

63. *Time*, May 23, 1949, 27.

64. Woodhouse, 238.

65. Wainhouse, June 1957, 24.

66. McCaffery, 10.

67. FM 90-8, *Counterguerrilla Operations* (Washington, DC: Department of the Army, 1986), 1-21-3.

68. D. M. Condit et al., *Challenge and Response in Internal Conflict: The Experience in Europe and the Middle East* (Washington, DC: American University, 1967), 516.

69. Wainhouse, 24; O'Ballance, 192–193.

70. Woodhouse, 259.

71. Ibid., 259; Condit, 516.

72. O'Ballance, 189, 192.

73. Woodhouse, 259, 261.

74. Andreas Papandreou, *Democracy at Gunpoint: The Greek Front* (Garden City, NY, Doubleday, 1970), 72.

75. O'Ballance, 195–196.

76. Papandreou, 73.

77. Woodhouse, 231.

78. Abbott, 32–33; Woodhouse, 254–255.

79. O'Ballance, 195–196.

80. Stavrianos, 203.

81. Woodhouse, 232.

82. O'Ballance, 198–199.

83. Ibid., 199–200.

84. Ibid., 200.

85. "Greece: Winged Victory," *Time*, October 24, 1949, 32; O'Ballance, 201.

86. John Iatrides, "Revolution or Self-Defense? Communist Goals, Strategy, and Tactics in the Greek Civil War," *Journal of Cold War Studies* 7, no. 3 (Summer 2005): 29.

87. Amikan Nachmani, *International Intervention in the Greek Civil War: The United Nations Special Committee on the Balkans, 1947–1952* (Santa Barbara, CA: Praeger Publishers, 1990), 147.

88. Iatrides, 33; Woodhouse, 274.

89. Paterson, 157.

90. Woodhouse, 275.

91. Ibid., 289.

92. Shrader, 514–515.

93. Abbott, 26.

Chapter 2

1. Roger Spiller, *"Not War But Like War": The American Intervention in Lebanon* (Fort Leavenworth, KS: Combat Studies Institute, 1981), 2–4.

2. Ibid.; Jack Shulimson, *Marines in Lebanon, 1958* (Washington, DC: Headquarters, U.S. Marine Corps, 1966), 1.

3. Don Perez, *The Middle East Today*, 2 ed. (Hinsdale, IL: Dryden Press, 1971), 329.

4. Dwight Eisenhower, "Special Message to the Congress on the Situation in the Middle East," January 5, 1957, available at "American Presidency Project" http://www.presidency.ucsb.edu/ws/index.php?pid=11007&st=&st1=#ixzz1LJwwpYaY (accessed 3 May 2011).

5. Spiller, 10.

6. Ibid., 13.

7. Walter LaFeber, *America, Russia, and the Cold War* (New York: John Wiley and Sons, 1968), 179.

8. Yates, *Lebanon*, 131.

9. Ibid., 127.

10. Lawrence Yates, "The US Military Intervention in Lebanon, 1958: Success without a Plan," in *Turning Victory into Success: Military Operations after the Campaign*, ed. Brian De Toy (Fort Leavenworth, KS: Combat Studies Institute, 2004), 128; Spiller, 38.

11. Yates, *Lebanon*, 132.

12. Roby Barrett, *The Greater Middle East and the Cold War: US Foreign Policy under Eisenhower and Kennedy* (New York: I. B. Tauris, 2007), 61–62.

13. Yates, *Lebanon*, 132.

14. Spiller, 13.

15. Yates, *Lebanon*, 127.

16. Robert Murphy, *Diplomat Among Warriors: The Unique World of a Foreign Service Expert* (Garden City, NY: Doubleday & Company, 1964), 398.

17. Yates, *Lebanon*, 123.

18. Richard Saunders, "Military Force in the Foreign Policy of the Eisenhower Presidency," *Political Science Quarterly* 100, no. 1 (Spring 1985), 114.

19. Murphy, 404.

20. Saunders, 114.

21. Shulimson, 11.

22. Ibid., 12.

23. Ibid., 11.

24. Spiller, 20.

25. Shulimson, 33.

26. Spiller, 25.

27. Ibid., 45.

28. Shulimson, 17.

29. Spiller, 44.

30. Lawrence Yates, *Power Pack: U.S. Intervention in the Dominican Republic, 1965–1966*

(Fort Leavenworth, KS: U.S. Army Command & General Staff College, 1988), 40.

31. Gary Wade, *Rapid Deployment Logistics: Lebanon, 1958* (Fort Leavenworth, KS: Combat Studies Institute, 1984), x.

32. Spiller, 7–9.

33. Barrett, 65; Robert Divine, *Since 1945: Politics and Diplomacy in Recent American History* (New York: McGraw-Hill, 1985), 87.

34. Spiller, 17.

35. Ibid., 18.

36. Shulimson, 24.

37. Spiller, 25.

38. Ibid., 25.

39. Ibid., 33–34.

40. Ibid., 6.

41. Ibid., 42.

42. Andrew Birtle, *US Army Counterinsurgency and Contingency Operations Doctrine, 1942–1976* (Washington, DC: U.S. Government Printing Office, 2006), 189.

43. Wade, 80.

44. Shulimson, 31.

45. Spiller, 18.

46. Birtle, 184.

47. Shulimson, 17.

48. Spiller, 32–33.

49. Yates, *Power Pack*, 40.

50. Spiller, 1; Yates, *Lebanon*, 131.

51. Birtle, 188.

52. Ibid., 187.

53. Yates, *Lebanon*, 130.

54. Shulimson, 12–13.

55. Ibid., 22; Spiller, 25.

56. Yates, *Lebanon*, 129.

57. Divine, 87.

58. David Gray, *The US Intervention in Lebanon, 1958: A Commander's Reminiscence* (Fort Leavenworth, KS: Combat Studies Institute, 1984), 18.

59. Birtle, 187.

60. Shulimson, 22.

61. Ibid., 32.

62. Birtle, 187, 190; Shulimson, 32.

63. Gray, 43.

64. Shulimson, 32.

65. Spiller, 43.

66. Shulimson, 35.

67. Spiller, 43.

68. Ibid., 10.

69. Barrett, 65.

70. Ibid., 72. See also Shulimson, 6.

71. Spiller, 10.

72. Shulimson, 6, 24.

73. "Lebanon-UNOGIL," Available http://www.un.org/en/peacekeeping/missions/past/unogilbackgr.html (accessed May 17, 2011).

74. Spiller, 44.

75. Ibid., 28. See also Wade, 82.

76. Shulimson, 7, 26; Spiller, 47.

77. Spiller, 6.

78. Shulimson, 5.

79. Spiller, 7.

80. Shulimson, 20; Yates, *Lebanon*, 128.

81. Shulimson, 14–15.

82. Ibid., 19.

83. Murphy, 401; Shulimson, 20.

84. Spiller, 23–25.

85. Shulimson, 12.

86. Yates, *Lebanon*, 129. See also Shulimson, 19.

87. Shulimson, 27.

88. Ibid., 23.

89. Ibid., 28.

90. Birtle, 186–187; Shulimson, 26–27.

91. Birtle, 188.

92. Yates, *Lebanon*, 128.

93. See Spiller, 22, for a description of the incident between McClintock and Hadd. Shulimson, 36, chocks it up to "an incomplete liaison between the American diplomat on the scene and the military commanders." See also Gray, 31.

94. Murphy, 404.

95. Ibid., 404–406; Yates, *Lebanon*, 130.

96. Murphy, 405; Birtle, 188–189.

97. Yates, *Lebanon*, 130–131; Shulimson, 36.

98. "Lebanon-UNOGIL."

99. Ibid.

100. Barret, 66.

101. Birtle, 186.

102. See Ibid., 186, for a discussion of the Lebanese role in safeguarding the Americans and Quincy Wright, "United States Intervention in the Lebanon," in *The American Journal of International Law* 53, no. 1 (Jan., 1959): 118 for an explanation of the legal requirement for an intervention based on the right of individual defense.

103. Birtle, 186.

104. Murphy, 405; Yates, *Lebanon*, 130.

105. Birtle, 186.

106. Murphy, 404.

107. Shulimson, 33.

108. Murphy, 408.

109. Yates, *Lebanon*, 130; Britle, 187; Spiller, 44.

110. Murphy, 401.

111. Ibid., 408.

112. Shulimson, 22.

113. Ibid., 27.

114. Spiller, 44.

115. Birtle, 188.

116. Wright, 114.

117. Murphy, 409.

118. Divine, 102.

119. John Marlowe, *Arab Nationalism and British Imperialism* (London: Cresset Press, 1961), 146.

120. Yates, *Lebanon*, 131.

121. Shulimson, 26.

Chapter 3

1. Bruce Palmer, *Intervention in the Caribbean: The Dominican Crisis of 1965* (Lexington: University Press of Kentucky, 1989), 24.

2. Ibid., 23.

3. Ibid., 25.

4. Lawrence Yates, *Power Pack: U.S. Intervention in the Dominican Republic, 1965–1966* (Fort Leavenworth, KS: U.S. Army Command & General Staff College, 1988), 53; Palmer, 26.

5. Yates, 74; Palmer, 19.

6. Palmer, 27–28.

7. Jerome Slater, *Intervention and Negotiation: The United States and the Dominican Revolution* (New York: Harper & Row, 1970), 116; Palmer, 5; Yates, 86.

8. Yates, 93.

9. Ibid., 35.

10. Abraham Lowenthal, *The Dominican Intervention* (Cambridge, MA: Harvard University Press, 1972), 127.

11. Palmer, 15.

12. Ibid., 1.

13. Ibid., 12.

14. Ibid., 69.

15. Ibid., 48.

16. Tad Szulc, as quoted in the Center for Strategic Studies, *Dominican Action, 1965: Intervention or Cooperation?* (Washington, DC: Georgetown University, July 1966), 84.

17. Lawrence Greenberg, *United States Army Unilateral and Coalition Operations in the 1965 Dominican Republic Intervention* (Washington, DC: U.S. Army Center of Military History, 1987), 26.

18. Yates, 79–81.

19. Greenberg, 25–26.

20. Yates, 75.

21. Ibid., 102.

22. Ibid., 173.

23. The Center for Strategic Studies, ix.

24. See also Palmer 64–68 for an additional discussion of overall issues between the military and the press in both the Dominican Republic and Vietnam.

25. Palmer, 29.

26. Ibid., 29.

27. Edward Haughney, *OAS and the Use of Military Forces* (Carlisle Barracks, PA: U.S. Army War College, 1966), 34.

28. Slater, 76.

29. Haughney, 35; Center for Strategic Studies, 39.

30. Rudolph Barnes, "Military Legitimacy in OOTW: Civilians as Mission Priorities," *Special Warfare* (Fall 1999): 37; Palmer, 5.

31. John Costa, *The Dominican Republic: Intervention in Perspective* (Carlisle Barracks, PA: U.S. Army War College, May 2, 1968), 32.

32. Palmer, 77; Yates, 156.

33. Yates, 150.

34. Palmer, 78.

35. Ibid., 79.

36. Costa, 31–32.

37. Palmer, 71.

38. Ibid., ix.

39. Ibid., xi.

40. Ibid., 6.

41. Ibid., 45.

42. Ibid., 3, 156.

43. Ibid., 156.

44. Ibid., 155.

45. Ibid.

46. Michael Grow, *US Presidents and Latin American Interventions: Pursuing Regime Change in the Cold War* (Lawrence: University Press of Kansas, 2008), 90.

47. Yates, 40.

48. Palmer, 76.

49. Lowenthal, 107. Lowenthal also feels that interservice rivalry contributed to the expanding intervention. See also Yates, 66.

50. Palmer, 158.

51. Ibid., 76.

52. Grow, 87.

53. Ibid.

54. Grow, 88; 90.

55. Palmer, 76.

56. Yates, 77; Lowenthal, 116–117.

57. Yates, 91.

58. Ibid., 73.

59. Palmer, 44–45.

60. Yates, 140.

61. Palmer, 46.

62. Yates, 140.

63. "Swift as Eagles," *Army Information Digest*, July 1965, 8.

64. Lowenthal, 119. See also Slater, 74.

65. Yates,140.

66. Ibid.

67. Ibid., 142.

68. Palmer, 81.

69. Yates, 122.

70. Peter Chew, "On a Lonely Point," *Army*, June 1965, 94.

71. Yates, 142; Palmer, 52–53.

72. Yates, 142.

73. Palmer, 52.

74. Ibid., 48–49.

75. Ibid., 82.

76. Ibid., 83.

77. Ibid., 84.

78. Sam Sarkesian, *US National Security: Policymakers, Processes, and Politics* (Boulder, CO: Lynne Rienner Publishers, 1989), 91.

79. Palmer, 83.

80. Yates, 178. Even Jerome Slater, certainly

not an apologist for the intervention, admits that "the record seems to bear ... out" that the U.S. soldiers acted with great restraint. Slater, 115.

81. Chew, 93.

82. Charles Moskos, Jr. "Grace Under Pressure," *Army*, September 1966, 41.

83. Ibid., 42–43.

84. Chew, 94.

85. Moskos, 43.

86. Yates, 177–178.

87. Palmer, ix.

88. Barnes, 37.

89. Yates, 176–177.

90. Greenberg, 49.

91. Yates, 143.

92. Palmer, 51.

93. Greenberg, 53–55.

94. Yates, 159.

95. "Moving in was easy, but...." *U.S. News & World Report*, June 21, 1965, 75.

96. Ibid., 75.

97. Yates, 158.

98. Ibid., 160–162.

99. Roland Paris, *At War's End: Building Peace After Civil Conflict* (New York: Cambridge University Press, 2004), 188.

100. Palmer, 87.

101. Ibid., 85.

102. Paris, 188.

103. Ibid., 189.

104. Palmer, 89.

105. Ibid., 93.

106. Ibid., 97–98.

107. Paris, 189.

108. Paris, 189; Palmer, 131.

109. Palmer, 129–132.

110. Ibid., 107.

111. Ibid., 134.

112. Ibid.

113. Ibid.

114. Ibid., 137.

115. Sarah Kershaw, "Joaquín Balaguer, 95, Dies; Dominated Dominican Life," *New York Times*, July 15, 2002. Available at http://www.ny times.com/2002/07/15/world/joaquin-balaguer-95-dies-dominated-dominican-life.html (accessed May 16, 2011).

116. Richard Haggerty, ed., *Dominican Republic and Haiti: Country Studies* (Washington, DC: Headquarters, Dept. of the Army, 1991), 33–35; Yates, 179.

117. Paris, 196.

118. Palmer, 54.

119. Palmer, 55; Yates, 132.

120. Palmer, 102, 115.

121. Ibid., 120–121.

122. Ibid., 156–157.

123. Yates, 131.

124. Samuel Huntington, *Political Order in Changing Societies* (New Haven, CN: Yale University Press, 1968), 8.

125. Paris, 198.

126. Ibid., 207.

127. Palmer, 54; 102.

128. Ibid., 100.

129. Ibid., 111.

130. Paris, 208.

131. Palmer, 158.

132. See Ibid., 79, for commentary on how quickly the situation in Vietnam detracted attention from the Dominican Republic.

133. Haggerty, 33–35; Yates, 179.

134. Barnes, 39.

135. Palmer, 154.

Chapter 4

1. Philip Catton, *Diem's Final Failure: Prelude to America's War in Vietnam* (Lawrence, KS: University of Kansas Press, 2003), 52; Thomas Thayer, *War Without Fronts: The American Experience in Vietnam* (Boulder, CO: Westview Press, 1985) 237.

2. Ibid., 63–64.

3. Ibid., 67.

4. Ibid., 66–67.

5. Ibid., 68–69.

6. Ibid., 60–70.

7. Anthony James Joes, *The War for South Viet Nam, 1954–197* (New York: Praeger, 2001), 64; Catton, 73, 93–97.

8. Guenter Lewy, *America in Vietnam* (New York: Oxford University Press, 1978), 112; Robert Doughty, *American Military History and the Evolution of Western Warfare* (Lexington, MA: D. C. Heath and Company, 1996), 642–643; Stanley Karnow, *Vietnam: A History* (New York: Penguin, 1997), 272–273.

9. Lewy, 25.

10. Ibid., 112.

11. Dave Palmer, *Summons of the Trumpet: US-Vietnam in Perspective* (San Rafael, CA: Presidio Press, 1978), 221.

12. Thayer, 137.

13. Lewy, 25.

14. James William Gibson, *The Perfect War: Technology in Vietnam* (Boston: The Atlantic Monthly Press, 1986), 270–271.

15. Lawrence Yates, "A Feather in Their Cap? The Marines' Combat Action Program in Vietnam," in *US Marines and Irregular Warfare, 1898–2007: Anthology and Selected Bibliography*, edited by Stephen Evans (Quantico, VA: Marine Corps University Press, 2008), 148.

16. Gibson, 270–271; Phillip Davidson, *Vietnam at War: The History, 1946–1975* (Novato, CA: Presidio Press, 1988), 302; Palmer, 220–221.

17. Larry Cable, *Conflict of Myths: The De-*

velopment of American Counterinsurgency Doctrine and the Vietnam War (New York: New York University Press, 1986), 250.

18. Scoville, 24; Jeffrey Clarke, *The United States Army in Vietnam, Advice and Support: The Final Years, 1965–1973* (Washington, DC: Center of Military History, 1988), 171.

19. Thayer, 169; Maurice Matloff, *American Military History* (Washington, DC: Department of the Army, 1973), 640; Lewis Sorley, "The Quiet War: Revolutionary Development," *Military Review* (Nov 1967): 13–19; William Willoughby, "Revolutionary Development," *Infantry* (Nov–Dec 1968): 5–11; Louis Swenson, "The Revolutionary Development Program," *Infantry* (Jan–Feb 1968): 28–31; Samuel Smithers, "Combat Units in Revolutionary Development," *Military Review* (Oct 1967): 37–41.

20. Gibson, 273–274; Lewy, 89.

21. George Herring, *America's Longest War: The United States and Vietnam, 1950–1975* (New York: Newberry Award Records, 1979), 158.

22. Lewy, 52; Dale Andrade and James Willbanks, "CORDS/Phoenix: Counterinsurgency Lessons from Vietnam for the Future," *Military Review* (March–April 2006): 78.

23. Yates, 150, 156.

24. Ibid., 156.

25. Erwin Brigham, "Pacification Measurement," *Military Review* (May 1970): 51–53; Maurice Roush, "The Hamlet Evaluation System," *Military Review* (September 1969): 12–13; Gibson, 305.

26. Lewy, 134.

27. Gibson, 313.

28. Ibid., 312; Gregory Daddis, *No Sure Victory: Measuring U.S. Army Effectiveness and Progress in the Vietnam War* (New York: Oxford University Press, 2011), 149–150.

29. Andrew F. Krepinevich, *The Army and Vietnam* (Baltimore: The Johns Hopkins University Press, 1986), 253.

30. Lewy, 137.

31. Davidson, 614.

32. See William Colby, *Lost Victory: A Firsthand Account of America's Sixteen-Year Involvement in Vietnam.* (New York: Contemporary Books, 1990), 271, for a discussion of the impact of the withdrawal decision.

33. *New York Times*, April 9, 1970, as quoted in Thompson; Donald Frizzell, *The Lessons of Vietnam* (New York: Crane, Russak, and Company: 1977), 218.

34. Komer, "Clear, Hold and Rebuild," *Army* 20, no. 5 (May 1970): 22.

35. Ibid., 22–23.

36. Matloff, 639.

37. Matloff, 639; Andrade and Willbanks, 79; Allan Millet and Peter Maslowski, *For the Common Defense: A Military History of the United States of America* (New York: Free Press, 1984), 556; Thompson and Frizzell, 214.

38. Gibson, 282; Komer, "Pacification: A Look Back ... and Ahead," *Army* 20, no. 6 (June 1970): 24.

39. Gibson, 271.

40. Ibid., 273.

41. Brigham, 49–50; Gibson, 305–308; Thayer, 138–139.

42. Gibson, 305.

43. Ibid., 313.

44. Ibid.

45. Joint Pub 1–02, *Department of Defense Dictionary of Military and Associated Terms* (Washington, DC: Joint Chiefs of Staff, 2010), 289.

46. See Shon McCormick, "A Primer on Developing Measures of Effectiveness," *Military Review* (July–August 2010): 63–64 for the continuing difficulty the military has in determining MOEs that measure largely qualitative factors.

47. Andrade and Willbanks, 80.

48. Robert Komer, "Clear, Hold and Rebuild," 16.

49. Yates, 147.

50. Thomas Scoville, *Reorganizing for Pacification Support* (Washington, DC: Center of Military History, 1982), 3.

51. Lewy, 89.

52. Andrade and Willbanks, 78.

53. Ibid., 81.

54. Scoville, 25.

55. Ibid., 25–26.

56. Komer, "Clear, Hold, and Rebuild," 18.

57. Andrade and Willbanks, 81; Gibson, 272; Lewy, 123.

58. Lewy, 124.

59. Robert Komer, "Pacification," 24.

60. Scoville, 384; Willoughby, 9; Andrade and Willbanks, 82–83; Coffey, 12.

61. Lewy, 124–125.

62. Ibid., 125.

63. Komer, "Clear, Hold, and Rebuild," 20.

64. Thompson and Frizzell, 231; Lewy, 124.

65. Komer, "Pacification," 24.

66. Ibid., 24.

67. Ibid., 27.

68. Ibid., 23.

69. Ibid., 27.

70. Komer, "Clear, Hold, and Rebuild," 19.

71. Komer, "Pacification," 23.

72. Maxwell Taylor, *Swords and Plowshares* (New York: W. W. Norton, 1972), 340. For other commentary on the lack of security, see Herring, 159; Lewy, 89; Willoughby, 6; Thayer, 137; John Cleland, "Principle of the Objective and Vietnam," *Military Review* (July 1966): 86; Edwin Chamberlain, "Pacification," *Infantry* (November–December 1968): 32–39; Cable, 257.

73. Yates, 148.

74. Ibid., 148–149; Al Hemingway, *Our War*

Was Different: Marine Combined Action Platoons in Vietnam (Annapolis, MD: Naval Institute Press, 1994), 178; Anthony James Joes, *Resisting Rebellion: the History and Politics of Counterinsurgency* (Lexington: University Press of Kentucky, 2006), 115.

75. Yates, 149; Lewy, 116–117; Andrew Brittle, *US Army Counterinsurgency and Contingency Operations Doctrine, 1942–1976* (Washington, DC: Center of Military History, 2006), 399–400; Swenson, 28; R. E. Williamson, "A Briefing for Combined Action," *Marine Corps Gazette*, March 1968, 41–43.

76. William Westmoreland, *A Soldier Reports* (Garden City, NY: Doubleday and Company, 1976), 166.

77. Yates, 148.

78. Lewy, 117.

79. James Olson and Randy Roberts, *Where the Domino Fell: America and Vietnam, 1945 to 1990* (New York: St. Martin's Press, 1991), 144.

80. John Tolson, *Vietnam Studies: Airmobility, 1961–1971* (Washington, DC: Department of the Army, 1989), 181.

81. Lewy, 143.

82. Julian Ewell and Ira Hunt, *Sharpening the Combat Edge: The Use of Analysis to Reinforce Military Judgment* (Washington, DC: Dept. of the Army, 1995), 160.

83. Millet and Maslowski, 556.

84. Ibid., 556.

85. Andrade and Willbanks, 85–86.

86. Ibid., 86.

87. Ibid., 89.

88. Karnow, 602.

89. Millet and Maslowski, 556; Olson, 197; Andrade and Willbanks, 88; Palmer, 225.

90. Millet and Maslowski, 556; Olson, 197; Palmer, 225.

91. Ivan Arreguin-Toft, "How the Weak Win Wars," *International Security* 26, no. 1 (Summer 2001).

92. Ibid., 109, 117–118.

93. Ibid., 118.

94. Ibid., 119.

95. Andrade and Willbanks, 168; Arreguin-Toft, 119.

96. Arreguin-Toft, 120.

97. "Vietnamese Civic Action Program," *Military Review* (December 1967), 102.

98. Brittle, 397.

99. Gibson, 282.

100. Ibid., 283.

101. Doughty, 639.

102. Lewis Sorley, *Honorable Warrior: General Harold K. Johnson* (Lawrence, KS: University Press of Kansas, 1998), 239–240.

103. Komer, "Pacification," 20.

104. Komer, "Clear, Hold, and Rebuild," 23.

105. Colby, 365.

106. Lewy, 63.

107. Smithers, 41.

108. Lewy, 88.

109. Ibid., 63.

110. Chamberlain, 39.

111. Thompson and Frizzell, 223–224.

112. Yates, 154.

113. Komer, "Clear, Hold, and Rebuild," 24.

114. Coffey, 16.

115. Palmer 164.

116. Lewy, 89.

117. Harold Johnson, extract from speech August 21, 1967, New Orleans, LA, *Military Review* 47, no. 12 (December 1967): back matter.

118. Arreguin-Toft, 120.

Chapter 5

1. Max Boot, *The Savage Wars of Peace: Small Wars and the Rise of American Power* (New York: Basic Books, 2002), 232.

2. Ibid., 233–235.

3. Ibid., 235.

4. Ibid., 235–241.

5. Ibid., 242.

6. Ibid.

7. Ibid., 242–243.

8. Ibid., 244–247.

9. Ibid., 249–251.

10. Ibid., 250.

11. Ibid., 251; Roland Paris, *At War's End: Building Peace after Civil Conflict* (New York: Cambridge University Press, 2004), 114.

12. Paris, 115; Michael Grow, *US Presidents and Latin American Interventions: Pursuing Regime Change in the Cold War* (Lawrence: University Press of Kansas, 2008), 114.

13. Grow, 115; Paris, 115.

14. Grow, 120–121.

15. Ibid., 121.

16. Ibid., 122.

17. Ibid., 116–117.

18. Ibid., 118.

19. Ibid., 118–120.

20. Ibid., 122.

21. Ibid., 123; Peter Schweizer, *Reagan's War: The Epic Story of His Forty-Year Struggle and Final Triumph over Communism* (New York: Doubleday, 2002), 204.

22. Grow, 123.

23. *Public Papers of the Presidents of the United States: Ronald Reagan, 1982* (Washington, DC: Government Printing Office, 1983), 360.

24. Schweizer, 155.

25. Ibid., 154.

26. James Scott, "Interbranch Rivalry and the Reagan Doctrine in Nicaragua," *Political Science Quarterly* 112, no. 2 (Summer 1997): 237.

27. Schweizer, 204.

28. Ibid.

29. Grow, 125.

30. Alexander Haig, *Caveat: Realism, Reagan, and Foreign Policy* (New York: Macmillan, 1984), 95–96.

31. Haig, 96.

32. Schweizer, 205.

33. Grow, 133–134.

34. Ibid., 134.

35. Ibid., 134–135; Kagan, 202.

36. Schweizer, 205.

37. Peter Kornbluth, *Nicaragua: The Price of Intervention* (Washington, DC: Institute of Political Studies, 1987), 136.

38. Robert Turner, *Nicaragua v. United States: A Look at the Facts* (Washington, DC: Pergamon-Brassey's, 1987), 19.

39. Kornbluth, 136.

40. Ibid., 139.

41. Ibid., 136.

42. Arthur Lykke, "Toward an Understanding of Military Strategy," in *Military Strategy: Theory and Application* (Carlisle, PA: U.S. Army War College, 1989), 6–7.

43. Scott, 237.

44. "Currents: US vs Nicaragua," *US News & World Report*, 28 April 1986, 8.

45. "Honduras Receives US Assistance to Repel Sandinista Attacks," Department of State Bulletin, May 1986, 86. Hereafter "Hondo Receives US Assistance."

46. Larry Martz, "Echoes of an Old War," *Newsweek*, 7 April 1986, 34–35.

47. James Wallace, "Next Stop for U.S. Forces?" *U.S. News and World Report*, 28 April 1986, 26; "Hondo Receives US Assistance," 86; Mark Whitaker, "More Contradictions," *Newsweek*, 14 April 1986, 20.

48. Wallace, 26.

49. Peter Range, "The End Game in Nicaragua," *U. S. News and World Report*, 28 March 1988, 17; Robert Zinti, "The Contra Tangle," *Time*, 28 March 1988, 15.

50. Jill Smolowe, "Pouncing on a Transgressor," *Time*, 7 April 1986, 24; Martz, 35; Whitaker, 20–21.

51. Harry Anderson, 36.

52. "Hondo Receives U. S. Assistance," 86.

53. Smolowe, 24.

54. "Contra Victory," *National Review*, 25 April 1986, 17; Smolowe, 25.

55. "Contra Victory," 18; Wallace, 26; Martz, 34–35.

56. Warner, 36; Martz, 34; Smolowe, 25.

57. Smolowe, 25.

58. Martz, 34; Smolowe, 25.

59. Caspar Weinberger, *Fighting For Peace: Seven Critical Years in the Pentagon* (New York: Warner Books, 1990), 375.

60. Roy Gutman, *Banana Diplomacy: The Making of American Policy in Nicaragua, 1981–1987* (New York: Simon and Shuster, 1988), 148; Grow, 129–130.

61. U.S. Department of State, Foreign Service Institute, "Low-Intensity Conflict: Support for Democratic Resistance Movements" (np: Center for the Study of Foreign Affairs, 1988), 22. Hereafter "Low-Intensity Conflict."

62. Thomas Walker, *Revolution and Counterrevolution in Nicaragua* (Boulder, CO: Westview Press, 1991), 298–299.

63. Grow, 124.

64. Todd Greentree, "The United States and the Politics of Conflict in the Developing World: A Policy Study" (np: Center for the Study of Foreign Affairs, 1990), 25, 35.

65. Grow, 130–131.

66. Kornbluth, 139.

67. Grow, 131–132.

68. Gutman, 73.

69. Kornbluth, 139.

70. Ibid., 140.

71. Holly Sklar, *Washington's War on Nicaragua* (Boston: South End Press, 1988), 147–148.

72. Ibid., 146.

73. Kornbluth, 143.

74. Ibid., 141.

75. Ibid., 143.

76. FM 7-98, *Operations in a Low-Intensity Conflict* (Washington, DC: Headquarters, Dept. of the Army, 1992), 5–6.

77. Kornbluth, 144.

78. Grow, 132.

79. Robert Kagan, *A Twilight Struggle: American Power and Nicaragua, 1977–1990* (New York: Free Press, 1996), 204–205.

80. Harry Anderson, "The Contras Under the Gun," *Newsweek*, 28 March 1988, 38; Kornbluth, 147; "Low-Intensity Conflict," 26.

81. K. J. Holsti, *International Politics: A Framework for Analysis* (Englewood Cliffs, NJ: Prentice-Hall, 1992), 12.

82. Sklar, 145.

83. Kornbluth, 148.

84. Ibid., 147; Stephen Kinzer, *Blood of Brothers: Life and War in Nicaragua* (New York: G. P. Putnam's Sons, 1991), 131.

85. Kagan, 303; Sklar, 162–164; Robert Turner, *Nicaragua v. United States: A Look at the Facts* (Washington, DC: Pergamon-Brassey's, 1987), 140–141.

86. Kornbluth, 155; Sklar, 267.

87. "Hondo Receives U. S. Assistance," 86.

88. Frank McNeil, *War and Peace in Central America* (New York: Charles Scribner's Sons, 1988), 223.

89. Richard Stengel, "A Restrained Show of Force," *Time*, 28 March 1988, 16.

90. "Sandinista Offensive," Department of State Bulletin, May 1988, 73.

91. Ibid., 73.

92. Stengel, 16; Peter Range, "The End Game in Nicaragua," *US News & World Report*, 28 March 1988, 17; Harry Anderson 36; "Sandinista Offensive," 73.

93. "Sandinista Offensive," 73.

94. Range, 16–17; Harry Anderson, 37.

95. "Sandinista Offensive," 75; Kreischer, 37; Range, 17.

96. FM 7-98, 5-8.

97. Range, 17.

98. Stengel, 16.

99. "Sandinista Offensive," 74.

100. Stengel, 16.

101. FM 7-8, 5-8.

102. FM 90-26, *Airborne Operations* (Washington, DC: Headquarters, Dept. of the Army, 1990), 1–5.

103. Ned Ennis, "Exercise Golden Pheasant," *Military Review* (March 1989), 23.

104. Kornbluth, 152.

105. FM 7-98, 5-2.

106. Kreisher, 38; Ennis, 23.

107. Kreisher, 39.

108. Harry Anderson, 37.

109. FM 7-98, 5-6.

110. Kreisher, 39; Ennis, 22–23.

111. Ennis, 24.

112. Stengel, 16.

113. "Nicaraguan Complaint against United States Discussed in Council," *UN Chronicle*, 29 June 1988, 59.

114. Range, 16; Harry Anderson, 38.

115. Sklar, 386.

116. Range, 16.

117. Stengel, 16.

118. Thomas Anderson, "Politics and the Military in Honduras," *Current History*, December 1988, 431.

119. Jill Smolowe, "There Is No Plan B," *Time*, 25 April 1988, 35.

120. Harry Anderson, 37–38.

121. Range, 16–18; Stengel, 16.

122. Stengel, 17; Martz, 34–35.

123. Range, 16; Harry Anderson, 36; Zinti, 15.

124. Ennis, 26.

125. Schweizer, 127.

126. Haig, 129.

127. *Public Papers of the Presidents of the United States: Ronald Reagan, 1983* (Washington, DC: Government Printing Office, 1984), 605, 607.

128. Schweizer, 206.

129. "Nicaraguan Resistance and Sandinistas Reach Agreement," *Department of State Bulletin*, May 1988, 74; Stengel, 17.

130. Stengel, 17.

131. Kinzer, 387.

132. Charles Lane, "Who 'Won' Nicaragua?" *Newsweek*, 12 May 1990, 37.

133. Ceasar Sereseres, "The Nicaragua Resistance: A Case Study in U.S. Foreign Policy and Unconventional Warfare, 1981–1990" (Irvine, CA: University of California, 1990), 3; Lane, 37; Turner, 2.

134. Kinzer, 387.

135. Ibid., 387–388.

136. Ibid., 388.

137. Ibid., 391.

138. Harry Anderson, 38.

139. Lane, 37.

140. Thomas Walker, *Reagan versus the Sandinistas: The Undeclared War on Nicaragua* (Boulder, CO: Westview Press, 1987), 15.

141. Speaking of the damage done to US international credibility to persevere, Alexander Haig wrote, "Vietnam and its aftermath had made a deep impression." Haig, 96.

142. John Hunt, "Hostilities Short of War," *Military Review*, March 1993, 46.

Chapter 6

1. James Mead, "Lebanon Revisited," *Marine Corps Gazette*, September 1983, 64.

2. John Boykin, *Cursed Is the Peacemaker: The American Diplomat versus the Israeli General, Beirut 1982* (Belmont, CA: Applegate Press, 2002), 266.

3. The Department of Defense Commission was headed by retired Admiral Robert Long, and some sources refer to its findings as the Long Report. In this study, it is referred to as the Department of Defense Commission Report.

4. "United Nations Interim Force in Lebanon," http://www.un.org/en/peacekeeping/missions/unifil/background.shtml (accessed June 7, 2011); Daniel Bolger, *Savage Peace: Americans at War in the 1990s* (Novato, CA: Presidio Press, 1995), 169.

5. Robert Divine, *Since 1945: Politics and Diplomacy in Recent American History* (New York: McGraw-Hill, 1985), 204–208.

6. John Blum, et al., *The National Experience: Part Two; A History of the United States since 1865* (New York: Harcourt, Brace, Jovanovich, 1981), 854.

7. Thomas Paterson, et al., *American Foreign Policy: A History Since 1900* (New York: D. C. Heath and Company, 1991), 609–610.

8. Blum, 856.

9. Paterson, 632; Blum, 871–873.

10. "United Nations Interim Force in Lebanon."

11. Bolger, 169.

12. Blum, 873–876, 880–88; Paterson, 662.

13. Bolger, 169.

14. Ibid., 170–171; "United Nations Interim Force in Lebanon"; Caspar Weinberger, *Fighting*

for Peace (New York: Warner Books, 1990), 143. Hereafter, Weinberger, "Fighting."

15. Weinberger, "Fighting," 143.

16. See Boykin for a detailed and sympathetic account of Habib's efforts.

17. Bolger, 171; Weinberger, "Fighting," 143–144.

18. Bolger, 171; Weinberger, "Fighting," 144.

19. Boykin, 262–263; Bolger, 171; Weinberger, "Fighting," 144.

20. Bolger, 171.

21. Weinberger, "Fighting," 144–145.

22. Boykin, 311–312. See also Bolger, 198 and 200; Glenn Dolphin, *24 MAU: 1983, A Marine Looks Back at the Peacekeeping Mission in Beirut, Lebanon* (Baltimore: Publish America, 2005), 142; Edgar O'Ballance, *Civil War in Lebanon, 1975–92* (New York: St. Martin's Press, 1998), 132–133.

23. Bolger, 172; Weinberger, "Fighting," 150.

24. Boykin, 267.

25. Bolger, 172; Boykin, 267–269; Weinberger, "Fighting," 150–151.

26. Eric Hammel, *The Root: The Marines in Lebanon, August 1982–February 1984* (St. Paul, MN: Zenith Press, 1999), 14.

27. Bolger, 172; Boykin, 271.

28. Boykin, 272.

29. Robert Jordan, "They Came in Peace," *Marine Corps Gazette*, July 1984, 57.

30. For a detailed discussion, see Peter Rodman, *Presidential Command: Power, Leadership and the Making of Foreign Policy from Richard Nixon to George W. Bush* (New York: Alfred A. Knopf, 2009).

31. Hammel, 219.

32. Petit, 125.

33. John Garofano, *The Intervention Debate: Towards a Posture of Principled Judgment* (Carlisle, PA: Strategic Studies Institute, 2002), 19.

34. George Shultz, "Low-Intensity Warfare: The Challenge of Ambiguity," Department of State, *Current Policy*, No. 783, January 1986.

35. George Shultz, *Turmoil and Triumph: My Years as Secretary of State* (New York: Scribner's, 1993), 350. Hereafter Shultz, *Turmoil and Triumph*.

36. Weinberger, "Fighting," 159.

37. Ibid., 159.

38. Ibid.

39. Ibid., 150–152.

40. Ibid., 154; Hammel, xxiii..

41. Weinberger, "Fighting," 154.

42. Shultz, *Turmoil and Triumph*, 650.

43. Weinberger, "Fighting," 155–156.

44. Jordan, 57.

45. Weinberger, "Fighting," 156.

46. Chris Lawson, "Peacekeeping Turned Sour 10 Years Ago, Too," *Army Times*, October 25, 1993, 11.

47. "DoD Commission Reports on Beirut Terrorist Attack," *Marine Corps Gazette*, February 1984, 12. Hereafter "DoD Commission."

48. Weinberger, "Fighting," 151.

49. See Arthur Lykke, "Toward an Understanding of Military Strategy," in *Military Strategy: Theory and Application* (Carlisle, PA: U.S. Army War College, 1989), 3–8 as discussed in the previous chapter.

50. Bolger, 174.

51. Ibid., 174.

52. Ibid.

53. Ibid., 173.

54. Dolphin, 46.

55. Hammel, 38.

56. Bolger, 182.

57. Ibid., 204.

58. Ibid., 206, 174.

59. Jordan 57.

60. Weinberger, "Fighting," 152.

61. Ibid., 151–152.

62. Dolphin, 46.

63. Bolger, 173.

64. "DoD Commission," 12.

65. FM 100-5, *Operations* (Washington, DC: Headquarters, Dept. of the Army, 1993), 13–7.

66. Weinberger, "Fighting," 152.

67. FM 100-5, 13-7.

68. Weinberger, "Fighting," 153.

69. FM 100-5, 13-7.

70. "The Application of Peace Enforcement Operations at the Brigade and Battalion White Paper" (Fort Benning, GA: U.S. Army Infantry School, 1994), 1.

71. FM 100-5, 13-0; Bruce Auster, "From Beirut to Somalia," *US News & World Report*, October 25, 1998, 34.

72. "DoD Commission," 10.

73. Ibid., 10; Mead, 71.

74. Mead, 73.

75. Mead, 73; Jordan, 56.

76. Bolger, 184.

77. "DoD Commission," 12.

78. Mead, 72.

79. Weinberger, "Fighting," 155–157. See also Bolger, 180–181.

80. Boykin, 307.

81. Ibid., 307. See also Ibid., 274–276, for a discussion of the Syrian and Israeli points of view going into the negotiations.

82. Hammel, 82–83.

83. Jordan, 57.

84. "DoD Commission," 12.

85. Bolger, 186–188.

86. Boykin, 310.

87. "Remarks of President Reagan and President Amin Gemayel of Lebanon Following Their Meetings, July 22, 1983," University of Texas Archives, http://www.reagan.utexas.edu/archives/speeches/1983/72283b.htm (accessed June 8, 2011).

88. Jordan, 59.
89. Boykin, 311.
90. Bolger, 188.
91. Jordan, 59; Bolger, 189–191.
92. House Armed Services Committee, *Review of the Adequacy of Security Arrangements for Marines in Lebanon*, 98 Congress, 1 session, December 15, 1983, 450.
93. Bolger, 191, 193.
94. Michael Petit, *Peacekeepers at War: A Marine's Account of the Beirut Catastrophe* (Boston: Faber and Faber, 1986), 113–114.
95. Bolger, 192.
96. Hammel, 215.
97. Ibid., 135.
98. Bolger, 194–195.
99. Dolphin, 143.
100. Hammel, 177.
101. Petit, 122.
102. Bolger, 195; Boykin, 310–311.
103. Bolger, 196–197.
104. Jordan, 61.
105. Ibid.
106. Hammel, 216.
107. Boykin, 311.
108. Petit, 132.
109. "Letter to the Speaker of the House and the President Pro Tempore of the Senate Reporting on United States Participation in the Multinational Force in Lebanon," September 29, 1982. University of Texas Archives. http://www.reagan.utexas.edu/archives/speeches/1982/92982e.htm (accessed June 10, 2011).
110. Weinberger, "Fighting," 154. See also Hammel, 18.
111. Bolger, 174.
112. Weinberger, "Fighting," 152.
113. "DoD Commission," 10.
114. Bolger, 174.
115. Hammel, 53.
116. Ibid.
117. Ibid., 54–55.
118. Bolger, 183.
119. Ibid., 177–178.
120. Boykin, 254. See also Boykin, 277 and 290–292, for early American problems with the Israelis.
121. "Letter to the Speaker of the House and the President Pro Tempore of the Senate Reporting on United States Participation in the Multinational Force in Lebanon," September 29, 1982.
122. Bolger, 178.
123. Hammel, 57.
124. Mead, 70; Bolger, 179.
125. Robin Wright, *Sacred Rage* (New York: Touchstone Simon and Schuster, 2001), 107.
126. Bolger, 180.
127. Mead, 72.
128. Bolger, 182.
129. Auster, 35.
130. Bolger, 192.
131. FM 100-5, 13-7.
132. Bolger, 192.
133. "The Application of Peace Enforcement Operations at the Brigade and Battalion White Paper," 1.
134. Weinberger, "Fighting," 154.
135. Ibid., 152.
136. Petit, 136.
137. Jordan, 61.
138. Hammel, 281.
139. "DoD Commission," 11.
140. Ibid., 11, 12; Bolger, 193, 208.
141. Jordan, 62.
142. "DoD Commission," 12.
143. Lawson, 11.
144. Hammel, 279.
145. Weinberger, "Fighting," 160.
146. Ibid., 157.
147. Jordan, 62; Auster, 35.
148. "DoD Commission," 11.
149. Weinberger, "Fighting," 157–158.
150. Bolger, 203.
151. House Committee on Appropriations, *Situation in Lebanon and Grenada: Hearings before a Subcommittee of the House Committee on Appropriations,* 98 Congress, 1 session, November 8, 1983, 19.
152. Kenneth Banta, "Visibility vs. Vulnerability," *Time*, November 7, 1983, 39.
153. "DoD Commission," 11.
154. Ibid., 13.
155. Bolger, 176–177.
156. Petit, 103.
157. Jordan, 62.
158. Ibid.
159. "DoD Commission," 12.
160. Jordan, 62. See also Petit, 183.
161. Dolphin, 46; Hammel, 433.
162. Dolphin, 46.
163. Petit, 99–100.
164. "DoD Commission," 12.
165. Herman Broadstone, "Rules of Engagement in Military Operations Other Than War, From Beirut to Bosnia," *Small Wars Journal*, http://smallwarsjournal.com/documents/broadstone.pdf (accessed June 12, 2011).
166. Benis Frank, *US Marines in Lebanon 1982–1984* (Washington, DC: History and Museums Division, Headquarters U.S. Marine Corps, 1987), 63.
167. "DoD Commission," 12.
168. Banta, 39.
169. Jordan, 62.
170. Hammel, 292–293; Bolger, 211.
171. Bolger, 211.
172. Jordan, 63.
173. John Abizaid, "Lessons for Peacekeepers," *Military Review* 73 (March 1993): 18.
174. Jordan, 62.

175. Ibid., 62; Petit, 184.
176. Jordan, 61, 62.
177. James Kelly, "Aftermath in Bloody Beirut," *Time*, November 7, 1983, 32.
178. Petit, 183.
179. Hammel, 421.
180. Kelly, 38.
181. O'Ballance, 133–134; Weinberger, "Fighting," 166–167.
182. Divine, 242.
183. Hammel, 423.
184. Weinberger, "Fighting," 167.
185. Hammel, xxii.
186. Caspar Weinberger, "The Uses of Military Power," *Defense 85*, January 1985, 2. Hereafter, Weinberger, "Power."
187. Ibid., 10.
188. Ibid., 3.
189. Ibid., 9.
190. Ibid., 3.
191. Ibid., 10.
192. Ibid., 8–9.
193. Ibid., 10.
194. Edwin Arnold, "The Use of Military Power in Pursuit of National Interests," *Parameters* (Spring 1994): 7–8.
195. Weinberger, "Power," 10; David Jablonsky, "The Persistence of Credibility: Interests, Threats and Planning for the Use of American Military Power," in *US Army War College Guide to Strategy*, ed. Joseph Cerami and James Holcomb (Carlisle, PA: U.S. Army War College, 2001), 45.
196. Hammel, 215.
197. Ibid.
198. Based on the by-name list of "US Servicemen Killed in Lebanon September 1982–February 1984" in Ibid., 435–438. There were, of course, non-military personnel killed as well.

Chapter 7

1. Kimberly Martin, "Warlordism in Comparative Perspective," *International Security* 31, no. 3 (Winter 2006): 41.
2. Helen Metz, ed., *Somalia: A Country Study* (Washington, DC: Headquarters, Dept. of the Army, 1993), xiv, xxx–xxxiv; Frederick Fleitz, *Peacekeeping Fiascoes of the 1990s: Causes, Solutions, and U.S. Interests* (Westport, CN: Praeger, 2002), 130–131; "UN-mandated Force Seeks to Halt Tragedy: Operation Restore Hope," *UN Chronicle*, March 1993, 14.
3. S. L. Arnold, "Somalia: An Operation Other Than War," *Military Review* (December 1993), 35; *U.S. Army Forces, Somalia, 10th Mountain Division (LI), AAR Summary* (Fort Drum, NY: Headquarters, 10th Mountain Division, 1993), 25. Hereafter, *10th Mountain AAR*.
4. Kenneth Allard, *Somalia Operations:*

Lessons Learned. (Washington, DC: National Defense University Press, 1995), 28.
5. Edwin Arnold, "The Use of Military Power in Pursuit of National Interests," in *Parameters* (Spring 94): 5–7. Several alternatives to the Weinberger Doctrine were put forward in the aftermath of the Cold War. President George Bush's Chairman of the Joint Chiefs of Staff, General Colin Powell, argued that force should be used only as a last resort, there should be a clear-cut military objective, that the military objective must be measurable, and that military force should only be used in an overwhelming fashion. While similar in most ways to the Weinberger Doctrine, Powell's criteria significantly omitted the requirement of vital interest. However, others such as President Bill Clinton's Secretary of Defense Les Aspin did not feel that Powell's criteria went far enough in recognizing the changed world environment. At particular issue was the idea of using the military only as a last resort. Aspin and others argued for a more activist role in what is known as the "limited objective school." The heart of this thinking is that the military can be applied in one place to compel an adversary to change his behavior elsewhere. President Bush was also one of those who viewed the military as one of the means available at any time to achieve national interests, not only the means of last resort. See Ibid., 8–9.
6. Ibid., 10–11.
7. Michael Mandelbaum, "The Reluctance to Intervene," *Foreign Policy* 95 (Summer 1994): 10.
8. Nik Gowing. "Real Time Television Coverage of Armed Conflicts and Diplomatic Crises: Does It Pressure or Distort Foreign Policy Decisions?" (The Joan Shorenstein Center for Press, Politics, and Public Policy, 1994), 49.
9. Craig Hines, "Pity, Not U. S. Security, Motivated Use of GIs in Somalia, Bush Says," *The Houston Chronicle*, 24 Oct 1999.
10. *10th Mountain AAR*, 1.
11. Speech by Anthony Lake to the TransAfrica Forum, Washington, DC June 29, 1995, in *US Department of State Dispatch* 6, no. 27 (July 3, 1995): 539.
12. David Pearce, *Wary Partners—Diplomats and the Media* (Washington, DC: Congressional Quarterly, 1995), 18.
13. "Confrontation in the Gulf: Transcript of President's Address to Joint Session of Congress," *New York Times*, 12 September 1990, http://www.nytimes.com/1990/09/12/us/con frontation-gulf-transcript-president-s-address-joint-session-congress.html.
14. Robert Bauman and Lawrence Yates, *"My Clan Against the World": US and Coalition Forces in Somalia; 1992–1994* (Fort Leavenworth, KS: Combat Studies Institute Press, 2004), 24; Robert

Oakley, "An Envoy's Perspective," *Joint Forces Quarterly* (Autumn 1993), 45.

15. Russell Watson, "It's Our Fight Now," *Newsweek,* 14 December 1992, 31.

16. Donald Snow, *Peacekeeping, Peacemaking and Peace Enforcement: The US Role in the New International Order* (Carlisle, PA: U.S. Army War College, 1993), 3.

17. *10th Mountain Division AAR*, 4.

18. Ibid.*,*34.

19. Baumann, 24.

20. *10th Mountain Division AAR,* 49.

21. The two principle components of JTF Somalia were 16,200 marines from the I Marine Expeditionary Force and 10, 200 soldiers from the 10 Mountain Division. See Baumann, 31.

22. Baumann, 85–88.

23. Ibid., 100.

24. Ibid., 101.

25. James Dobbins, et al., *America's Role in Nation-Building: From Germany to Iraq* (Santa Monica, CA: RAND, 2003), 59–60.

26. "Senator calls for Somalia pullout," *Columbus Ledger-Enquirer,* 14 July 1993. In fact, on October 15, 1993, the U.S. Senate adopted an amendment proposed by Byrd to cut off funds for military operations in Somalia after March 31, 1994 unless the president obtained additional spending authority from Congress. See P. L. 103–109, Section 8151.

27. See Kenneth Allard, "Lessons Unlearned: Somalia and Joint Doctrine," *Joint Forces Quarterly* (Autumn 1995): 109 for a characterization of operations in Somalia as "muddling." Hereafter cited as Allard, "Lessons Unlearned." See Donald Snow, *When America Fights: The Use of US Military Force* (Washington, DC: CQ Press, 2000), 111 for a criticism of the halfhearted nature of U.S. state-building efforts in Somalia.

28. Bruce Auster and Louise Lief, "What Went Wrong in Somalia?" *U. S. News & World Report,* 18 October 1993, 37.

29. *10th Mountain Division AAR,* 7. See also pages 20 and 48.

30. Oakley, 47–48. "Technicals" were crew-served weapons mounted on trucks and other vehicles. Their name originated from their drivers' providing "technical assistance" as security for relief agencies.

31. Fleitz, 131.

32. Baumann, 34–35.

33. Ibid., 155. See also Allard, 65.

34. Baumann, 68.

35. Ibid., 68–69, 124–125.

36. Jonathan Dworken, "Rules of Engagement: Lessons from Restore Hope," *Military Review* (September 1994): 30.

37. Baumann, 94.

38. Ibid., 126.

39. Allard, 13.

40. "Report of the Commission of Inquiry Established Pursuant to Resolution 885 (1993) to Investigate Armed Attacks on UNOSOM II Personnel," 117, UN Doc. S/1994/653 (June 1, 1994, reprinted in *The United Nations and Somalia*), 376.

41. Ruth Spaller, "Combat: 3 Bn 75 Rangers Face Ultimate Challenge in Somalia," *The Bayonet,* 12 November 1993.

42. Dworken, "Rules of Engagement," 28.

43. Allard, 71.

44. Ibid., 65.

45. Baumann, 131; TC 7–98–1, *Stability and Support Operations Training Support Package* (Washington, DC: Headquarters, Dept. of the Army, 1997), 2–445.

46. *10th Mountain Division AAR,* 55.

47. Oakley, 51.

48. Joseph Hoar, "A CINC's Perspective," *Joint Forces Quarterly* (Autumn 1993): 63.

49. Fleitz, 38.

50. John Hillen, "Peace(keeping) in Our Time: The UN as a Professional Military Manager," *Parameters* (Autumn 1996): 22.

51. Flietz, 9, 38; Hillen, 23.

52. Allard, 43.

53. FM 100-5, 13-7.

54. Allard, 89–90.

55. Jonathan Stevenson, "Hope Restored in Somalia?" *Foreign Policy,* no. 91 (Summer 1993): 150.

56. Robert Oakley, PBS FRONTLINE interview, "Ambush in Mogadishu," at http://www.pbs.org/wgbh/pages/frontline/shows/ambush/interviews/oakley.html

57. Baumann, 83.

58. Ibid., 37, 44.

59. Ibid., 48.

60. Ibid., 49.

61. Ibid., 68.

62. Ibid., 63. See also Allard, 13.

63. Allard, 61.

64. *10th Mountain Division AAR,* 39.

65. Hoar, 58. See also Stevenson, 139, and Allard, 68.

66. Allard, 8–9.

67. Dennis Jett, *Why Peacekeeping Fails* (New York: St. Martin's Press, 1999), 133.

68. Baumann, 82.

69. James Dobbins, et al., *The Beginner's Guide to Nation-Building* (Santa Monica, CA: RAND, 2007), 3.

70. Norman Cooling, "Operation Restore Hope in Somalia: A Tactical Action Turned Strategic Defeat," *Marine Corps Gazette,* September 2001, 95.

71. Allard, 13.

72. Thomas Montgomery, PBS FRONTLINE interview, "Ambush in Mogadishu," at http://

www.pbs.org/wgbh/pages/frontline/shows/amb
ush/interviews/montgomery.html.

73. S. L. Arnold, 33.

74. William Wunderle, *Through the Lens of Cultural Awareness: A Primer for US Armed Forces Deploying to Arab and Middle Eastern Countries* (Fort Leavenworth, KS: Combat Studies Institute, 2006), 133–134.

75. Lawrence Yates, "Military Stability and Support Operations: Analogies, Patterns and Recurring Themes," *Military Review* 72, no. 4 (July–Aug. 1997): 57.

76. Yates, 57.

77. Oakley FRONTLINE interview.

78. Allard, 13.

79. Jett, 134–135.

80. *10th Mountain Division AAR*, 7, 52–53.

81. Jonathan Dworken, "Restore Hope: Coordinating Relief Operations," *Joint Forces Quarterly* (Summer 1995): 16.

82. Dobbins, *Beginner's Guide*, xxiii

83. "US Frees Somali capital," *Columbus Ledger-Enquirer*, 10 December 1992.

84. *10th Mountain Division AAR*, 4–5.

85. Ibid., 35.

86. Ibid.

87. Ibid., 36.

88. Ibid., 34.

89. Ibid., 36.

90. Ibid., 35–36.

91. Baumann, 70–71.

92. Ibid., 73.

93. Montgomery FRONTLINE interview; Baumann, 116, 155.

94. Chris Lawson, "Peacekeeping Turned Sour 10 Years Ago, Too," *Army Times,* October 25, 1993, 11.

95. Ibid., 11. See also Bruce Auster, "From Beirut to Somalia," *US News & World Report,* October 25, 1993, 33–35.

96. Bill Clinton, Speech to the Nation, 7 Oct 1993.

97. George Church, "Anatomy of a Disaster," *Time,* 18 Oct 1993, 46.

98. *10th Mountain Division AAR*, 35.

99. Ibid., 20.

100. Andrew Natsios, *US Foreign Policy and the Four Horsemen of the Apocalypse: Humanitarian Relief in Complex Emergencies* (Westport, CN: Praeger, 1997), 142. See also Allard, 67.

101. *10th Mountain Division AAR*, i.

102. Dworken, "Restore Hope," 19–20.

103. Baumann, 79.

104. Naksios, 143.

105. Baumann, 53–54, 76–77; Allard, 69–70.

106. James Fearon and David Laitin, "Neotrusteeship and the Problem of Weak States," *International Security* 28, no. 4 (Spring 2004): 32.

107. *10th Mountain Division AAR*, 74.

108. Ibid., 73.

109. Ibid.

110. Allard, 56.

111. *10th Mountain Division AAR*, 73.

112. "UNOSOM Objectives Affirmed, Despite Continuing Violence," *UN Chronicle*, December 1993, 25.

113. "U.N. Special Envoy Calls for Unity among Peacekeepers in Somalia," *Columbus Ledger-Enquirer*, 16 July 1993.

114. "The Pitfalls of Peacekeeping," *Newsweek*, 26 July 1993, 32.

115. "U.N. Special Envoy Calls for Unity among Peacekeepers in Somalia," *Columbus Ledger-Enquirer*, 16 July 1993.

116. Marguerite Michaels, "Peacemaking War," *Time*, July 26, 1993, 48. The Italians ultimately requested to be pulled out of Mogadishu and were assigned a less volatile sector in northern Somalia. See "US Troops Fire on Marchers," *Columbus-Ledger Enquirer*, 13 August 1993.

117. "The Pitfalls of Peacekeeping," 32.

118. Samuel Huntington, *The Clash of Civilizations and the Remaking of the World Order* (New York: Simon & Schuster, 1996), 131.

119. Michaels, 48.

120. Ibid.

121. Jett, 50; Allard, 32–35.

122. Charles Ferry, "Mogadishu, October 1993: Personal Account of a Rifle Company XO," *Infantry* (September–October 1994): 26.

123. Ibid., 27.

124. Ibid.

125. Ibid.

126. Ibid.

127. Ibid., 28.

128. Ibid., 29.

129. Ibid., 30.

130. Ibid., 31.

131. J. B. Burton, "MOUT in Mogadishu" (presentation to the Infantry Officers Advanced Course, Fort Benning, GA, November 5, 1993).

132. Tom Donnelly and Katherine McIntire, "Anatomy of a Firefight: Rangers in Somalia," *Army Times*, 15 October 1993, 18.

133. Eric Schmitt, "Reinforcements for U. S. Troops Delayed 9 Hours," *New York Times*, 6 October 1993.

134. Ibid., A7.

135. Allard, 60.

136. Baumann, 156–157. See also Allard, 57–58.

137. Baumann, 157.

138. Jett, 174.

139. Ibid., 173–174.

140. Ibid., 147–148.

141. Edward Luttwark, "Wrong Place, Wrong Time," *New York Times*, 22 July 1993.

142. Oakley says, "My own personal estimate

is that there must have been 1,500 to 2,000 Somalis killed and wounded that day." Oakley FRONTLINE interview.

143. David Rieff, "A New Age of Imperialism?" *World Policy Journal* 16, no. 2 (Summer 1999): 5.

144. Max Boot, *The Savage Wars of Peace: Small Wars and the Rise of American Power* (New York: Basic Books, 2002), 329.

145. Montgomery FRONTLINE interview.

146. Walter Clarke. PBS FRONTLINE interview, "Ambush in Mogadishu" http://www.pbs.org/wgbh/pages/frontline/shows/ambush/interviews/clarke.html.

147. Michael Maren, "Somalia: Whose Failure?" *Current History: A Journal of Contemporary World Affairs* 95, no. 601 (May 1996): 202.

148. Jett, 143.

149. Ibid., 151.

150. Francis Fukuyama, *State-Building: Governance and World Order in the 21st Century* (Ithaca, NY: Cornell University Press, 2004), 38–41.

151. Dobbins, *America's Role*, 68 and 69.

152. Jett, 3.

153. Ibid., 170.

154. Stephen Walt, "Two Cheers for Clinton's Foreign Policy," *Foreign Affairs* 79, no. 2: 77; Douglas Brinkley, "Democratic Enlargement: The Clinton Doctrine," *Foreign Policy*, no. 106 (Spring 1997): 119; Jett, 42–43.

155. Jett, 4, 169–170.

156. Sarah Childress and Abdinasir Mohamed, "Somali Troops Gird for Battle with Militants," *The Wall Street Journal*, 9 February 2010.

157. Ibid.

158. James Wombwell, *The Long War against Piracy: Historical Trends* (Fort Leavenworth, KS: Combat Studies Institute Press, 2010), 144.

159. Ibid., 153.

160. Ibid., 149, 154.

161. Ibid., 156.

162. S. L. Arnold, 31.

163. Fukuyama, 99.

164. Allard, 89–90.

165. Ibid., 93.

166. Allard, 91.

167. Fukuyama, 100.

168. Ibid.

169. Ibid., 37.

Chapter 8

1. Walter Kretchik, Robert Baumann, and John Fishel, *Invasion, Intervention, "Intervasion": A Concise History of the US Army in Operation Uphold Democracy* (Fort Leavenworth, KS, 1998), 18–19.

2. Ibid., 19–20.

3. J. Christopher Kovats-Bernat, "Fac-

tional Terror, Paramilitarism and Civil War in Haiti: The View from Port-au-Prince, 1994–2004," *Anthropologica* 48, no. 1: 130.

4. Kretchik, 33; Richard Melanson, *American Foreign Policy since the Vietnam War: The Search for Consensus from Nixon to Clinton* (Armonk: NY: M. E. Sharpe, 1996), 262–263.

5. Kretchik, 34.

6. Ibid., 34.

7. Kate Doyle, "Hollow Diplomacy in Haiti," *World Policy Journal* 11, no. 1 (Spring 1994): 54.

8. Kretchik, 34–35.

9. An "accurate representation of the original text" of the Governor's Island Accord is found at Kretchik, 247–248.

10. UNSCR 847, September 23, 1993. http://daccess-dds-ny.un.org/doc/UNDOC/GEN/N93/515/30/PDF/N9351530.pdf?OpenElement (accessed May 12, 2011).

11. James Pulley, Stephen Epstein, and Robert Cronin, "JTF Haiti: A United Nations Foreign Internal Defense Mission," *Special Warfare*, July 1994, 3.

12. Kretchik, 37.

13. Ibid., 35.

14. Doyle, 55.

15. Kretchik, 36–37; Peter Riehm, "The USS *Harlan County* Affair," *Military Review* 77, no. 4 (July–August 1994): 32.

16. Doyle, 55.

17. Kretchick, 32.

18. Ibid., 35.

19. Ibid., 35. See also Riehm, 31–32.

20. Kretchik, 36.

21. Riehm, 32; Kretchik, 36.

22. Pulley, 9.

23. Ibid., 8.

24. Doyle, 55.

25. Riehm, 32.

26. See Kevin Dougherty, "Mission Analysis in OOTW," *Combat Training Center (CTC) Quarterly Bulletin 3d Qtr, FY 95* (Fort Leavenworth, KS: Center for Army Lessons Learned, 1995) for a more detailed discussion of this phenomenon.

27. Pulley, 5.

28. Kretchik, 38–40.

29. Riehm, 32; Kretchin, 40.

30. Riehm, 34.

31. Christopher Mitchell, "US Policy toward Haitian Boat People, 1972–93," *Annals of the American Academy of Political and Social Science* 534 (July 1994): 74; Melanson, 262.

32. Mitchell, 75.

33. Ibid.

34. Melanson, 262.

35. "Two Decades Later, Mariel Boat Lift Refugees Still Feel Effects of Riot," *Los Angeles Times*, May 5, 2001. http://articles.latimes.com/

2001/may/05/news/mn-59567 (accessed May 12, 2011).

36. "Cuban Refugee Crisis," *Arkansas Encyclopedia of History and Culture,* http://www.encyclopediaofarkansas.net/encyclopedia/entry-detail.aspx?entryID=4248 (accessed May 12, 2011).

37. Steven Greenhouse, "Freewheeling Ways Pay Off for the White House," *New York Times,* September 11, 1994.

38. Robert Keohane and Joseph Nye, *Power and Independence,* 2nd ed. (Cambridge, MA: Center for International Affairs, Harvard University with Harper Collins Publishers, 1989), 26.

39. Glenn Hastedt, *American Foreign Policy: Past, Present, Future* (Upper Saddle River, NJ: Pearson, 2009), 266.

40. Ibid., 274.

41. Raymond Copson, *The Congressional Black Caucus and Foreign Policy* (Hauppauge, NY: Nova Science Pub, 2003), 38.

42. Hastedt, 274.

43. Melanson, 263.

44. Tom Masland, "Should We Invade Haiti?" *Newsweek,* July 18, 1994, 42.

45. Melanson, 263.

46. Jeffrey Record, "A Note on Interests, Values, and the Use of Force," *Parameters* (Spring 2001): 16.

47. Michael Mandelbaum, "Foreign Policy as Social Work," *Foreign Affairs* 75, no. 1 (Jan.–Feb., 1996), 17.

48. Ibid., 22.

49. Hastedt, 274.

50. Mandelbaum, 22.

51. Ian Martin, "Haiti: Mangled Multilateralism," *Foreign Policy,* no. 95 (Summer, 1994): 80–81; Pulley, 8.

52. Ibid., 85.

53. Doyle, 53.

54. Pulley, 3–4.

55. Riehm, 32; Kretchik, 35–36.

56. Pulley, 7.

57. Ibid.

58. Ibid.

59. Martin, 78–79.

60. Pulley, 7.

61. Ibid., 9.

62. UNSCR 847, September 23, 1993, http://daccess-dds-ny.un.org/doc/UNDOC/GEN/N93/515/30/PDF/N9351530.pdf?OpenElement (accessed May 12, 2011); Kretchik, 37.

63. Riehm, 33; Kretchin, 38.

64. Ibid.

65. Riehm, 33; Kretchin, 39.

66. Riehm, 33; Kretchin, 38.

67. Riehm, 33–34; Kretchin, 39–40.

68. Riehm, 34; Kretchin, 40.

69. Riehm, 34–35; Kretchin, 40–41.

70. Riehm, 35; Kretchin, 41.

71. Pulley, 9.

72. Riehm, 35; Kretchin, 41.

73. Richard Millet, "Panama and Haiti," in *US and Russian Policy Making with Respect to the Use of Force,* ed. Jeremey Azrael and Emil Payin (Santa Monica, CA: RAND Corporation, 1996), 154.

74. Riehm, 34.

75. Pulley, 8.

76. Martin, 79.

77. Pulley, 8.

78. Riehm, 34:Kretchik, 40.

79. Riehm, 34.

80. Steven Holmes, "Bid to Restore Haiti's Leader is Derailed," *New York Times,* October 13, 1993, http://www.nytimes.com/1993/10/13/world/bid-to-restore-haiti-s-leader-is-derailed.html?pagewanted=2&src=pm (accessed May 13, 2011).

81. See Doyle, 54, for a discussion on misplaced faith in Cedras.

82. Adam Siegel, *The Intervasion of Haiti* (Alexandria, VA: Center for Naval Analyses, 1996), 6.

83. Anthony Lewis, "Abroad at Home; Resolution Matters," *New York Times,* September 19, 1994, http://www.nytimes.com/1994/09/19/opinion/abroad-at-home-resolution-matters.html?pagewanted=2&src=pm (accessed May 13, 2011).

84. Riehm, 35.

85. Paul Horvitz, "Christopher Calls Plan by Senator 'Offensive' to the U.S. Constitution: White House Acts to Block Dole Move over Haiti," *New York Times,* October 19, 1993, http://www.nytimes.com/1993/10/19/news/19iht-haiti_9.html (accessed May 13, 2011).

86. Jeffrey Berejikian, "Model Building with Prospect Theory: A Cognitive Approach to International Relations," *Political Psychology* 23, no. 4 (December 2002), 759.

87. Robert Jervis, "Political Implications of Loss Aversion," *Political Psychology* 13, no. 2 (June 1992): 194.

88. Martin, 86.

89. Doyle, 56.

90. Linda Miller, "The Clinton Years: Reinventing US Foreign Policy?" *International Affairs* 70, no. 4 (Oct., 1994): 627–628.

91. Masland, 43.

92. Mandelbaum, 21.

Chapter 9

1. Carl von Clausewitz, *On War,* trans. Michael Howard and Peter Paret (Princeton, NJ: Princeton University Press, 1989), 579.

2. FM 100-5, 13-4.

3. Ibid., 13–4.

4. Peter Jakobsen, *Nordic Approaches to Peace Operations: A New Model in the Making,* Cass Series on Peacekeeping (New York: Routledge, 2006), 2.

Bibliography

Abizaid, John. "Lessons for Peacekeepers." *Military Review* 73 (March 1993): 11–19.

Allard, Kenneth. "Lessons Unlearned: Somalia and Joint Doctrine." *Joint Forces Quarterly* (Autumn 1995): 105–109.

_____. *Somalia Operations: Lessons Learned.* Washington, DC: National Defense University Press, 1995.

Anderson, Harry. "The Contras under the Gun." *Newsweek*, March 28, 1988.

Anderson, Thomas. "Politics and the Military in Honduras." *Current History* (December 1988): 425–431.

Andrade, Dale, and James Willbanks. "CORDS/ Phoenix: Counterinsurgency Lessons from Vietnam for the Future." *Military Review* (March–April 2006): 77–91.

"The Application of Peace Enforcement Operations at the Brigade and Battalion White Paper." Fort Benning, GA: US Army Infantry School, 1994.

Arnold, Edwin. "The Use of Military Power in Pursuit of National Interests." *Parameters* (Spring 1994): 4–12.

Arnold, S. L. "Somalia: An Operation Other Than War." *Military Review* (December 1993): 26–35.

Arreguin-Toft, Ivan. "How the Weak Win Wars." *International Security* 26, no. 1 (Summer 2001): 93–128.

Auster, Bruce. "From Beirut to Somalia." *US News & World Report*, October 25, 1993.

Auster, Bruce, and Louise Lief. "What Went Wrong in Somalia?" *US News & World Report*, October 18, 1993.

Banta, Kenneth. "Visibility vs. Vulnerability." *Time*, November 7, 1983.

Barnes, Rudolph. "Military Legitimacy in OOTW: Civilians as Mission Priorities." *Special Warfare*, Fall 1999, 32–43.

Barrett, Roby. *The Greater Middle East and the Cold War: US Foreign Policy under Eisen-*

hower and Kennedy. New York: I. B. Tauris, 2007.

Bauman, Robert, and Lawrence Yates. *"My Clan Against the World": US and Coalition Forces in Somalia; 1992–1994.* Fort Leavenworth, KS: Combat Studies Institute Press, 2004.

Bennett, Andrew, and Colin Elman. "Case Study Methods." In *The Oxford Handbook of International Relations,* edited by Christian Reus-Smit and Duncan Snidal, 499–517. New York: Oxford University Press, 2008.

Berg, Bruce. *Qualitative Research Methods for the Social Sciences.* Boston: Allyn and Bacon, 2001.

Berejikian, Jeffrey. "Model Building with Prospect Theory: A Cognitive Approach to International Relations." *Political Psychology* 23, no. 4 (December 2002): 759–786.

Birgisson, Karl Th. "United Nations Special Commission on the Balkans." In *The Evolution of UN Peacekeeping: Case Studies and Comparative Analysis,* edited by William Durch, 77–83. New York: St. Martin's Press, 1993.

Birtle, Andrew. *US Army Counterinsurgency and Counterinsurgency Operations Doctrine, 1942–1976.* Washington, DC: Center of Military History, 2006.

Black, C. E. "Greece and the United Nations." *Political Science Quarterly* 63, no. 4 (December 1948): 551–568.

Blaufarb, Douglas. *The Counterinsurgency Era: US Doctrine and Performance 1950 to the Present.* New York: The Free Press, 1977.

Blum, John, et al. *The National Experience: Part Two; A History of the United States since 1865.* New York: Harcourt, Brace, Jovanovich, 1981.

Bolger, Daniel. *Savage Peace: Americans at War in the 1990s.* Novato, CA: Presidio, 1995.

Boot, Max. *The Savage Wars of Peace: Small Wars and the Rise of American Power.* New York: Basic Books, 2002.

Boykin, John. *Cursed Is the Peacemaker: The American Diplomat Versus the Israeli General,*

Beirut 1982. Belmont, CA: Applegate Press, 2002.

Brasel, Richard. "Operation Joint Endeavor: Operational Guidance from the Principles of Operations Other Than War." Paper, Naval War College, 1996.

Brigham, Erwin. "Pacification Measurement." *Military Review,* May 1970, 47–55.

Brinkley, Douglas. "Democratic Enlargement: The Clinton Doctrine." *Foreign Policy,* no. 106 (Spring 1997): 111–127.

Broadstone, Herman. "Rules of Engagement in Military Operations Other Than War, From Beirut to Bosnia." *Small Wars Journal.* Accessed June 12, 2011. http://smallwarsjournal.com/documents/broadstone.pdf.

Burton, J. B. "MOUT in Mogadishu." Presentation to the Infantry Officers Advanced Course, Fort Benning, GA, November 5, 1993.

Catton, Philip. *Diem's Final Failure: Prelude to America's War in Vietnam.* Lawrence: University Press of Kansas, 2003.

Center for Strategic Studies. *Dominican Action-1965: Intervention or Cooperation?* Washington, DC: Georgetown University, 1966.

Chamberlain, Edwin. "Pacification." *Infantry* (November–December 1968):32–39.

Chamberlin, Stephen. "The Greek Situation." Report to Chief of Staff Army, October 20, 1947.

Chew, Peter. "On a Lonely Point." *Army,* June 1965, 92–94.

Childress, Sarah, and Abdinasir Mohamed. "Somali Troops Gird for Battle with Militants." *The Wall Street Journal,* 19 February 2010.

Church, George. "Anatomy of a Disaster." *Time,* 18 Oct 1993, 40–50.

Clarke, Jeffrey. *The United States Army in Vietnam, Advice and Support: The Final Years, 1965–1973.* Washington, DC: Center of Military History, 1988.

Clarke, Walter. "Ambush in Mogadishu." PBS Frontline. http://www.pbs.org/wgbh/pages/frontline/shows/ambush/interviews/clarke.html (accessed 22 June 2010).

Clausewitz, Carl von. *On War.* Edited by Michael Howard and Peter Paret. Princeton: Princeton University Press, 1976.

Cleland, John. "Principle of the Objective and Vietnam." *Military Review* (July 1966): 82–86.

CNN.com. "Senate Passes Iraq Withdraw Bill; Veto Threat Looms." http://www.cnn.com/2007/POLITICS/04/26/congress.iraq/index.html?eref=rss_topstories (accessed April 26, 2007).

Coffey, Ross. "Revisiting CORDS: The Need for Unity of Effort to Secure Victory in Iraq." *Military Review* (March–April 2006): 8–18.

Colby, William. *Lost Victory: A Firsthand Account of America's Sixteen-Year Involvement in Vietnam.* New York: Contemporary Books, 1990.

Commander, TRADOC. "Commander TRADOC's Philosophy on Term "Operations Other Than War.'" Personal For message DTG 272016Z Oct 95. Released by Colonel Robert Killebrew, HQ TRADOC, 31 March 1997.

Condit, D. M., et al. *Challenge and Response in Internal Conflict: The Experience in Europe and the Middle East.* Washington, DC: American University, 1967.

"Contra Aid." *Congressional Digest* (March 1988): 67–71, 96.

"Contra Victory." *National Review,* April 25, 1986, 17–18.

"Confrontation in the Gulf: Transcript of President's Address to Joint Session of Congress." *New York Times,* 12 September 1990. http://www.nytimes.com/1990/09/12/us/confrontation-gulf-transcript-president-s-address-joint-session-congress.html (accessed April 21, 2010).

Cooling, Norman. "Operation Restore Hope in Somalia: A Tactical Action Turned Strategic Defeat." *Marine Corps Gazette* (September 2001): 92–106.

Copson, Raymond. *The Congressional Black Caucus and Foreign Policy.* Hauppauge NY: Nova Science Pub., 2003.

Costa, John. "The Dominican Republic: Intervention in Perspective." Carlisle Barracks, PA: US Army War College, 1968.

Cowan, John. "Operation Provide Comfort: Operational Analysis for Operations Other Than War." Paper, Naval War College, 1995.

"Cuban Refugee Crisis." *Arkansas Encyclopedia of History and Culture.* http://www.encyclopediaofarkansas.net/encyclopedia/entry-detail.aspx?entryID=4248 (accessed May 12, 2011).

Daddis, Gregory. *No Sure Victory: Measuring US Army Effectiveness and Progress in the Vietnam War.* New York: Oxford University Press, 2011.

Davidson, Phillip. *Vietnam at War: The History, 1946–1975.* Novato, CA: Presidio Press, 1988.

Divine, Robert. *Since 1945: Politics and Diplomacy in Recent American History.* New York: McGraw-Hill, 1985.

Dobbins, James, et al. *America's Role in Nation-Building: From Germany to Iraq.* Santa Monica, CA: RAND, 2003.

_____, et al. *The Beginner's Guide to Nation-Building.* Santa Monica, CA: RAND, 2007.

_____, et al. *The UN's Role in Nation-Building: From the Congo to Iraq.* Santa Monica, CA: RAND, 2005.

"DoD Commission Reports on Beirut Terrorist Attack." *Marine Corps Gazette* (February 1984): 10–13.

Dolphin, Glenn. *24 MAU: 1983, A Marine Looks*

Back at the Peacekeeping Mission in Beirut, Lebanon. Baltimore, MD: Publish America, 2005.

Donnelly, Tom, and Katherine McIntire. "Anatomy of a Firefight: Rangers in Somalia," *Army Times,* 15 October 1993.

Dougherty, Kevin. "Mission Analysis in OOTW." In *Combat Training Center (CTC) Quarterly Bulletin 3d Qtr, FY 95.* Fort Leavenworth, KS: Center for Army Lessons Learned, 1995.

Doughty, Robert. *American Military History and the Evolution of Western Warfare.* Lexington, MA: D. C. Heath and Company, 1996.

Doyle, Kate. "Hollow Diplomacy in Haiti." *World Policy Journal* 11, no. 1 (Spring 1994): 50–58.

Dunlap, Charles, Jr. "The Origins of the American Military Coup of 2012." *Parameters* (Winter 1992–1993): 2–20.

Dworken, Jonathan. "Restore Hope: Coordinating Relief Operations." *Joint Forces Quarterly* (Summer 1995): 14–20.

_____. "Rules of Engagement: Lessons from Restore Hope." *Military Review* (September 1994): 26–34.

Edwards, Sean. *Swarming and the Future of Warfare.* Santa Monica, CA: RAND, 2005.

Eich, Dieter, and Carlos Rincon. *The Contras.* San Francisco: Synthesis Publications, 1984.

Eisenhower, Dwight. "Special Message to the Congress on the Situation in the Middle East" (January 5, 1957). "American Presidency Project" http://www.presidency.ucsb.edu/ws/index.php?pid=11007&st=&st1=#ixzz1LJwwpYaY (accessed 3 May 2011).

Ennis, Ned B. "Exercise Golden Pheasant." *Military Review* (March 1989): 20–26.

Ewell, Julian, and Ira Hunt. *Sharpening the Combat Edge: The Use of Analysis to Reinforce Military Judgment.* Washington, DC: Department of the Army, 1995.

Fastabend, David. "The Categorization of Conflict." *Parameters* (Summer 1997): 75–87.

Feaver, Peter, and Richard Kohn. "The Gap: Soldiers, Civilians, and Their Mutual Misunderstanding." *National Interest* 61 (Fall, 2000): 29–37.

Ferry, Charles. "Mogadishu, October 1993: Personal Account of a Rifle Company XO." *Infantry* (September–October 1994): 23–31.

Fleitz, Frederick. *Peacekeeping Fiascoes of the 1990s: Causes, Solutions, and US Interests,* Westport, CN: Praeger, 2002.

FM 3–0, *Operations.* Washington, DC: Headquarters, Department of the Army, 2001.

FM 3–07, *Stability Operations and Support Operations.* Washington, DC: Headquarters, Department of the Army, 2003.

FM 3–24, *Counterinsurgency.* Washington, DC: Headquarters, Department of the Army, 2006.

FM 7–98, *Low-Intensity Conflict.* Washington, DC: Headquarters, Department of the Army, 1992.

FM 90–8, *Counterguerrilla Operations.* Washington, DC: Headquarters, Department of the Army, 1986.

FM 90–26, *Airborne Operations.* Washington, DC: Headquarters, Department of the Army, 1990.

FM 100–5, *Operations.* Washington, DC: Headquarters, Department of the Army, 1986.

FM 100–5, *Operations.* Washington, DC: Headquarters, Department of the Army, 1993.

FM 100–19, *Domestic Support Operations.* Washington, DC: Headquarters, Department of the Army, 1993.

FM 100–20, *Low Intensity Conflict.* Washington, DC: Headquarters, Department of the Army, 1981.

FM 100–23, *Peace Operations.* Washington, DC: Headquarters, Department of the Army, 1994.

Frank, Benis. *US Marines in Lebanon 1982–1984.* Washington, DC: History and Museums Division, Headquarters US Marine Corps, 1987.

Fulton, John. "The Debate About Low-intensity Conflict." *Military Review* (February 1986): 60–67.

Garofano, John. "The Intervention Debate: Towards a Posture of Principled Judgment." Carlisle, PA: Strategic Studies Institute, 2002.

George, Alexander, and Andrew Bennett. *Case Studies and Theory Development in Social Sciences.* Cambridge, MA: MIT Press, 2005.

Gibson, James William. *The Perfect War: Technology in Vietnam.* Boston, MA: The Atlantic Monthly Press, 1986.

Gray, David. *The US Intervention in Lebanon, 1958: A Commander's Reminiscence.* Fort Leavenworth, KS: Combat Studies Institute, 1984.

"Greece: A First-class War." *Time,* 24 July 1950.

"Greece: Winged Victory." *Time,* 24 October 1949.

"Greece: With Will to Win." *Time,* 23 May 1949.

Greenberg, Lawrence. *United States Army Unilateral and Coalition Operations in the 1965 Dominican Republic Intervention.* Washington, DC: US Army Center of Military History, 1987.

Greenhouse, Steven. "Freewheeling Ways Pay Off for the White House." *New York Times,* September 11, 1994.

Greentree, Todd. *The United States and the Politics of Conflict in the Developing World.* Washington, DC: Center for the Study of Foreign Affairs, 1990.

Grow, Michael. *US Presidents and Latin Ameri-*

can Interventions: Pursuing Regime Change in the Cold War. Lawrence: University Press of Kansas, 2008.

Growing, Nik. *Real Time Television Coverage of Armed Conflicts and Diplomatic Crises: Does it Pressure or Distort Foreign Policy Decisions?* Cambridge, MA: Joan Shorenstein Center for Press, Politics, and Public Policy, 1994.

Gurley, Michael. "Operation Earnest Will." Paper, US Naval War College, 1995.

Gutman, Roy. *Banana Diplomacy: The Making of American Policy in Nicaragua, 1981–1987.* New York: Simon and Schuster, 1988.

Hackworth, David. *The Vietnam Primer: Lessons Learned.* Sechelt, BC: Twin Eagles, 2003.

Haggerty, Richard, ed. *Dominican Republic and Haiti: Country Studies.* Washington, DC: Headquarters, Department of the Army, 1991.

Haig, Alexander. *Caveat: Realism, Reagan, and Foreign Policy.* New York: Macmillan, 1984.

Hammel, Eric. *The Root: The Marines in Lebanon, August 1982–February 1984.* St. Paul, MN: Zenith Press, 1999.

Handbook for Military Support to Pacification. San Francisco: Headquarters, United States Military Assistance Command, Vietnam, 1968.

Hastedt, Glenn. *American Foreign Policy: Past, Present, Future.* Upper Saddle River, NJ: Pearson, 2009.

Haughney, Edward. "OAS and the Use of Military Forces." Carlisle Barracks, PA: US Army War College, 1966.

Hemingway, Al. *Our War Was Different: Marine Combined Action Platoons in Vietnam.* Annapolis, MD: Naval Institute Press, 1994.

Herring, George. *America's Longest War: The United States and Vietnam, 1950–1975.* New York: Newberry Award Records, 1979.

Hickey, Gerald. *Accommodation and Coalition in South Vietnam.* Santa Monica, CA: RAND Corporation, 1972.

Hillen, John. "Peace(keeping) in Our Time: The UN as a Professional Military Manager." *Parameters* (Autumn 1996): 17–34.

_____. "UN Collective Security: Chapter Six and a Half." *Parameters* (Spring 1994): 27–37.

Hoar, Joseph. "A CINC's Perspective." *Joint Forces Quarterly* (Autumn 1993): 56–63.

Holmes, Steven. "Bid to Restore Haiti's Leader is Derailed." *New York Times*, October 13, 1993. http://www.nytimes.com/1993/10/13/world/bid-to-restore-haiti-s-leader-is-derailed.html?pagewanted=2&src=pm (accessed May 13, 2011).

Holsti, K. J. *International Politics: A Framework for Analysis.* Englewood Cliffs, NJ: Prentice-Hall, 1992.

"Honduras Receives US Assistance to Repel Sandinista Attacks." *Department of State Bulletin.* (May 1986): 86–87.

Horvitz, Paul. "Christopher Calls Plan By Senator 'Offensive' to the U.S. Constitution: White House Acts to Block Dole Move over Haiti." *New York Times*, October 19, 1993. http://www.nytimes.com/1993/10/19/news/19iht-haiti_9.html (accessed May 13, 2011).

Hosmer, Stephen, and George Tanham. *Countering Covert Aggression.* Santa Monica, CA: RAND, January 1986.

House Armed Services Committee. *Review of the Adequacy of Security Arrangements for Marines in Lebanon,* 98th Cong., 1st sess., 1983.

House Committee on Appropriations. *Situation in Lebanon and Grenada: Hearings before a Subcommittee of the House Committee on Appropriations.* 98th Cong., 1st sess., 1983.

Howard, Michael. *The Theory and Practice of War.* Bloomington: University of Indiana Press, 1975.

Hunt, John. "Emerging Doctrine for LIC." *Military Review* (June 1991): 51–60.

_____. "Hostilities Short of War." *Military Review* (March 1993): 41–50.

Huntington, Samuel. *The Clash of Civilizations and the Remaking of the World Order.* NY: Simon & Schuster, 1996.

_____. *Political Order in Changing Societies.* New Haven, CN: Yale University Press, 1968.

Iatrides, John. "Revolution or Self-Defense? Communist Goals, Strategy, and Tactics in the Greek Civil War." *Journal of Cold War Studies* 7, no. 3 (Summer 2005): 3–33.

JP 1–02, *Department of Defense Dictionary of Military and Associated Terms.* Washington, DC: Joint Chiefs of Staff, 2010.

JP 3–0, *Doctrine for Joint Operations.* Washington, DC: Chairman of the Joint Chiefs of Staff, 2001.

JP 3–07, *Joint Doctrine for Military Operations Other Than War.* Washington, DC: Joint Chiefs of Staff, 1995.

Jablonsky, David. "The Persistence of Credibility: Interests, Threats and Planning for the Use of American Military Power." In *US Army War College Guide to Strategy*, edited by Joseph Cerami and James Holcomb, 43–54. Carlisle, PA: US Army War College, 2001.

Jakobsen, Peter. *Nordic Approaches to Peace Operations: A New Model in the Making.* Cass Series on Peacekeeping. New York: Routledge, 2006.

Jervis, Robert. "Political Implications of Loss Aversion." *Political Psychology* 13, no. 2 (June 1992): 187–204.

Jett, Dennis. *Why Peacekeeping Fails.* New York: St. Martin's Press, 1999.

Joes, Anthony James. *Resisting Rebellion: The History and Politics of Counterinsurgency.*

Lexington: University Press of Kentucky, 2006.

_____. *The War for South Viet Nam, 1954–1975.* New York: Praeger, 2001.

Johnson, Harold. Speech August 21, 1967, New Orleans, LA. *Military Review* 47, no. 12 (December 1967): back matter.

Joint US Military Advisory and Planning Group, Greece. *History of the JUSMAPG.* Headquarters, JUSMAPG, 1949.

Jomini, Antoine-Henri de. *Summary of the Art of War or A New Analytical Compend of the Principal Combinations of Strategy, of Grand Tactics and of Military Policy.* New York: G. P. Putnam & Co. 1854.

Jones, Frank. "Blowtorch: Robert Komer and the Making of Vietnam Pacification Policy." *Parameters* (Autumn 2005): 103–118.

Jones, Howard. *"A New Kind of War": America's Global Strategy and the Truman Doctrine in Greece.* New York: Oxford University Press, 1989.

Jordan, Amos, William Taylor, and Lawrence Korb. *American National Security: Policy and Process.* Baltimore, MD: The Johns Hopkins University Press, 1989.

Kagan, Robert. *A Twilight Struggle: American Power and Nicaragua, 1977–1990.* New York: Free Press, 1996.

Karnow, Stanley. *Vietnam: A History.* New York: Viking Press, 1983.

Kelly, James. "Aftermath in Bloody Beirut." *Time,* November 7, 1983.

Keohane, Robert, and Joseph Nye. *Power and Independence.* 2nd ed. Cambridge, MA: Center for International Affairs, Harvard University with Harper Collins Publishers, 1989.

Kershaw, Sarah. "Joaquín Balaguer, 95, Dies; Dominated Dominican Life." *New York Times,* July 15, 2002. http://www.nytimes.com/2002/07/15/world/joaquin-balaguer-95-dies-dominated-dominican-life.html (accessed May 16, 2011).

Kimmens, Andrew. *Nicaragua and the United States.* New York: H. W. Wilson Company, 1987.

Kinzer, Stephen. *Blood of Brothers: Life and War in Nicaragua.* New York: G. P. Putnam's Sons, 1991.

Klein, Joe. "A Grip-But No Grins." *Newsweek,* 13 Nov 1995, 52–53.

Komer, Robert. "Clear, Hold, and Rebuild." *Army* 20, no. 5 (May 1970): 16–24.

_____. "Pacification: A Look Back...And Ahead." *Army* 20, no. 6 (June 1970): 20–29.

Kornbluth, Peter. *Nicaragua: The Price of Intervention.* Washington, DC: Institute of Policy Studies, 1987.

Kovats-Bernat, J. Christopher. "Factional Terror, Paramilitarism and Civil War in Haiti:

The View from Port-au-Prince, 1994–2004." *Anthropologica* 48, no. 1: 117–139.

Kreisher, Otto. "Operation Golden Pheasant." *Army* (May 1988): 36–39.

Krepinevich, Andrew. *The Army and Vietnam.* Baltimore, MD: The Johns Hopkins University Press, 1986.

Kretchik, Robert Baumann, and John Fishel. *Invasion, Intervention, "Intervasion": A Concise History of the US Army in Operation Uphold Democracy.* Fort Leavenworth, KS: Command and General Staff College Press, 1998.

Kupperman, Robert, and Associates, Inc. *Low Intensity Conflict, Vol. 1, Main Report,* AD-A 137260. Fort Monroe, VA.: US Army Training and Doctrine Command, 1983.

Kurlantzick, Joshua. "Mission Expanding." *Military Officer,* May 2004, 552–60.

LaFeber, Walter. *America, Russia, and the Cold War.* New York: John Wiley and Sons, 1968.

Lake, Anthony. Speech to the TransAfrica Forum, Washington, DC June 29, 1995. *US Department of State Dispatch* 6, no.27 (July 3, 1995): 539.

Lane, Charles. "Who 'Won' Nicaragua?'" *Newsweek,* March 12, 1990, 37.

Lawson, Chris. "Peacekeeping Turned Sour 10 Years Ago, Too." *Army Times,* October 25, 1993, 11.

Leaf, Louise, and Bruce Auster. "The Unmaking of Foreign Policy." *US News & World Report,* 18 October 1993, 30–37.

"Letter to the Speaker of the House and the President Pro Tempore of the Senate Reporting on United States Participation in the Multinational Force in Lebanon," September 29, 1982. University of Texas Archives. http://www.reagan.utexas.edu/archives/speeches/1982/92982e.htm (accessed June 10, 2011).

Lewis, Anthony. "Abroad at Home: Resolution Matters." *New York Times,* September 19, 1994. http://www.nytimes.com/1994/09/19/opinion/abroad-at-home-resolution-matters.html?pagewanted=2&src=pm (accessed May 13, 2011).

Lewy, Guenter. *America in Vietnam.* New York: Oxford University Press, 1978.

"Low-Intensity Conflict: Support for Democratic Resistance Movements." Washington, DC: Foreign Service Institute, 1988.

Lowenthal, Abraham. *The Dominican Intervention.* Cambridge, MA: Harvard University Press, 1972.

Luttwark, Edward. "Wrong Place, Wrong Time." *New York Times,* 22 July 1993.

Lykke, Arthur. "Toward an Understanding of Military Strategy." In *Military Strategy: Theory and Application,* 3–8. Carlisle, PA: US Army War College, 1989.

MacDonald, Hugh. "The Dominican Crisis

1965." Carlisle Barracks, PA: US Army War College, 1967.

Mages, Robert. "Without the Need of a Single American Rifleman: James Van Fleet and His Lessons Learned as Commander of the Joint United States Military Advisory and Planning Group during the Greek Civil War, 1948–1949." In *The US Army and Irregular Warfare, 1775–2007*, edited by Richard Davis, 195–212. Washington, DC: Center of Military History, 2007.

Malik, J. Mohan. "The Evolution of Strategic Thought." In *Contemporary Security and Strategy*, edited by Craig Snyder, 13–52. New York: Routledge, 1999..

Mandelbaum, Michael. "Foreign Policy as Social Work." *Foreign Affairs* 75, no. 1 (Jan- Feb, 1996): 16–32.

_____. "The Reluctance to Intervene." *Foreign Policy* 95 (Summer 1994): 10.

Maren, Michael. "Somalia: Whose Failure?" *Current History: A Journal of Contemporary World Affairs* 95, no. 601 (May 1996): 201–205.

Marlowe, John. *Arab Nationalism and British Imperialism*. London: Cresset Press, 1961.

Martin, Ian. "Haiti: Mangled Multilateralism." *Foreign Policy*, no. 95 (Summer, 1994): 72–89.

Martin, Kimberly. "Warlordism in Comparative Perspective." *International Security* 31, no. 3 (Winter 2006): 41–73.

Martz, Larry. "Echoes of an Old War." *Newsweek*, April 7, 1986.

Masland, Tom. "Should We Invade Haiti?" *Newsweek*, July 18, 1994.

Matloff, Maurice. *American Military History*. Washington, DC: Department of the Army, 1973.

Matthews, Lloyd. "The Politician as Operational Commander." *Army*, March 1996, 29–36.

McCaffrey, William. "Gen. Van Fleet: One of the Last the Stars Fell On." *Army*, Dec. 1992, 8–11.

McCormick, Shon. "A Primer on Developing Measures of Effectiveness." *Military Review* (July–August 2010): 60–66.

McNeil, Frank. *War and Peace in Central America*. New York: Charles Scribner's Sons, 1988.

Mead, James. "Lebanon Revisited." *Marine Corps Gazette* (September 1983): 64–73.

Melanson, Richard. *American Foreign Policy since the Vietnam War: The Search for Consensus from Nixon to Clinton*. Armonk: New York: M. E. Sharpe, 1996.

Metz, Helen, ed. *Somalia: A Country Study*. Washington, DC: Headquarters, Department of the Army, 1993.

Michaels, Marguerite. "Peacemaking War." *Time*, 26 July 1993, 48.

Mill, John Stuart. *A System of Logic: Ratiocinative and Inductive*. Honolulu, HI: University Press of the Pacific, 2002.

Miller, Linda. "The Clinton Years: Reinventing US Foreign Policy?" *International Affairs* 70, no. 4 (Oct., 1994): 621–634.

Millet, Allan, and Peter Maslowski. *For the Common Defense: A Military History of the United States of America*. New York: The Free Press, 1984.

Millet, Richard. "Panama and Haiti." In *US and Russian Policy Making with Respect to the Use of Force*, edited by Jeremey Azrael and Emil Payin, 137–161. Santa Monica, CA: RAND Corporation, 1996.

Mitchell, Christopher. "US Policy toward Haitian Boat People, 1972–93." *Annals of the American Academy of Political and Social Science* 534 (July 1994): 69–80.

Molnar, Andrew, et al. *Undergrounds in Insurgent, Revolutionary, and Resistance Warfare*. Washington, DC: American University, 1963.

Montgomery, Thomas. "Ambush in Mogadishu." PBS Frontline interview. http://www.pbs.org/wgbh/pages/frontline/shows/ambush/interviews/montgomery.html (accessed 21 June 2010).

Moskos, Charles, Jr. "Grace Under Pressure." *Army*, September 1966, 41–44.

"Moving in Was Easy, But...." *US News & World Report*, June 21, 1965, 75.

Murphy, Robert. *Diplomat among Warriors: The Unique World of a Foreign Service Expert*. Garden City, New York: Doubleday & Company, 1964.

Nachmani, Amikan. *International Intervention in the Greek Civil War: The United Nations Special Committee on the Balkans, 1947–1952*. Santa Barbara, CA: Praeger Publishers, 1990.

National Security Strategy of Engagement and Enlargement. Washington, DC: The White House, 1995.

"The Nations: Captain of the Crags." *Time*, April 5, 1948.

Natsios, Andrew. *US Foreign Policy and the Four Horsemen of the Apocalypse: Humanitarian Relief in Complex Emergencies*. Westport, CN: Praeger, 1997.

Negrete, Bernardo. "Grenada: A Case Study in Military Operations Other Than War." Paper, Army War College, 1996.

"Nicaraguan Complaint against United States Discussed in Council." *U.N. Chronicle* (29 June 1988): 59.

"Nicaraguan Resistance and Sandinistas Reach Agreement." *Department of State Bulletin* (May 1988): 74–76.

Oakley, Robert. "An Envoy's Perspective." *Joint Forces Quarterly* (Autumn 1993): 44–55.

_____. "Ambush in Mogadishu." PBS Frontline

interview. http://www.pbs.org/wgbh/pages/frontline/shows/ambush/interviews/oakley.html (accessed 21 June 2010).

O'Ballance, Edgar. *Civil War in Lebanon, 1975–92.* New York: St. Martin's Press, 1998.

_____. *The Greek Civil War: 1944–1949.* New York: Praeger, 1966.

Olson, James, and Randy Roberts. *Where the Domino Fell: America and Vietnam, 1945 to 1990.* New York: St. Martin's Press, 1991.

Palmer, Bruce. *Intervention in the Caribbean: The Dominican Crisis of 1965.* Lexington: University Press of Kentucky, 1989.

Palmer, Dave Richard. *Summons of the Trumpet: US-Vietnam in Perspective.* San Rafael, CA: Presidio Press, 1978.

Papandreou, Andreas. *Democracy at Gunpoint: The Greek Front.* Garden City, NY, 1970.

Pardo-Maurer, R. *The Contras, 1980–1989: A Special Kind of Politics.* New York: Praeger, 1990.

Paris, Roland. *At War's End: Building Peace after Civil Conflict.* New York: Cambridge University Press, 2004.

Paterson, Thomas. *On Every Front: The Making of the Cold War.* New York: W. W. Norton & Company, 1979.

_____, et al. *American Foreign Policy: A History Since 1900.* New York: D. C. Heath and Company, 1991.

Pearce, David. *Wary Partners—Diplomats and the Media.* Washington, DC: Congressional Quarterly, 1995.

Perez, Don. *The Middle East Today,* 2nd ed. Hinsdale, IL: Dryden Press, 1971.

Perlman, Michael. "The Rise and Fall of LIC Doctrine and Instruction." *Military Review* (September, 1988): 78–79.

"Perry: US troops needed in Bosnia." *The Benning Leader,* 20 Oct. 1995, 13.

Petit, Michael. *Peacekeepers at War: A Marine's Account of the Beirut Catastrophe.* Boston, MA: Faber and Faber, 1986.

Pogue, Forrest. *George C. Marshall: Statesman, 1945–1959.* New York: Viking Penguin, 1989.

Public Papers of the Presidents of the United States: Ronald Reagan, 1982. Washington, DC: Government Printing Office, 1983.

Public Papers of the Presidents of the United States: Ronald Reagan, 1983. Washington, DC: Government Printing Office, 1984.

Pulley, James, Stephen Epstein, and Robert Cronin. "JTF Haiti: A United Nations Foreign Internal Defense Mission." *Special Warfare* (July 1994): 2–9.

Quirk, Joel. "Historical Methods." In *The Oxford Handbook of International Relations,* edited by Christian Reus-Smit and Duncan Snidal, 518–536. New York: Oxford University Press, 2008.

Range, Peter. "The End Game in Nicaragua."

US News and World Report, March 28, 1988, 16–18.

Rauch, Steven. "Southern (Dis)Comfort: British Phase IV Operations in South Carolina and Georgia, May–September 1780." In *The US Army and Irregular Warfare, 1775–2007,* edited by Richard Davis, 33–58. Washington, DC: Center of Military History, 2007.

Record, Jeffrey. "A Note on Interests, Values, and the Use of Force." *Parameters* (Spring 2001): 15–21.

"Remarks of President Reagan and President Amin Gemayel of Lebanon following Their Meetings, July 22, 1983." University of Texas Archives http://www.reagan.utexas.edu/archives/speeches/1983/72283b.htm (accessed June 8, 2011).

"Report of the Commission of Inquiry Established Pursuant to Resolution 885 (1993) to Investigate Armed Attacks on UNOSOM II Personnel," 117, UN Doc. S/1994/653 (June 1, 1994, reprinted in *The United Nations and Somalia*).

Rieff, David. "A New Age of Imperialism?" *World Policy Journal* 16, no. 2 (Summer 1999): 1–10.

Riehm, Peter. "The USS *Harlan County* Affair." *Military Review* 77, no. 4 (July–August 1994): 31–37.

Rodman, Peter. *Presidential Command: Power, Leadership and the Making of Foreign Policy from Richard Nixon to George W. Bush.* New York: Alfred A. Knopf, 2009.

Romjue, John. *From Active Defense to AirLand Battle: The Development of Army Doctrine 1973–1982.* Fort Monroe, VA: United States Army Training and Doctrine Command, 1984.

Roush, Maurice. "The Hamlet Evaluation System." *Military Review* (September 1969): 10–17.

"Sandinista Offensive." *Department of State Bulletin.* May 1988: 73–74.

Sarkesian, Sam. "Low-Intensity Conflict: Concepts, Principles, and Policy Guidelines." *Air University Review* 36, no. 2 (January–February 1985): 4–23.

_____. *US National Security: Policymakers, Processes, and Politics.* Boulder, CO: Lynne Rienner, 1989.

Saunders, Richard. "Military Force in the Foreign Policy of the Eisenhower Presidency." *Political Science Quarterly* 100, no. 1 (Spring 1985): 97–116.

Savolainen, Jukka. "The Rationality of Drawing Big Conclusions Based on Small Samples: In Defense of Mill's Methods." *Social Forces* 72, no. 4 (June 1994): 1217–1224.

Schmitt, Eric. "Reinforcements for US Troops Delayed 9 Hours." *New York Times,* 6 October 1993.

Scott, James. "Interbranch Rivalry and the Reagan Doctrine in Nicaragua." *Political Science Quarterly* 112, no. 2 (Summer 1997): 237–260.

Scoville, Thomas. *Reorganizing for Pacification Support.* Washington, DC: Center of Military History, 1982.

"Senator Calls for Somalia Pullout." *Columbus Ledger-Enquirer,* 14 July 1993.

Sereseres, Caesar. *The Nicaraguan Resistance: A Case Study in US Foreign Policy and Unconventional War; 1981–1990.* Irvine, CA: University of California, 1990.

Shinn, Rinn. *Greece: A Country Study.* Washington, DC: American University, 1986.

Shrader, Charles. *The Withered Vine: Logistics and the Communist Insurgency in Greece.* New York: Praeger, 1999.

Shulimson, Jack. *Marines in Lebanon, 1958.* Washington, DC: Headquarters, US Marine Corps, 1966.

Shultz, George. "Low-Intensity Warfare: The Challenge of Ambiguity." Department of State, *Current Policy,* No. 783, January 1986.

_____. *Turmoil and Triumph: My Years as Secretary of State.* New York: Scribner's, 1993.

Siegel, Adam. *The Intervasion of Haiti.* Alexandria, VA: Center for Naval Analyses, 1996.

Sklar, Holly. *Washington's War on Nicaragua.* Boston, MA: South End Press, 1988.

Slater, Jerome. *Intervention and Negotiation: The United States and the Dominican Revolution.* New York: Harper & Row, 1970.

Small Wars Manual, US Marine Corps, 1940. Washington, DC: Government Printing Office, 1940.

Smithers, Samuel. "Combat Units in Revolutionary Development." *Military Review* (October 1967): 37–41.

Smolowe, Jill. "Pouncing on a Transgressor." *Time,* April 7, 1986.

_____. "There is No Plan B." *Time,* April 25, 1988.

Snow, Donald. *Peacekeeping, Peacemaking and Peace Enforcement: The US Role in the New International Order.* Carlisle, PA: US Army War College Strategic Studies Institute, 1993.

_____. *When America Fights: The Use of US Military Force.* Washington, DC: CQ Press, 2000.

Sorley, Lewis. *Honorable Warrior: General Harold K. Johnson and the Ethics of Command.* Lawrence: University of Kansas, 1998.

_____. "The Quiet War: Revolutionary Development." *Military Review* (November 1967): 13–19.

Spaller, Ruth. "Combat: 3rd Bn 75th Rangers Face Ultimate Challenge in Somalia." *The Bayonet,* 12 November 1993.

Spiller, Roger. "*Not War But Like War*": *The American Intervention in Lebanon.* Fort Leavenworth, KS: Combat Studies Institute, 1981.

Stengel, Richard. "A Restrained Show of Force." *Time,* March 28, 1988.

Stevenson, Jonathan. "Hope Restored in Somalia?" *Foreign Policy,* no. 91 (Summer 1993): 138–154.

Stavrianos, L. S. *Greece: American Dilemma and Opportunity.* Chicago: Henry Regnery, 1952.

Story, Ann, and Aryea Gottlieb. "Beyond the Range of Military Operations." *Joint Forces Quarterly* (Autumn 1995): 99–104.

Strube, Richard. "Operations Other Than War and Their Ramifications for US Military Capability." *Army* (January 1997): 9–12.

Summers, Harry, Jr. *On Strategy: A Critical Analysis of the Vietnam War.* Novato, CA: Presidio, 1982.

Swenson, Louis. "The Revolutionary Development Program." *Infantry* (Jan–Feb 1968): 28–31.

"Swift as Eagles." *Army Information Digest,* July 1965, 5–8.

Taw, Jennifer Morrison, and Robert Leicht. "The New World Order and Army Doctrine: The Doctrinal Renaissance of Operations Short of War?" Santa Monica, CA: RAND, 1992.

Taylor, Maxwell. *Swords and Plowshares.* New York: W. W. Norton, 1972.

TC 7–98–1, *Stability and Support Operations Training Support Package.* Washington, DC: Headquarters, Department of the Army, 1997.

Thayer, Thomas. *War Without Fronts: The American Experience in Vietnam.* Boulder, CO: Westview Press, 1985.

Thompson, Robert. *Revolutionary War in World Strategy, 1945–1969.* New York: Taplinger, 1970.

Thompson, W. Scott, and Donald Frizzell. *The Lessons of Vietnam.* New York: Crane, Russak, and Company, 1977.

Tolson, John. *Vietnam Studies: Airmobility, 1961–1971.* Washington, DC: Department of the Army, 1989.

TRADOC Pamphlet 525–44, *Military Operations: US Army Operational Concept for Low Intensity Conflict.* Fort Monroe, VA: Headquarters, TRADOC, 1986.

Tucker, David. "Facing the Facts: The Failure of Nation Assistance." *Parameters* (Summer 1993): 34–40.

Turner, Robert. *Nicaragua v. United States: A Look at the Facts.* Washington, DC: Pergamon-Brassey's, 1987.

"Two Decades Later, Mariel Boat Lift Refugees Still Feel Effects of Riot." *Los Angeles Times,* May 5, 2001. http://articles.latimes.com/2001/may/05/news/mn-59567 (accessed May 12, 2011).

"U.N. Special Envoy Calls for Unity among Peacekeepers in Somalia." *Columbus Ledger-Enquirer,* 16 July 1993.

"UN-mandated Force Seeks to Halt Tragedy:

Operation Restore Hope." *UN Chronicle*, March 1993.

"UNOSOM Objectives Affirmed, Despite Continuing Violence." *UN Chronicle*, December 1993, 24–27.

UNSCR 847, September 23, 1993. http://dac cess-dds-ny.un.org/doc/UNDOC/GEN/ N93/515/30/PDF/N9351530.pdf?OpenEle ment (accessed May 12, 2011).

U.S. Army Forces, Somalia: *10th Mountain Division (LI); After Action Report, Summary.* Fort Drum, NY: Headquarters, 10th Mountain Division, 1993.

"US Frees Somali Capital." *Columbus Ledger-Enquirer,* 10 December 1992.

"US Troops Fire on Marchers." *Columbus-Ledger Enquirer,* 13 August 1993.

U.S. Department of State. *Foreign Relations of the United States, 1948. Eastern Europe; The Soviet Union.* Vol. 4. Washington, DC: US Government Printing Office, 1947. http://digicoll.lib rary.wisc.edu/cgi-bin/FRUS/FRUS-idx?type= turn&entity=FRUS.FRUS1948v04.p005 6&id=FRUS.FRUS1948v04&isize=M&q1= Van%20Fleet (accessed March 30, 2010).

US News & World Report. October 29, 1948, 24.

Van Fleet, James. "How We Won in Greece." Speech to the Institute for Research in the Humanities and University Extension, University of Wisconsin, Madison, WI, April 11, 1967.

"Vietnamese Civic Action Program." *Military Review* (December 1967): 102.

Wade, Gary. *Rapid Deployment Logistics: Lebanon, 1958.* Fort Leavenworth, KS: Combat Studies Institute, 1984.

Wainhouse, Edward. "Guerrilla War in Greece, 1946–49: A Case Study." *Military Review* (June 1957): 17–25.

Walcott, John. "Taking the Point on Central America." *Newsweek,* April 14, 1988.

Walker, Thomas. *Reagan versus the Sandinistas: The Undeclared War on Nicaragua.* Boulder, CO: Westview Press, 1987.

_____. *Revolution and Counterrevolution in Nicaragua.* Boulder, CO: Westview Press, 1991.

Wallace, James. "Next Stop for US Forces?" *US News and World Report,* April 28, 1986.

Walt, Stephen. "Two Cheers for Clinton's Foreign Policy." *Foreign Affairs* 79, no. 2: 63–79.

"War Risks in Greek-aid Plans." *US News & World Report,* March 5, 1948.

Warner, Margaret. "Thunder on the Right at the White House." *Newsweek,* April 7, 1986.

Watson, Russell. "It's Our Fight Now." *Newsweek,* 14 December 1992.

Weinberger, Caspar. *Fighting for Peace: Seven Critical Years in the Pentagon.* New York: Warner Books, 1990.

_____. "The Uses of Military Power." *Defense 85,* January 85: 2–11.

Westmoreland, William. *A Soldier Reports.* Garden City, NY: Doubleday and Company, 1976.

Whitaker, Mark. "More Contra-dictions." *Newsweek,* April 14, 1988.

Williams, Bruce. Interview with General James A. Van Fleet, US Army Military History Institute, Senior Officer Debriefing Program, Carlisle Barracks, PA, vol. 3.

Williamson, R. E. "A Briefing for Combined Action." *Marine Corps Gazette* (March 1968): 41–43.

Willoughby, William. "Revolutionary Development." *Infantry* (Nov–Dec 1968): 5–11.

Wittner, Lawrence. *American Intervention in Greece.* New York: Columbia University Press, 1982.

Wombwell, James. *The Long War against Piracy: Historical Trends.* Fort Leavenworth, KS: Combat Studies Institute Press, 2010.

Woodhouse, C. M. *The Struggle for Greece, 1941–1949.* London: Hart-Davis, MacGibbon, 1976.

Wright, Donald, and Timothy Reese. *On Point II: Transition to the New Campaign: The United States Army in Operation Iraqi Freedom, May 2003–January 2005.* Fort Leavenworth, KS: Combat Studies Institute Press, 2008.

Wright, Quincy. "United States Intervention in the Lebanon." *The American Journal of International Law* 53, no. 1 (Jan., 1959): 112–125.

Wright, Robin. *Sacred Rage.* New York: Touchstone Simon and Schuster, 2001.

Wunderle, William. *Through the Lens of Cultural Awareness: A Primer for US Armed Forces Deploying to Arab and Middle Eastern Countries.* Fort Leavenworth, KS: Combat Studies Institute, 2006.

Yates, Lawrence. "A Feather in Their Cap? The Marines' Combat Action Program in Vietnam." In *US Marines and Irregular Warfare, 1898–2007: Anthology and Selected Bibliography,* edited by Stephen Evans, 147–157. Quantico, VA: Marine Corps University Press, 2008.

_____. "Military Stability and Support Operations: Analogies, Patterns and Recurring Themes." *Military Review* 72, no. 4 (July-Aug. 1997): 51–61.

_____. *Power Pack: US Intervention in the Dominican Republic, 1965–1966.* Fort Leavenworth, KS: US Army Command & General Staff College, 1988.

_____. "The US Military Intervention in Lebanon, 1958: Success without a Plan." In *Turning Victory Into Success: Military Operations after the Campaign,* edited by Brian De Toy, 123–133. Fort Leavenworth, KS: Combat Studies Institute, 2004.

Zinti, Robert. "The Contra Tangle." *Time,* March 28, 1988.

Zotos, Stephanos. *Greece: The Struggle for Freedom.* New York: Thomas Crowell, 1967.

Index